*Horry County, South Carolina
1730-1993*

Horry County, South Carolina

1730–1993

Catherine H. Lewis

Foreword by Charles Joyner

University of South Carolina Press

© 1998 University of South Carolina

Published in Columbia, South Carolina, by the
University of South Carolina Press

Manufactured in the United States of America
02   5 4 3 2

Library of Congress Cataloging-in-Publication Data

Lewis, Catherine Heniford.
  Horry County, South Carolina, 1730–1993 / Catherine H. Lewis.
    p. cm.
  Includes index.
  ISBN 1-57003-207-6
  1. Horry County (S.C.)—History. I. Title.
  F277.H6L48 1998
  975.7'87—dc21   97-21012

For Riley Evan Lewis and Claire Catherine Lewis

The tale of South Carolina's least known county is so remarkable, so pregnant with interest, that it reads like romance.

James Henry Rice,
The (Columbia, S.C.) State, July 19, 1903

Civilization is a stream with banks. The stream is sometimes filled with blood from people killing, stealing, shouting and doing the things historians usually record, while on the banks, unnoticed, people build homes, make love, raise children, sing songs, write poetry and even whittle statues. The story of civilization is the story of what happened on the banks. Historians are pessimists because they ignore the banks for the river.

Will Durant,
Life Magazine, October 18, 1963

Contents

List of Illustrations   viii

Foreword   ix

Preface   xv

Chronology   xx

Abbreviations   xxv

1 Wonderful, Rich, *and* Varied   1

2 In Order of Appearance   36

3 Ladies and Gentlemen   91

4 Self-Help as a Way of Life   140

5 The Civil War and Its Aftermath   170

6 Memorable Murderers   180

7 You Would Not Expect It in Horry!   187

Acknowledgments   198

Index   207

Illustrations

Following Page *116*

Mouzon Map of Georgetown District, 1775
William Hemingway's map of Conwayborough, 1802
Harlee's map of Horry District, 1820
Little River area, showing sites of historical interest
Horry County seal
Steamboats *F. G. Burroughs* and *Ruth*
Peter Horry, Huguenot planter who fought under General Francis Marion
The second Horry County Courthouse, shown in the late nineteenth century
Tokens used to pay workers
Tobacco farmers
The third Horry County Courthouse, built in 1908
Loris, about 1895
Downtown Myrtle Beach
Ocean Forest Hotel, Myrtle Beach
Franklin Gorham Burroughs and Adeline Cooper Burroughs
Henry Buck
Confederate memorial near the corner of Sixth Avenue and Elm Street
John P. Derham house at Green Sea
Lieutenant Governor Robert Scarborough
Beaty funeral notice
Colonel Doc Allen Spivey
Burroughs School, opened in 1906
Conwayborough Academy
The Gully Store, located at Ninth Avenue and Elm Street in Conway
Edmund Bigham on his way to court, 1926
The *Henrietta*, launched at Bucksville in 1875
The *Henrietta* being built at Bucksville
Advertisement for the Homewood Colony

Foreword

Charles Joyner

Horry County begins on the porch of Holliday's General Store in Gallivant's Ferry and extends east to the surf in front of the Myrtle Beach Pavilion. Physically it is more nearly part of North Carolina (with which it shares a land border) than of South Carolina (from which it is separated by the Peedee River, except for a stretch of about two miles across Waccamaw Neck that serves as a land border with Georgetown County). Roughly the size of Rhode Island, Horry is the largest county in South Carolina, but it was one of the least populous as late as the 1930s.

Horry is my home. It has been the home of my ancestors for nearly three centuries, since John and Mary Paul began raising crops and children on Hunting Swamp in the eighteenth century. In the beginning, long before John and Mary Paul, what would become Horry County was virgin forest, filled with thick impenetrable stands of oak and gum, cypress and cane, tall pines and great moss-draped live oaks, bordered on its Atlantic coast by a wide white beach and interspersed here and there inland with blackwater swamps—the lair of the alligator and the cottonmouth moccasin. There was an especially large fen between the beach and the rest of the county. On the early maps it was called the Great Impassable Swamp. It remained impassable until construction of the inland waterway in the 1930s drained it and construction of Highway 501 in the 1950s crossed it. Some contend that its impassable state has been restored in the 1990s by the traffic congestion on Highway 501.

There were already people here when the first Spaniards and Africans came. Like generations of natives to follow, they graciously welcomed the tourists with oyster roasts and southern hospitality; and they regaled their visitors with tall tales of giants, treasures, and men with tails who had to sit in chairs with holes in the seats. The Spaniards solemnly accepted their hospitality, claimed their continent, and carried them off to slavery in the West Indies.

Foreword

Unilke the rest of South Carolina, Horry County was settled by people drifting down from North Carolina rather than moving up from Charleston. Many of the descendants of those early settlers with their English and French and German and especially Scotch-Irish names still live in the county—Alford and Bellamy, Causey and Dawsey, Graham and Grainger, Hardee and Harper, Rabon and Sarvis, Vaught and Vereen.

The early settlers brought little with them except their creative imaginations. They dotted the landscape with towns and hamlets, to which they gave colorful names as a way of making their new homes more interesting. They bestowed Biblical names upon such communities as Antioch, Bethlehem, Ebenezer, Gethsemane, Hebron, Jerusalem, Macedonia, Pisgah, Rehobeth, Salem, Sharon, and Zion; and their faith was also reflected in others such as Hardshell, True Vine, Free Will, and Camp Ground. They seem to have felt more affection for those places than for the ones they dubbed Hell Gate and Hell's Neck. Horry folk could make a place seem a little more exotic by giving it such a name as Athens, Klondike, or Exile. But when they named a place Free Welcome, Good Hope, Pleasant Home, Happy Home, Sweet Home, New Home or Homewood Colony, they imparted a feeling of *belonging*. And they felt a little safer, perhaps, whenever they were near Jack's Lookout. Some imposed their own names on such places as Grantsville, Toddville, Bucksville, Bucksport, and Port Harrelson. But what was in their minds when they decided that some places should have such names as Flag Patch, Shoo Fly, Ketchuptown, Playcard, and St. Delight?

The towns and hamlets were populated by horses and mules as well as by men and women. For nearly two centuries it was impossible for those human inhabitants to go from one town or hamlet to another unless they walked or rode one of those horses or mules. Over such land routes as Good Luck Road, New Hope Road, and Race Path, their trips must have seemed a lot more interesting than over plain old Ditch Bank Road, less dangerous than over Bear Bone Trail, and more comfortable than over Rough and Ready Road. And if they got tired on the journey, they could rest in the shade of Sweet Gum, Maple, Canepatch, or Dogwood Neck; Cedar Grove, Hickory Grove, or Oak Grove; Pine Grove, Silent Grove, or the Free Woods. They could take the high ground at Glass Hill, Bunker Hill, Hickory Hill, or Windy Hill; at Mt. Vernon, Mt. Olive, Mt. Gilead, Mt. Beulah, Mt. Calvary, or Mt. Triumph. Or they could sink in such quagmires as Boggy Branch, Cartwheel Branch, or Sweetwater Branch; Watering Hole Branch, Knotty Branch, or Wasp Branch; Gravelly Gully, Drinking Gully, or just *the* Gully; White Oak Swamp, Pawley Swamp, or Halfway Swamp; Honey Camp Swamp, Big Breakfast Swamp, or Bug Swamp; not to mention Bear Swamp, Folly Swamp, Dead Man's Swamp, or Do Damn Swamp. Some folks said that Horry County was so boggy that buzzards had to fly high over the swamps lest their shadows be caught in the mire.

The Atlantic ocean poked fingers of saltwater in the Horry coast at Cane Patch Swash, Deep Hand Swash, Eight Mile Swash, Singleton's Swash, and Withers Swash. And the county boasted substantial freshwater bodies at Bass Lake, Eddy Lake, Rose Lake, and Horseshoe Lake; Cedar Creek, Hook Creek, and Drowning Creek, bordered by such places as Red Bluff, Star Bluff, Dog Bluff, and Bear Bluff. Horry fold crossed the Waccamaw and Peedee rivers at Gallivant's Ferry, Bull Creek Ferry, Potato Bed Ferry, or Peachtree Ferry (all handpowered) to land at such places as Enterprise Landing, Cartwheel Landing, and Polecat Landing.

The county is home to a series of mysterious natural phenomena known as the Carolina Bays—strange elliptical depressions in the landscape that are filled with water except during droughts. The early settlers gave these curious craters such colorful names as Flat Bay, Spring Bay, and Kate's Bay; Lucas Bay, Grassy Bay, and Wolf Bay; Fifteenth Bay, Bethany Bay, and Juniper Bay; Wolf Pit Bay, Polecat Bay, Buzzard's Bay, and Bitch Bay. Long Bay, on the other hand, refers to the whole concave Atlantic shoreline of Horry County.

Horry County has imbibed its share, perhapse more than its share, of paradox. It has stood off to the edge of South Carolina—both literally and figuratively. Unlike the state's other coastal counties, Horry was never plantation country. Its rivers were too far from the ocean and their banks were too high to support rice plantations (except for a few just above the Georgetown County line, owned by Georgetown rice planters). And its soil was too light and fine for King Cotton. While other coastal counties developed capital-A Aristocratic societies of great rice and cotton plantations and wealthy planters with massive slave forces, Horry developed a little-d democratic society of small farms with corn and sweet potatoes and small farmers with more kids than slaves. In the nineteenth century more than eighty of every ten Georgetonians were Africans or the descendants of Africans, while at the same time more than eight of every ten Horryites were Europeans, or the descendants of Europeans.

Politically, Horry voters went against the grain of antebellum South Carolina. They sent unionists to the legilsature and resisted the simplistic lures of nullification and secession. Surely the origins of Horry unionism owed less to the county's preference for nation over state than to its waterbound isolation from either. Not for nothing was it called the Independent Republic. The White House in Washington was a long way from the court house in Conwayboro, but the State House in Columbia seemed almost as remote. And when Columbia seemed close, it often seemed *too* close. Horry folk resented the propaganda of Yankee abolitionists, but they resented even more the pressure exerted upon them by the slaveholders who dominated the South Carolina legislature to make them conform.

Unionist sentiment remained very strong among Horry folk until the final disunion crisis. Once their state stepped over the abyss of secession, however, they loyally followed it into disaster. Although (as one Horryite put it) "I have no quarrel with the Yankees," the county gave more volunteers to the Confederacy than it had eligibles. In defense of home and family, Horry boys signed up *en masse*, especially in the Tenth South Carolina Regiment, which was largely made up of Horryites. The Confederacy in its wisdom sent them to Tennessee, beneath whose bloodsoaked battlefields many of them would remain.

Horry politics after the war contined to differ from the rest of South Carolina. It was the only county in the state to remain Democratic throughout Reconstruction. Horry voters enthusiastically joined in the campaign to elect Wade Hampton governor in 1876; but unlike other Carolinians they did so to maintain Democratic rule, not to restore it.

"The Four T's"—turpentine, timber, tobacco, and tourism—marked the stages of Horry's economic history. Turpentine and other naval stores were most prominent in the colonial and antebellum periods, especially around Little River. Timbering began before the Civil War around Bucksport but spread across the county in the closing decades of the century as turpentine waned. Small amounts of tobacco began to be cultivated near Gallivant's Ferry in the 1850s, but Bright Leaf and the flue-curing process swept the county in the 1890s, and the production and marketing of tobacco continued to dominate Horry agriculture until the late twentieth century.

It was the flourishing tourist economy of the late twentieth century that transformed Horry from one of the poorest counties in the state into perhaps South Carolina's leading generator of revenue. The rise of tourism brought both prosperity and problems to Horry's "Grand Strand"—consisting of Cherry Grove, Ocean Drive, and Crescent Beach (now consolidated into North Myrtle Beach), Atlantic Beach, Surfside, Garden City, and especially Myrtle Beach. Starting in the 1930s and accelerating after World War II, Horry's beaches were flooded with visitors, settlers, and money—at least for three months out of each year. Resort natives sometimes complained that "they work us to death all summer and starve us to death all winter."

Foreword

The "season" had become a year-round phenomenon by the end of the century, however, with the proliferation of golf courses, shopping complexes, theaters and entertainment parks.

As late as the 1950s the county's population, even in the coastal resort area, remained fairly homogeneous. By the 1990s, however, surging growth generated not only extraordinary geographic, ethnic, racial, and religious diversity, but also extraordinary growing pains. Coastal resorts were crowded with people exercising their inalienable right to the pursuit of happiness— in their own individual ways. They included tourists who came to have a good time, entrepreneurs who came to find economic success, and retirees who came to find peace and quiet. Occasionally their ambitions reinforced one another, but more often they proved incompatible. Nonetheless all of them—old and young, natives and newcomers, in their similarities and in their diversity, in their selfishness and in their generosity, in their contentiousness and in their concord—have helped to make Horry County the fascinating place that Catherine Lewis reveals it to be in this book.

No one is better qualified to have written these historical sketches than Catherine Henniford Lewis. She has deep roots in the county, and for more than thirty years she has been central to the study of its history. It is difficult to imagine what that study would have been like without her. It certainly would not be what it is. Before she retired as Librarian of the Horry County Memorial Library in Conway, she developed its local history collection into the preeminent archive of research materials on Horry County history and one of the state's leading local history collections. Since her retirement, she has edited and published (with Ashley P. Cox, Jr.), a series of major historical source publications (fifteen volumes thus far), including early land plats, abstracts of nineteenth-century marriage and death notices, an index to the 1860 Census, World War I Draft Registrations, and numerous volumes of cemetery inventories. As longtime editor of the *Independent Republic Historical Quarterly,* the publication of the Horry County Historical Society, she elicited and published manuscripts and documents that would otherwise have remained unknown beyond the families who had preserved them. With Randall Wells she conducted videotaped interviews with more than fifty of the county's "living libraries" for Coastal Carolina University's Horry County Oral History Project.

Not only has she been the essential catalyst for the study of the county's history, but as a columnist for the *Sun News* (the Myrtle Beach daily newspaper), as a teacher in Coastal Carolina University's Third Quarter series, as a popular conductor of historical tours for Coastal Carolina University and

Foreword

Horry-Georgetown Technical College, and as a frequent lecturer to community groups, she has popularized and humanized the history of her county for a large audience of natives and newcomers alike. Everyone who is interested in the history of Horry County is indebted to Catherine Lewis not only for her diligent development of source material but also for her perceptive insights into their meaning.

Preface

I grew up in Loris in Horry County. Even before I graduated from library school at the University of North Carolina in 1948 I had talked to a member of the governing commission of the Horry County Memorial Library about becoming the county librarian. There were to be two more similar conversations before a vacancy and my availability coincided some twelve years later.

No sooner had I settled into my new office in 1960 than I became aware of the need to know the history of the county in sufficient depth to provide good reference service. Never mind that there was little or nothing available to provide the answers.

Fortunately, the unofficial historian of the county, the late Senator Paul Quattlebaum, was an honorary member of the library commission. His lifelong avocation had been the collection and cultivation of local history. He had files of printed materials, research, and correspondence, in addition to his broad and deep personal knowledge. He had already published what was then regarded as the definitive book on the Spanish exploration of the area, *The Land Called Chicora*. He was always generous in providing information when I called on him.

I overheard him say early in my tenure that I was the first county librarian whom he didn't have to train, because I was a native. That assumption had two major flaws. I really had more intuition and curiosity than actual knowledge of the history of Horry County. It is true that I grew up in Loris, the center of the northern reaches of the county. It is true that I lived there before and after I was born, but I was born in Richmond, Virginia, my mother's native city. In the strictest use of the word, therefore, I cannot be called a native of Horry County. But, as we say, I'm "near enough as makes no never mind."

The enabling legislation for the library system gives its public library a broad and generous mandate: to provide "free library service to the entire people" of the county. Some of the later fine print in the act included the responsibility of providing access to the history of the county.

The Library Commission had from the beginning interpreted the law to mean the sponsorship of a book written by a qualified historian. Easier said than done! The task had been turned down by more than one academic. Fewer records for Horry were held by the South Caroliniana Library at the University of South Carolina and the South Carolina Department of Archives and History than for any other county in the state. Our own courthouse records had not been well organized or even carefully preserved. Academics, therefore, were understandably reluctant to undertake the work.

Although I continued to seek a qualified person to adopt the project, I told the governing commission that we could, in the meantime, try to collect as much material as possible, safeguard it, and make it accessible. In so doing we might make the project more attractive to a researcher and we would, at least to some extent, be fulfilling the legislative mandate.

The library already owned crumbling newspaper files which had been in the Woodward family's hands. (H. H. Woodward Sr. was for many years the editor of the *Horry Herald*.) I bargained with the University of South Carolina's South Caroliniana Library to pay half the costs of microfilming them. We discovered in the process—and to our great delight—that among them were copies of papers dating back to 1861. There were gaps which have never been filled, but here was a treasure of information now in a format which could be made available for research. In the next year or so I set myself the task of reading them and making notes for my own reference.

Then one day, while I was exploring a Fibber McGee supply closet, I found in a sealed box, hidden from sight for years, materials placed in the library by the family of Dr. James A. Norton. Among them were three manuscripts, each similar to the others yet unique, in which he had tried to organize notes his father, Dr. Evan Norton, and his brother, the lawyer Van Norton, and he himself had collected about the history of Horry County. I could scarcely believe it.

Excited as I was, I failed to understand the apprehension with which some people greeted my great news. I learned that Dr. Norton had told people that he intended to tell the history, warts and all, and lay bare past scandals. It turned out that he was teasing. He did hope to produce a serious study of the Independent Republic, but he bogged down again and again in his own highly personal views of cause and effect. Still, it was wonderful to have his essays and his opinions, and I learned a great deal

Preface

from him. Although he died in 1950 and I never knew him, I feel an affection and affinity for this man who loved the history of Horry.

The establishment of the Horry County Historical Society in 1966 and its decision to begin publication of the *Independent Republic Quarterly* beginning in 1967 gave impetus to the growing interest in local history. The *Quarterly* provided a forum for the collection and publication of local history and a stimulus to people to share documents, pictures, and family and institutional records. The *Quarterly* is now (1998) in its thirty-second volume, an invaluable cupboard of Horry County history.

In the mid-1960s, I began to give talks about Horry County history to clubs and other organizations. They turned out to be popular beyond their merit. I can't even imagine now how I had the temerity. Lately I came across the first typewritten notes I used for these talks. They were in the form of a chronology into which I had plugged what I knew at the time. I have continued to add to this as I established new information through reading or research. The most recent version of this chronology is included in this book to help the reader establish a context for the essays.

In retirement I have been able to pursue my interest in Horry's past through research, writing, lecturing, and giving tours. Whenever I write an article, give a lecture, or conduct a tour, someone I encounter will add a fact, or tale, or piece of lore to my collection. These activities are a happy, if unforeseen, outcome of a job which provided me with a livelihood for nearly twenty-eight years. As one of my librarian sons remarked not too long ago, "They don't tell you in library school that it is such fun."

I have been encouraged to put into book form some of the history about which I have been lecturing and writing for years. Now is as good a time as any to do it. I have selected from material I have written for a number of purposes and published in various places, edited it, and added new pieces.

I try to be accurate, given the state of research or availability of information at the time. If information, however questionable, gets into print, it tends to be viewed as Holy Writ, but new information is being unearthed all the time. Sometimes it supports what had been conventional wisdom, sometimes it refutes it. Old tales, even when based on history, have been burnished and embellished by many retellings, each reporter shaping the details to add to the dramatic effect of the story. I have included notes about sources to help readers, but have tried to keep them from being intrusive.

I am indebted to all those Horry County people who have shared the

Preface

joy of learning about its history, who have contributed to the *Independent Republic Quarterly*, and who have preserved the old stories and documents handed down in their families. Meeting and talking with them has been the fun part of compiling the information in this volume.

I have already acknowledged the role of the Norton papers and the files of the *Horry Herald* and other newspapers. I must also thank the staffs of the South Carolina Department of Archives and History Research Room, the Horry County Memorial Library headquarters in Conway, and Chapin Memorial Library in Myrtle Beach for their diligence in providing materials I have needed. The local history collection in the county library is still the best available.

If the Horry County Historical Society had not existed, I doubt that I would have had the incentive to do this study which has enriched my life. I admire those members and officers who have kept the work going for three decades. Long may the Society flourish!

In recent years the Waccamaw Center for the Study of Southern History and Culture at Coastal Carolina University has sponsored an oral history project which has made and "banked" for future study interviews with Horry people of all backgrounds. Randall Wells, who managed the project, and I are fortunate to have had the opportunity to interview many knowledgeable and interesting people. Under its distinguished director, Dr. Charles W. Joyner, the center is attracting academics to the study of local history.

The Pee Dee Heritage Center, which began at Coker College in Hartsville and has gradually attracted other cosponsors, has also focused scholarly attention on our history. It provides an excellent lecture series and has sponsored an important history of tobacco culture in this region.

I am indebted to those publications in which much of this material has appeared over a twenty year period, specifically the *Independent Republic Quarterly*, the *West Horry Journal*, the *Sun News*, and *Sandlapper Magazine*. I also thank Conway Hospital for providing the opportunity for two lectures, those on Robert Conway and on the history of medical care before the Conway Hospital was established.

It was not until 1993 that I seriously considered the idea of putting this collection of short articles, essays, and lectures together. My brothers, Davis Heniford Jr. of Loris and North Myrtle Beach and Lewis W. Heniford of Carmel, California, encouraged me to undertake the project. Lewis critiqued much of this material while he was in Horry on his vacation in 1994.

Dr. Charles W. Joyner encouraged me to submit the manuscript to the University of South Carolina Press. I would like to thank Ashley P. Cox Jr., my partner in Waccamaw Records, for proofreading what was almost the final version.

The Horry County Museum provided invaluable assistance with the illustrations. Stewart Pabst, the assistant curator, and William H. Keeling, the director, have been generous with their time, expertise, and collections.

Finally I am grateful to all those people who helped me run down a copy of T. M. Jordan's 1930 map of the coast. Dr. Marcus Smith and Mrs. Ernest Southern put me in touch with his son, Jack Jordan, who provided a copy.

We need to appreciate and affirm our own story! Horry County history, though certainly different, is just as valid as that of Georgetown, Charleston, or any other county of the state—and perhaps more interesting than most. It certainly has been colorful, filled with people of character and industry, as well as a generous supply of eccentrics and oddballs. I encourage others to write, to do research, to preserve the letters, documents, pictures, and memorabilia in their possession which will enable future historians to do a better job of interpreting the history of the Independent Republic. Someone yet to appear will undertake the much needed task of writing a sound, readable history of Horry County. If what I have done contributes to that enterprise, I shall be pleased.

A Brief Chronology of Horry County History

10,000 B.C.	Estimated earliest human habitation of the area.
A.D. 1521	Spaniards explore the land called Chicora.
1670	British settle Charles Town. Under the Lords Proprietors, present-day Horry was part of Craven County.
1730	Robert Johnson, first royal governor, includes Kingston Township on the Waccamaw in a plan to develop the province.
1732	Site of Kingston is laid out by Alexander Skene and Chief Justice Robert Wright.
1735	First land grants in Horry area.
1740	Reverend George Whitefield travels the coast road, January 1-2.
1760	John Bartram, naturalist, visits and records his discoveries.
1776-83	American Revolution. Small engagements at Bear Bluff and Black Lake. General Francis Marion, the "Swamp Fox," is said to have camped at Kingston overnight on his way to the Battle of Black Mingo, September 1780.
1783	Kingston Village ordered to be "laid out" again (Act 1183).
1785	Kingston County designated as a subdivision of Georgetown District.
1785, 1791, 1795, 1801	Bishop Francis Asbury visits Kingston.
1791	George Washington spends the night of April 17 with Jeremiah Vereen. The historic marker on Highway 17 south of North Myrtle Beach which commemorates the event has been lost.
1801	Horry District is named for Brig. Gen. Peter Horry (1743-1815). The village of Kingston is designated the county seat and renamed Conwayborough for Brig. Gen. Robert Conway (ca. 1753-1823).

Chronology

1802	First board of commissioners (Thomas Livingston, Samuel F. Floyd Jr., Samuel Foxworth, William Hemingway, William Williams, John Graham Sr., Thomas Fearwell, and Robert Conway) meets for the first time, January 3, and authorizes a courthouse on Fifth Avenue and sale of lots.
1807	First post office is established in Conwayborough.
1820	Population 5,015. *Mills' Atlas* shows 20 schools, 6 meeting houses.
1824-1825	Second courthouse (presently Conway City Hall), designed by Robert Mills, costs $9,500. The jail, built later, costs $8,000.
1828	Henry Buck of Bucksport, Maine, builds his home at Upper Mill, now on the Historic Register. He establishes commercial lumber industry along the lower Waccamaw River.
1830s	Commercial production of naval stores becomes important.
1840	Population 5,755. Post offices at Conwayborough, Green Sea, Bayboro, Galivants Ferry, and Bucksport (Port Harrelson).
1857	Conwayborough Academy Association builds a schoolhouse on Fifth Avenue, replacing an earlier building.
1860	Population 7,962. Ordinance of Secession, December 17, is signed by Horry delegates Thomas W. Beaty, William J. Ellis, and Benjamin E. Sessions.
1861-1865	Civil War. First newspaper, the *Horry Dispatch*, established. First steamboat on the Waccamaw River is the *Francis Marion*, a troopship. The age of steamboats on the Waccamaw lasts until after World War I.
1863	Federal Navy captures Fort Randall on January 5, but it is recaptured by Confederate defenders.
1876	End of the Reconstruction Era. Marker on oak tree at Fifth and Main St., Conway, commemorates Wade Hampton's speech during his campaign. F. G. Burroughs takes over the schools in Conwayborough. In the next few years he builds a new school house at Main St. and Kingston Lake Drive. The old Academy (built about 1857) becomes Whittemore Academy for blacks.
1883	General Assembly changes name of town from Conwayborough to Conway.

Chronology

1886	*Horry Herald* begins publication. Charleston earthquake felt in Horry County, August 31.
1887	On December 15, the railroad (built by the Chadbourn family) comes to Conway. A station along its route is named Loris.
1890s	Commercial tobacco cultivation begins. Homewood Colony attracts immigrants from the west. Naval stores decline.
1890	Population 19,256 (13,706 white; 5,550 black). Conway population: 677.
1893	Tidal wave, October 13.
1898	Conway incorporated. Population 705. Colonel C. P. Quattlebaum is elected first intendant (mayor).
1899	Seashore and Conway Railroad begins construction of a line from Conway to the beach. The first tobacco warehouse opens in Conway.
1900	Population, 23,364. New Town on coast renamed Myrtle Beach for the native shrub.
1902	Wooden bridge at Galivants Ferry opens access to the rest of South Carolina. It has one lane with turnouts. Loris incorporated; D. J. Butler, first mayor.
1906	New Burroughs School opens (Ninth and Main). A lot for a new courthouse is purchased. The first automobile comes to Conway. New town established at the end of the Conway, Coast & Western Railroad is named Aynor.
1907	Paul Quattlebaum's new company brings electric light to Conway.
1908	Present courthouse (Third and Elm, Beaty and Second) finished and dedicated, May 22, 1908. Construction cost is $24,950.40; contractor, H. P. Little. It has renovations and additions in 1927, 1964, and 1982-1983.
1914	The road to Myrtle Beach is built. Aynor incorporates.
1917-1918	World War I.
1919	Waccamaw Line of Steamers, established in 1880s, ceases operation.
1920s	First efforts to establish a tourist industry.

Chronology

1923	Statewide law ending free range for stock takes effect January 1.
1926	In March, Myrtle Beach Farms sells 65,000 acres to Woodside Brothers of Greenville for $850,000, to be paid in six installments through 1932. The venture ends in the Great Depression.
1928	Railroad tracks finally removed from Main Street, Conway.
1930	County population is 39,376, Conway's is 2,947. The Ocean Forest Hotel opens.
1936	Intracoastal Waterway completed, dedicated at Socastee, April 11.
1937	Bridge over the Waccamaw River at Conway opens.
1938	Myrtle Beach incorporated; W. L. Harrelson, mayor.
1940	Horry Electric Cooperative formed 24 April to bring electricity to rural Horry County.
1941	Myrtle Beach Air Force Base established.
1941-1945	World War II.
1948	Ocean Drive Beach is incorporated.
1950	Population 59,820. Loris Community Hospital opens May 15.
1953	Crescent Beach incorporated.
1954	Sun Fun Festival is held at Myrtle Beach for the first time. Hurricane Hazel hits, October 15. Coastal Carolina Junior College is established. County board of education becomes an elected body and the superintendent of education an appointive post. Horry County police is established.
1958	Ocean View Hospital opens in Myrtle Beach.
1959	Cherry Grove Beach incorporated.
1960	Population 68,247.
1964	Surfside Beach and Windy Hill Beach incorporated.
1965	Horry-Georgetown-Marion Technical College established. (Marion later drops out.) Myrtle Beach High School accepts its first black students.
1966	Atlantic Beach incorporated.

Chronology

1968	Ocean Drive Beach, Crescent Beach, Windy Hill Beach, and Cherry Grove Beach consolidate and become North Myrtle Beach.
1970	Population 69,998. School freedom of choice ended; unified system established. South Carolina celebrates the tricentennial of the founding of Charles Town.
1974	Ocean Forest Hotel destroyed on Friday, September 13.
1975	Home Rule Act passes.
1976	Briarcliffe Acres incorporated. First Horry County Council is elected.
1977	First Horry County Council is seated. Douglas Wendel, first county administrator, enters duty on July 1.
1980	Population 101,419.
1984	Horry County Railroad Line established to continue rail service to Myrtle Beach.
1985	Horry County celebrates 250 years since the area was opened for settlement.
1989	Hurricane Hugo, September 21–22.
1990	Population 144,053.
1993	Myrtle Beach Air Force Base closes in March.
	Coastal Carolina College, independent of the University of South Carolina, becomes Coastal Carolina University, July 1.
1996	Hurricanes Bertha (July 12) and Fran (September 5).

Abbreviations

AP	Edmund Kirke, *Among the Pines* (New York: J. R. Gilmore, 1862; reprint, *IRQ* 17:1)
BDSCS	*Biographical Directory of the South Carolina Senate, 1776-1985,* ed. N. Louise Bailey (Columbia: University of South Carolina Press, 1986)
CGHS	*Collections of the Georgia Historical Society*
Cooper	Mrs. Julian Cooper, "Socastee," in Clarke Willcox's *Musings of a Hermit*, 2nd ed. (Murrells Inlet: The Hermitage, 1967)
CT	*Charleston Times*
ESC	Robert L. Meriwether, *The Expansion of South Carolina, 1729-1765* (Kingsport, Tenn.: Southern Publishers, 1940)
HH	*Horry Herald*
IRQ	The *Independent Republic Quarterly*
JL	Francis Asbury, *Journal and Letters*, 3 vols. (Nashville, Tenn.: Abingdon Press, 1958)
LC	Ralph J. Roske and Charles Van Doren, *Lincoln's Commando: The Biography of Commander W. B. Cushing* (New York: Harper & Brothers, 1957)
SLSC	Thomas Cooper and David J. McCord, eds., *The Statutes at Large of South Carolina* (Columbia, S.C., 1837-41)

*Horry County, South Carolina
1730-1993*

1

Wonderful, Rich, *and* Varied

A BRIEF HISTORY OF A BIG COUNTY

As archaeologists interpret the remains of pre-European dwellings, villages, and middens in South Carolina, we are becoming more aware of the early dwellers along this coast. Men and women and their children appeared in this region 10,000 years ago or more. How and why they came we can only guess.

We are not sure that the first Europeans who came here were representatives of Spain, but we are sure that the Spaniards explored the South Carolina coast in the sixteenth century, although the exact track of their passage is in dispute. They discovered a native population at home in an environment they had inhabited for millennia. These Native Americans had a well-developed culture and sophisticated government. The Spaniards enslaved some of them and took them back to the West Indies. One fellow converted to the Catholic religion of his masters and took the name of Francisco Chicora. He told the eager explorers amusing and enticing tales of his homeland, which he called Chicora. Francisco told how his people could create giants out of quite ordinary individuals and of a tribe with stiff tails that forced them to make their seats with holes to accommodate the strange appendages. He also told of rich cities, plentiful gold, and gemstones.

Francisco's mischievous stories created trouble for his tribesmen. Gold-hungry Spaniards came back to the mainland to make further explorations. Native people in their path fell victim to pillaging, to diseases for which they had no immunity, and to captivity as slaves.

Horry County's claim to be in the path of exploration by the Spaniard Lucas Vasquez de Ayllon was made many years ago by Paul Quattlebaum in his *A Land Called Chicora*. Though not trained as a historian (he graduated from Clemson as an engineer), Quattlebaum had the interest and determination to search the archives of Spain for evidence that Ayllon made a journey of exploration from the Cape Fear region south and west along the coast to the mouth of Winyah Bay.

Recent scholarship has argued for a site in the Beaufort area for Ayllon's ill-fated settlement, San Miguel de Gualdape, but geography to some extent still favors Quattlebaum's argument. According to the expedition records, the Spanish ships sailed west from the mouth of the great river they called Jordan, which Quattlebaum assumed to be the Cape Fear River. A look at the map of the North Carolina and South Carolina coast shows that this area accords with that record.

Ayllon also recorded the site of his settlement as the point at which his expedition was hemmed in on either side by bodies of water as winter approached. Although archaeologists who have investigated what is now known as Waccamaw Neck have not found San Miguel, what they have proved is only that they have not found it!

A century and a half later English settlers in the Carolinas found small indigenous tribes of a much less advanced culture. Since these natives have left no written records, we know little about them, except what was observed by the Europeans and Africans who came here. The new settlers seized the natives' land, took the deerskins for export, and played one tribe against the other. Waccamaw, Pee Dee, Winyah, Socastee, Wampee, Waccawache—these names recall the area's pre-European inhabitants. Too soon after the European's arrival, in just one century, they disappeared. William Bull II, writing to the Earl of Hillsboro, November 30, 1770, made this poignant observation: "I cannot quit the Indians without mentioning an observation that has often raised my wonder. That in this Province, settled in 1670 ... Then swarming with tribes of Indians, there remain now, except the few Catawbas, nothing of them but their names, within three hundred miles of our seacoast ... nor any accounting to their extinction by war or pestilence equal to the effect."

The English came, frequently by way of Barbados, to the newly opened lands of the Carolinas. The center of their universe was Charleston, and scant attention was paid to areas too remote to be easily reached from the "Holy City."

Rivers and swamps and bays protected this corner of the wilderness from the first intrusion of settlers. Sixty years passed after the English settled Charles Town, the whole era of the Lords Proprietors, before the government of the province of Carolina turned its attention to this part of the frontier. The first royal governor, Robert Johnson, anxious to secure his borders with settlements, advanced a township scheme in 1730 to encourage interest in remote sections.

Finally in 1732 surveyors were sent to lay out Kingston Township on the Waccamaw River. Knowing that the land would soon be opened to settlers, a party of young men journeyed from Georgetown up the Waccamaw in 1734 to find land they could seek warrants to possess. Accompanied by a "young gentleman" from England (*CGHS,* rpt. *IRQ* 23:1, 8-20), they found their way upriver as far as Bear Bluff. From that point they turned back and camped on the high bluff beside the river where they knew the village seat of Kingston Township would be established. There they killed and barbecued a bear—the first recorded example of this fine old Horry tradition.

In the same year the "young gentleman" made another trip along the coast from Savannah to Wilmington. The lack of settlements along the Grand Strand was notable. He said he saw nothing between Murrells Inlet and Ashe's at Little River. The sand and the sea were here then as now but had not yet attracted people. He visited the source of the Waccamaw River before returning south, retracing his earlier path.

Six years later a man of the cloth came into the same area from the north. The Rev. George Whitefield arrived late in the afternoon on New Year's Day, 1740, in the village at Little River. He found the inhabitants celebrating with fiddling and dancing. The preacher exhorted them to abandon their frivolous ways but met resistance, particularly from one woman who urged the fiddler to keep playing. Nevertheless, his preaching finally resulted in the baptism of a child. Satisfied with this result, the preacher retired. As soon as he closed the door of his room, the fiddles began again. Whitefield spent the night but shook the dust of Little River from his feet the next morning. When his progress along the King's highway led him to the strand, his anger evaporated at the sight of the majestic ocean and the porpoises at play beyond the surf.

The people he found at Little River and the people who settled in the area from the ocean to the Little Pee Dee River were mostly British subjects. Why did they leave their homeland for the wilderness? Perhaps a sense of adventure motivated the bravest among them, but most of them came because they suffered economic and social deprivation at home. They were offered free land in the new world. This was not a hope many of them could have cherished in the lands from which they came. They did not come in organized groups to this isolated area, but as individuals and families. Although they were offered fifty acres for each member of the family, each servant, or each slave, these people, for the most part, had neither servants nor slaves. The hope of land ownership persuaded them, and they sought independence of landlords.

Little River was an early settlement, probably the earliest in the area, almost certainly predating the opening of Kingston Township to settlement. The fact that the young gentleman found hospitality at Ashe's meant that permanent residents were there in 1734. Little River was not so much a village as a vaguely defined community. Kingston village was designated the center of the township but had few inhabitants even in 1757, two decades into settlement and just two decades before the American Revolution. Generally the newcomers did not favor towns. Each family found for itself a likely spot and settled down to create a homestead. A trial deposition provides us with a chance description of the village of Kingston in 1768, less than a decade before the citizens of Charleston sought independence from the British monarch. William Hunter, master of a trading schooner, visited the village on the Waccamaw River and witnessed a remarkable fight. The drama of the deposition he made has been summarized as follows:

> John McDougal was justice of the peace in Kingston and also operated the local tavern. From a vantage point on the piazza of the public house Hunter observed a fierce quarrel develop between McDougal and one Joseph Jordan. A fight accompanied by fierce oaths broke out and horsewhips, swords, and knives came into play. In the course of the long altercation Jordan paused to eat the victuals set before him by the serving wench of the tavern, but the landlord refused him any punch with which to wash down the food. Jordan sent to the nearby house of a Mrs. Wilson for his drink. After this lunch break the fight was resumed, McDougal wounded Jordan, pursued him eighty yards to a smith's shop and there killed him. A Mrs. Gaddis dressed a slight cut in the hand of the justice of the peace. (*ESC*)

Early settlers carved homesteads from the wilderness. Most of them had come from the orderly countryside and structured society of the British Isles. Amid these woods and swamps, they were without any government representatives, without amenities of village or school or pub or church, without extended family, and without the direction of landed gentry, aristocrats, or clergy.

While they didn't have to contend with the Indians for possession of the land, they had little opportunity to study the skills which allowed the native peoples to live off the land. They did learn something of Indian foods and medicines, probably from remnants of the tribes who remained in the area. Many family trees contain Indian ancestors, evidence that not all of the original inhabitants had disappeared from this area.

Consider how great an accomplishment it was for them just to survive and put down roots in this new land. They adapted their skills to new conditions; they changed the land. They cleared small fields, hunted in the woods, fished the streams. They felled trees and built cabins and planted crops. They acquired animals that helped with the work, provided food and clothing, and shared the loneliness of the wilderness. They made clothes by spinning, weaving, and dyeing materials and sewing them by hand. They provided themselves with light by making candles. They doctored themselves with herbs and medicines made from natural substances. They made instruments for music and toys for entertainment. They adapted, invented, and concocted and "made do"—or did without.

Although life was hard, settlers had land and freedom. They raised families and fashioned a rich community life. They looked after each other and traded skills and chores. They didn't have money, but they had food, shelter, friends, work, and entertainment—all of which they provided for themselves.

When the commercial and political leaders of the colonies declared independence of the king and the American Revolution began, there were some who eagerly embraced the cause. When the news of "the shot heard 'round the world" was brought south from Massachusetts by a horseman, Isaac Marion was living at the Boundary House on the border between North and South Carolina. He provided a fresh mount and sent the word on to Georgetown and Charleston.

What happens when one government is rejected and there is none in place to assume responsibility? The Little River Committee of Safety provided an interim government for the region while the state of South Carolina was being organized. Other men in the area did not welcome the change and felt no obligation to join the rebels. Small clashes between local rebels and Tories took place. The engagement which took place at Bear Bluff on April 1, 1781, was doubtless the most important of these.

Those who answered the call of the new nation and went off to fight signed up in the local militia; a few went into units which were later incorporated into the South Carolina and Continental Lines. Those who survived and were still alive in 1820 have left accounts of their service in their applications for military pensions.

The greatest local hero was the "Swamp Fox," Francis Marion, who took control of the campaign against the British in this part of South Carolina after the fall of Charleston. During the campaign of 1780–1781, Marion's guerrilla tactics kept the British forces in the south from joining up with those in the north. The partisan leaders of South Carolina—Marion, Thomas Sumter (the "Gamecock"), and Francis Pickens (the "Fighting Elder")—are credited with harassing and debilitating the British forces and thus ultimately contributing to the surrender of Cornwallis at Yorktown.

The men Marion commanded were well suited to the hit-and-run tactics he employed. They were hunters with woodland skills, who could survive without outside support. They knew the swamps and forest trails. Many, especially those from west of the Pee Dees, had been victimized by the rapacious British officer Colonel Banastre Tarleton and others.

Marion's chief problem was uncertainty that his forces would be available when he needed them. His men signed up for service for terms as short as ninety days, returning home to look after their families and farms between periods of enlistment. He frequently had trouble getting supplies and once shared with a captured British officer a meal that consisted only of sweet potatoes. The wealthy planters of Waccamaw Neck furnished Marion with some provisions, so he doubtless crossed the lower part of Horry time and again. Most of the time he operated on the inland side of the Little Pee Dee. At one point Marion retreated into White Swamp across the line into North Carolina. As summer waned, he learned that Tarleton was raiding again in the Pee Dee. He gathered his men and started back to Williamsburg County. On the way he spent the night, according to his biographers, encamped "under the oaks" at Kingston and then crossed the Little Pee Dee the next day on his way to the Battle of Black Mingo. On Sept. 29, 1780, he defeated the Tories encamped near the Black Mingo Creek, even though the clatter of his horses' hooves on the bridge warned them of his coming.

After the Revolution more settlers began to move into this area. Their motivations probably varied with each individual and family. Many were still in search of free land, now from the hands of the state rather than the royal government. The men who fought in the Revolution were entitled to land grants. Some sought the freedom of a remote area; some no doubt hoped to escape their pasts and make a new start.

The militia for the control and defense of the township recorded eighty-six militiamen and fifty-seven male slaves eligible for service in 1767. The settlement at the village seat was so insignificant that the government (Act No. 1183, passed in 1783) directed commissioners "to lay out the lots in a town in Prince George's parish by the name of Kingston, agreeable to the plan thereof." "Plan" apparently referred to the work of the surveyors Alexander Skene and Justice Robert Wright, who laid out the village in 1732. Neither the map made in 1732 nor the one of 1783 is known to have survived.

Lacking the requisite population base, this remote part of the Georgetown judicial district had never reached parish status under the old royal government. Consequently, the people there never attained self-government during the colonial period; their elections were supervised by officials of the parishes of All Saints and Prince George Winyah. All legal business had to be conducted in Charleston before Act 1263 passed in 1783 finally created the Georgetown Court of Inferior Jurisdiction. This act previewed the eventual breakup of Georgetown Judicial District into Winyah (Georgetown), Liberty (Marion), Williamsburg, and Kingston (Horry) Districts (*SLSC*, 661).

Many came from over the North Carolina line; fewer from the south. Scots overflowed from their settlements in North Carolina. Families who had lived in Virginia and other colonies to the north moved south. It is simply astonishing how many Horry family histories begin "There were three brothers who came to this country from England [Scotland, Wales, or Ireland]. One stayed in the north, one went west and one came south."

In 1785 Robert Conway, a veteran of the Revolution, moved his wife and daughter to the Waccamaw region from Charleston. He obtained grants in and near Kingston, the district seat, and built a home on the waterfront there. Shortly thereafter twins, a boy and a girl, were added to the family. Conway quickly became prominent in the affairs of the area and was elected to represent it in the General Assembly.

Bishop Francis Asbury began to make missionary journeys through this area, crisscrossing the land from end to end and side to side, planting Methodist congregations wherever conditions were favorable. He kept a journal (*JL*) that recorded his texts and kept account of his reception—and in which he often described the countryside and the people. On one occasion he commented, "Cross where you will between these States [North and South Carolina], and it is a miserable pass for one hundred miles west. This country abounds with bays, swamps and drains: If there were no sinners, I would not go along these roads." Dr. Jamie Norton, a Conway Methodist in this century, commented that he didn't know exactly about the sinners, but he had an idea that the saints were pretty widely scattered.

In 1791, the first United States president, George Washington, decided to visit the southern states to cement relationships between them and the young federal government. He traveled without advance parties to prepare for his comfort along the way. He and his small party took their chances with whatever accommodations could be found.

Just above the North Carolina line he spent the night of April 16 with William Gause near Gause's Landing. When he entered South Carolina above Little River, he lunched with James Cochran, a Revolutionary War veteran, and pushed on to the home of Jeremiah Vereen near White Point Swash. He had been told that Vereen, also a Revolutionary War veteran, kept a public house for the accommodation of travelers. Vereen, however, refused payment for lodging and the next morning guided the president's party safely over big Singleton Swash, sending them on toward the wealthy rice plantations of Waccamaw Neck.

As the century turned from eighteenth to nineteenth, this was still a very remote, sparsely populated, poor region whose people spent most of their energies in wresting a livelihood from stream, forest, and a few cleared fields. What they could not get by hunting, fishing, cutting timber, tilling their small cleared plots, and tending some livestock, they did without. Doing without became a way of life.

Formal education was almost nonexistent. Medicine was mostly the province of granny women who delivered the babies and herb doctors who gathered their pharmaceuticals from the woods. Law and other professions were almost absent. The people produced out of materials at hand most of what they needed to exist but created nothing to sell. At the end of the eighteenth century, government and law enforcement were still remote. People lived by a rough code of personal ethics that required a man to keep his word, help his neighbor, and defend his own.

Going to court to record legal documents or to attend trial required a long journey across two major rivers and numerous creeks, swamps, and lakes. Landowners often had had no opportunity to record their claims to the land they had settled on and developed into farmsteads. Crimes committed in the area went unpunished because of the difficulty of getting witnesses to make the arduous trip to Charleston or Georgetown. They had no money to pay the expenses of a stay in town.

As the population of the county grew, the incentives to seek a court of its own grew. When news reached local landowners in 1793 that three Irishmen were seeking from the General Assembly a grant which would overlay one-third of the county, including much land already taken up by settlers, they petitioned the General Assembly for a court of their own. The grant was not allowed, but neither was a court authorized at that time.

Eight years later citizens of the county were better prepared. They signed up in impressive solidarity to renew their petition to the assembly to create a new court district. This time their plea was granted, and the new district was named for Peter Horry, a Revolutionary War officer whom they greatly admired. The courthouse town's name was changed from Kingston to Conwayborough in honor of the chairman of the committee that drafted the act to establish the court. It was signed into law on December 19, 1801. Commissioners appointed under the act were empowered to build a courthouse and jail. They employed William Hemingway to make a new map of the village divided into numbered lots. When these went on sale in 1802–1803, there were eager takers. People who lived in the area and people who were buying for speculative purposes signed up. They didn't always pay, however, and the commissioners had their hands full with collection problems during the next years.

The county maintained a commissioner of locations to oversee land grants. Titles for land that had been taken up in the eighteenth century were finally recorded officially in the deed books. The first federal census in which this district appeared as a separate entity was 1810. At that time 4,349 people, 33 percent of them black, were counted.

The forests had always been generous to the families who depended on their bounty. Wood provided housing and fuel for cooking and warmth. Animals provided skins and food. The waters of the swamps and rivers provided energy for milling, food for the table, and transportation. From the second and third decades of the nineteenth century the woods provided the basis for two great industries which dominated the area for the rest of the century—naval stores and lumber.

Naval stores comprise all the products that are distilled from the gum of the pine tree. Originally the production of tar was important for making ships and boats watertight (hence the name), but in the nineteenth century a whole new surge of industrial development was fueled by turpentine and other products from the pine. The naval stores industry came to the Horry District as the pine forests to the north were depleted. Tapping or scraping the pines to collect gum eventually killed the trees. As each area played out, the industry moved on south, taking with it a large number of migrants and prosperity to those who were enterprising enough to establish themselves as distillers and dealers.

The other was the production of lumber. The magnificent cypress, the pines and the hardwoods of this area were in great demand. Again, prosperity resulting from this industry fell upon the men who owned the sawmills. Neither turpentine nor timber conferred prosperity on the men who labored in the woods gathering the gum or cutting the logs. They were paid generally in tokens imprinted with the name of the issuing company and the value (from one cent to one dollar). Such tokens could only be redeemed in the commissary store owned by the issuer. Both industries were well established by the time the Civil War began.

Horry District had not developed a plantation economy for the production of rice, cotton, or indigo, although each was produced here in small quantities. Not being under the necessity of employing slave labor, it was not, like other low-country districts, a major slaveholding district. Although Horry sent representatives to the Secession Convention and supported in general the idea that a state could withdraw from the voluntary compact known as the United States, there was no great enthusiasm for war here. It was not until their homeland was threatened with Yankee invasion that the men of Horry signed up to fight. There is an old saying that eight hundred men were eligible for service and twelve hundred volunteered.

This time, unlike what happened during the Revolution, men signed up for the duration and were gone from their homes for long periods of time. While Horry was not devastated by battles fought on its land, it was ruined by neglect resulting from the absence of its men. Women and children who had to fend for themselves were often hard put to survive.

As the armies of the South fell apart toward the end, it became apparent to farmers in uniform that defeat was only a matter of time. Horry veterans found opportunities to return to the area. Technically they were deserters and could not openly rejoin their families. They hid in nearby swamps and contributed to the almost total breakdown of civil government and order by raiding nearby farmsteads for food and supplies. Units in which Horry men were enrolled suffered great casualties in battle and in hospitals. There are instances in which three, four, even five men from one family were sacrificed to the war. Many who survived were victims of various physical and emotional injuries that hampered their return to productive lives. They returned to farming, to turpentine and timber production, and to hardship and poverty extending through generations. As the longleaf pine forests began to decline and the naval stores industry began its inevitable southward migration, many of these workers went with it, further depleting the manpower of the county.

Although there was an attempt after the Civil War to restart public education, good schools hardly existed outside Conwayborough and Socastee. In the country, itinerant schoolteachers, some of them barely literate themselves, provided a few weeks of instruction in communities willing to house and pay them. Rough trails penetrated the forests, but transportation was still primarily by river. Cargo had to move on water. The canoes, small schooners, and rafts that plied the Waccamaw and the Little Pee Dee in the first part of the century were joined during the Civil War by paddlewheel steamers.

A few professionals began to establish themselves in the county seat. There was a growing community of doctors, lawyers, and trained ministers, but the opportunity for higher education was available to very few. Conway owed much of its prosperity to the courthouse and the people who were assembled to run the government and the businesses. Politicians gravitated to the county seat, many settling in to swell the number of permanent residents.

The town was a river port with an active waterfront. Through it flowed products of the woods and fields on their way to outside markets. Back through it came the goods bought with the proceeds of their sales. During the latter half of the nineteenth century people migrated into and out of this county. Some established themselves permanently. Some only paused on their way to other frontiers.

The coming of the railroad and telegraph from North Carolina to Conway in 1887 began the process of opening the county to the outside world. Loris became the first town not located on navigable water.

The nineteenth century ended with Horry County men serving in the Spanish American War, but few were gone for more than a few weeks. The naval stores industry, having depleted the pine forests here, began to move on to states farther south and west. Many men uprooted their families to follow the turpentine business to new locations. The great cypress forests of the swamps had been cut over, but there was still sufficient timber to support a forest industry.

Horry farmers were introduced to a new commercial crop, tobacco, which would at last put money in their pockets. For the first time any little farm could produce a cash crop. The farmers could sell it directly and benefit from the infusion of cash into their lives. Early leaders who hoped for profit in growing tobacco and in owning the auction warehouses where it was sold imported men from North Carolina to teach Horry farmers how to grow the crop. At first the local entrepreneurs who built the warehouses needed experienced men to run them and recruited men from North Carolina and Virginia. Auction markets sprang up in Conway, Loris, and Aynor. As the years passed, tobacco brought an unprecedented prosperity to the county, and these towns took on new vigor in the fall selling season.

Little railroads sprang up in every direction, primarily in support of the timber industry. The logging companies built tram roads through the woods to get their product out to the mills. The major transportation routes remained the rivers, however, until the 1920s, when road improvement became a statewide policy and bridges across the rivers began to connect Horry County to the outside world. One railroad line was built from Conway to the coast by the Burroughs and Collins Company. A settlement appeared there, which was first called New Town and then named Myrtle Beach for the wax myrtle, a native shrub that grows stubbornly and abundantly all over the county. A rail line from Conway west eventually resulted in the birth of the little town of Aynor.

The automobile came to Horry County about 1905. Among the first owners were doctors, who had been making house calls along rough roads in the country on horseback or in buggies. Now they could get about more rapidly in horseless carriages. Gradually the gasoline engine came to the farms, too. What the people needed now was better roads.

The land along the coast had supported some fisheries and small farms, but it was generally regarded as poor and unproductive. When its potential as a tourist attraction became apparent to the Woodside brothers of Greenville, they purchased a large tract from the Myrtle Beach Farms Company in 1926 to establish a resort. They built the famous "million dollar" Ocean Forest Hotel, which opened in 1930, and the first golf course, now Pine Lakes International. Although this first attempt at tourism failed during the Depression, awareness of the area would not go away, and development began slowly.

The assassination of a royal duke in Europe resulted in the "Great War to end war." Men from Horry, descendants of ancestors who had come from the British Isles and Europe, returned there to make the world safe for democracy. Most had never been away from home before they answered the draft.

After the war new professionals appeared on the scene ready to help the people of Horry improve their standard of living. Clemson College (now University) trained extension agents and vocational agriculture teachers for each county. They helped farmers improve the land and foster its productivity. They introduced new breeding stock to improve their hogs and cattle and new seeds to produce better crops.

Horry's first hospital was established in Conway by Dr. Homer H. Burroughs in 1913 and went out of business when he became disabled in

1922. A modern hospital was established in 1936 and began to attract a strong medical community. Public health nurses vaccinated schoolchildren against contagious diseases, taught midwives how to save mothers and children, and urged people to adopt good hygiene and safe food practices.

Adult education also began to lower the illiteracy rate in the county and offered a second chance for those willing to learn. Inspired by Miss Wil Lou Gray, who headed the state program, local leaders established classes and recruited students.

The Great Depression caused fewer hardships here than elsewhere. The people were scarcely a generation away from a barter economy, and they simply went back to their old ways. Most had food and shelter, though for everything else "make do" was again the order of the times. As the Depression began to lift, Horry County had more people, more business, more contact with the outside world. The Horry Electric Cooperative, which was formed in 1940, strung lines all over the county, bringing electric lights and modern appliances to the farm. Human resources improved as its educational system developed. Schools were consolidated; teachers were better trained.

Progress was interrupted by World War II. Again men left home and were forever changed by their experiences. Those who returned picked up the pieces and began to fashion a new Horry County. The Grand Strand became the engine that drove the economy of the county.

At the beginning of the Civil War era, the 1860 population, black and white, numbered 7,962. In 1960 the population of Horry County was 68,247. Horry County was beginning to be aware of the civil rights movement. Big money was becoming interested in Myrtle Beach, and major construction was about to begin. Tobacco was still king, but even then the industry was threatened by growing health consciousness across the nation. The Legislative Delegation was the final authority for the operation of local government. James P. Stevens of Loris served as senator with the "ABC" House Delegation—Eugene Altman, Lloyd Bell, and Robert Carter. None of them were from Conway, a break from traditional politics.

Coastal Carolina Junior College, a two-year institution, was a dream brought to birth in 1954 by a group of farsighted men in the professional and business community. It was under the aegis of the College of Charleston for three years. In the last year of its contract with the Charleston school, it was faced with the prospect of independence without the funding necessary to survive. A black junior college, Eastern Carolina Junior College, established about the same time at the old Whittemore High School had to close for the same reason. The drive to achieve fiscal stability for Coastal Carolina began with a referendum. The staff of the college joined with the founders to become a speakers bureau. Someone was ready to speak enthusiastically on behalf of the four mill tax levy any time three people would hold still to listen. Obviously the people of Horry County felt the same way, for they passed the levy with an eloquent majority. At the same time two major state-supported institutions began aggressive drives to establish branches around the state. Eventually the question of accreditation led the Horry County Higher Education Commission to turn the academic future of the college over to the University of South Carolina.

In 1960 the Legislative Delegation established the Horry County Development Board in the hope of increasing the industrial segment of the economy. This has been from the beginning an uphill battle, since the county lacked the necessary infrastructure to attract major plants. Geography was a factor because Horry County sits beside the ocean, automatically halving a manufacturer's potential marketing area. The county lacked the air, rail, and highway transport to offset this difficulty. It also lacked a labor force trained for industry. Its unskilled labor, though much in demand for the tourist industry and agriculture, had no experience on the production line. One needle plant operator in the 1960s bemoaned the tendency of his workers to take off on a fine day to go fishing. He had no complaint about the willingness or the good nature of his employees, but he failed to comprehend that a crop to be put in or to be harvested or a day on the river had priority over showing up for "public work." It took another all-out effort to mold a labor force capable of attracting industrial prospects. As they had with Coastal Carolina a decade earlier, the business and political leadership set out to obtain a technical school. Senator Ernest "Fritz" Hollings likes to tell about his achievement in establishing the network of technical education centers around South Carolina.

Former state senator James Stevens led Horry County's fight for a place in that system. Conway was not one of the sites in the state plan as originally conceived. Horry County leaders "camped" on the doorstep of the State Technical Education Commission, employing persuasion and political heft to get the state to agree to putting one of the schools there. They pledged the resources of county government to underwrite the school until it reached the minimum student population demanded by the state. Horry-Georgetown Technical College (as it is now called) developed a curriculum sensitive to the local economy and has never slowed down.

Wonderful, Rich, *and* Varied

In the decade of the sixties the population of Horry County grew only by 1,751, a figure which certainly did not alert people to the phenomenon of the 1970s. The potential for tourism began to attract all kinds of investments and with them the people to finance, build, manage, and provide service to this industry.

Then came national awareness of the "Sun Belt," and thousands of retirees turned their faces south. Horry County became a Mecca for those who looked for lower taxes, a relaxed lifestyle, and year-round temperate weather. The newcomers affected the life of the community with a tenacious energy that has brought changes in its social, religious, economic, and political institutions. Many of them are well educated and financially secure and have the leisure and the inclination to participate fully in local affairs. Although their coming has produced considerable strain on long-standing institutions, they have for the most part contributed to making them work.

County government has been severely strained to provide necessary services, an effort complicated by a historic change in the form of government itself. Before 1976 the county had been governed by a board of commissioners appointed by and subject to the will of the elected County Legislative Delegation. The senator was the final arbiter of all governmental decisions by virtue of his ability to lock up legislation as it moved from the House to the Senate.

This system fell to the civil rights movement that demanded one-man, one-vote representation at all levels of government. New rules eventually caused the state to be districted so that not every county had a resident senator and House districts tended to overlap county boundaries. When it became clear that internal county decisions might be in the hands of non-residents, the old form was doomed. In 1976 the General Assembly passed the Home Rule Act.

Horry County chose a council-administrator form of government. The years since have seen a continuing effort to make the government efficient and responsive—with indifferent results. The concentration of power under the old system vanished almost overnight. Elected and appointed officials alike have been trying ever since to put together sufficient coalitions of power to make home rule work.

The early years were marked by constant judicial and federal regulatory oversight. There were times when no one was sure that the local government was seated legally. Disputes nearly always ended up in court. Horry County gained the reputation for plowing new ground in the courts as home rule took form and substance. In the old days the Legislative Delegation had been assisted in the management of county functions by such elected officials as the clerk of court, treasurer, and auditor and by bodies of laypersons appointed by the delegation "provided that the Senator was a member of the majority." Most commissions had legislative mandates—that is, they were created by law passed in the General Assembly. Subject to the will and veto power of the delegation, to say nothing of its budget control, the members exercised considerable responsibility and discretion in managing various functions of government.

The public library system had a commission. So did the county police, the college, and the tech school. The system at its best broadened the leadership base, taking advantage of the experience, knowledge, and drive of individuals for the public good, and helped to defuse criticism of government by the population at large. The system was highly political. As one member of the House used to say, "We sure aren't going to appoint anyone who isn't a friend."

Under home rule the county council gradually exercised its option to dismiss all these bodies, though it has sometimes found it expedient to replace them with advisory groups in which each councilman has the right to appoint one member. It would be silly to suggest that this system is any less political than the old. Few of these groups have any power beyond that of making recommendations to the council for action.

One of the lingering problems of home rule is the tendency of elected council members to forget that their function is to make policy through ordinances and shape those policies through the budget process. Instead, they involve themselves in day-to-day operations and take on more and more of the functions that the law reserves to the professional administrator. This confuses and stultifies employees and results in poor morale and diminished efficiency.

The unresolved problems of home rule, gray areas that the legislation did not address, has caused untold tension within the government. The relationship of the council to the elected officials is but one case in point. Continued uncertainty about the limits and nature of its authority has come close at times to paralyzing the council. This transition unfortunately has coincided with the stress caused by population growth, the expanding tourist economy, and the uncertain future of agriculture as farmers contemplate the loss of tobacco as their chief crop.

Other factors also have created problems. Consider the growing tendency of the media to adopt an adversarial attitude toward government—matched, to be sure, by an opposing tendency of elected bodies to mistrust the media. Or take the cavalier way in which the General Assembly mandates locally funded programs without providing the financial means to implement them, leaving local government to pick up the tab. Or notice a growing tendency of the judiciary to mandate county action. The most obvious result, of course, is that council tends to be more reactive than creative, following mandates rather than planning for orderly overall development.

As much of Horry County's traditional way of life is being lost to or modified by the changes in the population and the economy, its past is becoming more precious to both the government and individuals. An awakening awareness of the value of preserving the past has resulted in the work of the Horry County Historical Society, in the establishment of the Horry County Museum and a government commission to oversee preservation and restoration as part of the planning and zoning function of county government, and, visibly, in the restoration of the Burroughs School. Conway's partnership of city government and business in the restoration of the downtown area is another encouraging sign.

There is also much more interest in preserving and safeguarding natural resources and reserving areas which can be studied and enjoyed by future generations. The establishment of the Vereen Gardens near Little River will preserve an estuarine ecology, and the Playcard Environmental Education Center will make available to students and public alike the remarkable variety of a black-water swamp. Two areas containing Carolina bays and large sections of the Waccamaw and Little Pee Dee River swamps are reserved.

Zoning is an elusive goal at the county level. Land near the coast is effectively controlled, but in the western rural area it is not. By consolidating water and sewer authorities of the unincorporated areas of the county, the council has laid the groundwork for the necessary infrastructure in the western and northern portions of the county, which have lagged behind the tourist-oriented coast.

There have been intermittent efforts to provide drama, music, and art over the years. The establishment of the Theater of the Republic was a watershed event, particularly in Conway. New residents have provided considerable stimulus to establish concert programs, dramatic performances, art exhibits, and writers' groups, finally resulting in the Horry Cultural Arts Council to encourage and coordinate the arts. On almost any day the person who wishes to attend a cultural event can find one, and such entertainment overshadows even beach activities along the coast. Dare one mention in the next breath the flourishing folk culture represented by the Loris Bog-Off, the Aynor Hoe-down, the Little River Blue Crab Festival, Afro-Fest at Coastal Carolina University, and Myrtle Beach's Sun Fun?

Old Horry hands may look back with some nostalgia to the Horry County in which they grew up, but few would return to those times. Optimism for the future lies in the vigor of the people who live there and their ability to cope. The county has much more variety and provides more attractive alternatives for earning a living and for leisure than ever before. Nobody promises the future will be easy, or that there won't be mistakes along the way, but surely its people will find it possible to keep Horry County a good place in which to live and work.

MIND THE H! A SONG OF OURSELVES

Newcomers, whether they come as vacationers or take up permanent residence, have trouble with the name of our county. Mostly they edge up to it carefully, fearful lest they give offense by pronouncing it just the way it looks. Or, they avoid uttering the name altogether.

It's the fault of those French! Within ten years of the settlement of Charleston, "where the Ashley and Cooper Rivers flow together to form the Atlantic Ocean," French Huguenots had begun to appear in the colony. Some came directly, some after sojourns in other countries. A colony which welcomed all religions drew these persecuted Protestants to this new land. By 1700, thirty years into South Carolina history, they comprised 12 percent of the white population.

The Calvinist Huguenots soon melded into the dominant Church of England (Episcopal), their clergy making the transition easily once they had mastered English. Educated, industrious, and ambitious, with a tradition in the trades and commerce which the colony needed, they were acceptable as marriage partners with the British majority. Gradually they spread out of Charleston into other areas, most notably along the Santee River. So many settled there that its south branch became known as the French Santee.

Not many of them came to the remote area which is present-day Horry County. One prominent exception is the Vereen family, who came early to the north coastal area and became prominent in the affairs of Little River and nearby areas. It was a fourth-generation Jeremiah Vereen (originally Varin) who welcomed President Washington and provided him shelter for an April night in 1791.

It is, therefore, somewhat remarkable that this county took its name from a Georgetown planter of Huguenot descent. When South Carolina declared war on the English monarch, Peter Horry and his brother Hugh joined Francis Marion. Col. Peter Horry became one of Marion's most trusted officers and commanded from time to time men from this area. After the war his journal, adapted by the famous Parson Weems, became the first biography of Marion and spread the fame of the "Swamp Fox" across the new country.

Horry never lived in this area, but was regarded as a great Revolutionary hero by the people. When they sought a courthouse district in 1801, they asked in their petition that it be named for him.

Even though the Huguenots themselves assimilated, there were still their names, which English tongues found difficult. The British had some pretty funny pronunciations of their own, but they gradually forced French names into shapes acceptable to them. The process continued into the post-Civil War era as freedmen chose their surnames, and spelling was generally simplified. Manigault, for example, is now sometimes spelled Manigo—which is approximately the way the French would be pronounced. We who live in the county named for Horry drop the H and stress both syllables. Along with names we have inherited from the Native Americans, Germans, and other groups, the Huguenot names are the subject of an amusing small book which may be recommended as a help to the uninitiated: *Correct Mispronunciations of Some South Carolina Names* (University of South Carolina Press, 1983), by Claude Henry and Irene Neuffer, a husband and wife team.

In Loris schools in the 1930s students were taught a little bit of doggerel to help them remember. As far as can be determined, Loris was the only place this was done, but there it was a frequent part of the daily assembly programs. Two verses and a refrain were sung to the tune of "Yankee Doodle" and went like this:

> There is a great big county
> In eastern South Carolina,
> And those too ignorant to know better
> Think that it is Horrie.
> Refrain:
> Oree, Oree, you're the stuff,
> It's Oree, it's not Horrie.
> Mind the H and don't pronounce it,
> Horry folks dislike it.
>
> Now, if you still call Oree Horrie,
> You must surely rue it.

> For there are those who know what's right
> And they'll think you unschoolly.
> (Repeat Refrain)

WHATEVER HAPPENED TO HUGERBOROUGH?

In 1734, a young English gentleman came up the Waccamaw River from Georgetown with a party of young men who were looking over the land with an eye to claiming prize parcels for themselves. They were aware that a township named Kingston had been laid out and that it would soon be opened for settlement. In 1730 Robert Johnson, royal governor of the province the Crown had recouped from the Lords Proprietors, had authorized townships on rivers of South Carolina from the Savannah to the North Carolina line. Surveyors were given specific instructions to locate them 100 miles from the first city. The township on the Waccamaw was laid out in 1732 by Alexander Skene and Justice Robert Wright. Now the stage was set to allow settlers to claim the promised free land.

The townships were designed to be a defense perimeter to safeguard Charlestown against the incursions of Spaniards and Indians, to further economic development, and to insure the dispersal of immigrants who were arriving in Charleston in ever greater numbers. Since planters were enlarging their rice fields and importing more and more slaves to cultivate them, it became important to encourage the immigration of white settlers to keep a safe balance between slave and free inhabitants. Encouragement was given to "poor white Protestants," who received land grants amounting to 50 acres each for every member of a family, including slaves and indentured servants. The government furnished modest supplies and free transportation to a township. When Kingston Township and its village seat were opened to settlement in 1735, there was no rush to occupy so remote a place. Families and individuals came to the area and settled in, but one estimate based on militia strength indicated there were probably not more than four hundred or so living in the township thirty years after it had been opened to settlers.

A trader who visited Kingston's river port in 1767 was required to give a deposition about a duel he witnessed there in which two men fought to the death of one. In describing the scene he mentioned perhaps a half dozen buildings clustered within sight of the wharves, two offering refreshment to wayfarers and one a smithy. After the Revolution more settlers were brought to the township by state grants. In 1801 Bishop Francis Asbury wrote that he preached to about one hundred persons in the village, "including the colored." Even in 1825, nine decades after the land was opened to settlers, Robert Mills reported the village had only about "twenty or twenty-five houses."

Increasing population and the distance from a courthouse which could record documents and impose order compelled local inhabitants to seek a court district of their own in 1793. They claimed the village of Kingston had certain features which recommended it as a courthouse town: it was on a navigable river, lots had been reserved for public buildings, and the site was altogether "most suitable." The appeal failed. Seven years later they sent petitions stressing growing lawlessness and the hardships imposed on them by the lack of a court sitting nearer than Georgetown. Nearly all adult males signed the petition, a virtual roll of the white adult male property owners at the time.

The drafters asked the state legislature to name the judicial district for Peter Horry, a Georgetown native of Huguenot descent, trusted colonel under Francis Marion in the Revolution and later brigadier general of the local militia. They asked that the district seat be renamed Hugerborough. The Hugers, who were of Huguenot descent, were prominent as planters, politicians, and Revolutionary heroes. The Marquis de Lafayette and the Baron de Kalb came to the home of Benjamin Huger when they landed on North Island in 1777. The Huger family was distinguished by several prominent members. As a student making the grand tour of Europe, Francis Kinloch Huger and a friend are said to have attempted to rescue Lafayette from prison. It may have been this bit of daring that excited the admiration of the signers of the 1801 petitions for a separate judicial district.

The petitions were assigned to a committee of representatives who were expected to render a favorable judgment. It was headed by Col. Robert Conway, himself a hero of the Revolution, who also had fought under Marion. The other members were John Nesmith of Georgetown and Erasmus Rothmaler of Prince George Winyah Parish. They found merit in the petitions and asked permission to draft a bill. Legislation in those days moved rapidly. A bill was reported out of committee, passed by the House of Representatives on December 17, 1801, sent to the Senate, passed and signed into law on December 19, 1801.

Too late the inhabitants of the new Horry District learned that the village had been renamed Conwayborough. Although Robert Conway was a popular and prominent local figure who had been several times elected to the General Assembly, news that the village would bear his name was not welcome to all at home. A second attempt to have the village named

Hugerborough failed the next year. Conwayborough it remained until 1883, when the General Assembly shortened the name to Conway, which had already been adopted by the Post Office. Unofficially the people had long since shortened it to Conwayboro and almost universally spoke of it as the 'Borough.

HORRY COUNTY COURTHOUSES

A courthouse has its own mystique, an aura no other building in the jurisdiction shares. It is a symbol of government, law, justice—the best of American traditions. Despite or perhaps because of its special functions, power struggles swirl about it. Political battles and personal ambitions gravitate to it. It draws those who want to serve and those who want to be served. Courthouse gossip can propel or destroy careers.

To make a court more accessible to the remote northeastern corner of South Carolina, the General Assembly at the request of the people established the Horry District in December 1801. The inhabitants had petitioned to gain relief from hardships suffered traveling to court in Georgetown. The enabling legislation appointed commissioners to see to the construction of the courthouse and a gaol, so necessary to the administration of justice.

The commissioners met initially on January 30, 1802, about six weeks after passage of the act. Samuel Floyd Jr., Samuel Foxworth, William Williams, John Graham Sr., Thomas Fearwell, and Robert Conway named Col. Thomas Livingstone chairman. Construction of the courthouse and gaol required a new survey of local land holdings. Two previous surveys had been done—one in 1732, preliminary to the establishment of the old Kingston Township and village, and one in 1783, prior to the establishment of a court. The commissioners ordered Thomas Fearwell and William Hemingway to resurvey the old metes [boundaries] of the village, then to designate lots. Fearwell and Hemingway produced the new survey as directed. Hemingway's signature is on this map, which is preserved at Conway City Hall.

The board agreed to reconvene the first Monday in March; however, the meeting actually took place somewhat later, on March 22. Although the Fearwell-Hemingway survey was still incomplete, the commissioners contracted the next day, March 23, with Richard Green Sr. And William Snow to build a courthouse and gaol on Fifth Avenue for five thousand dollars. They demanded that the contractor provide a ten-thousand-dollar bond and scheduled two payments to him during construction, the final two thousand dollars to be paid on their acceptance of the buildings. Subsequently, the board replaced Fearwell with Josiah Lewis. It declared the surveyors would be paid from the sale of lots. Since selling could not begin without a completed survey, the board obviously hoped to speed completion. Further, it had discovered a grant of 223 acres to Robert Conway on July 2, 1787. His land occupied the heart of the village! The commissioners bought that acreage on August 6, 1802.

The Board of Commissioners wanted a two-story wooden courthouse, 28 by 36 feet, set on brick pillars. The hip roof was to be covered with 21-inch, heart-of-cypress shingles. Further specifications for materials and embellishments indicated their intent that the buildings should be "of as good materials as the Court House in Marion District and finished in as Workmanlike manner." This last stipulation would prove critical. The jail, 30 by 36 feet, was to be made of brick with great attention to security. No pictures of either are on record.

Deadlines passed unmet. Court convened first in 1803, but apparently not in the new courthouse. The commissioners' side of the developing controversy is on record, but not a word of Green's side. Snow, Green's partner, apparently had dropped from their project. Seven years passed. On August 11, 1810, the board (now comprised of commissioners Livingston, Conway, Fearwell, Hemingway, Henry Durant, and Anthony Pawley) ordered their clerk to write Green regarding whether he had completed the buildings "according to contract" and to ask that he attend the board meeting on October 1, either to deliver the completed buildings to them or show cause why not. Minutes for that meeting do not mention Green, suggesting he did not attend.

More than two years later, on January 23, 1813, the board indicated a loss of patience. It summoned Green to appear on the fourth Monday of February. The record continues that in February they ordered him to appear prior to April 1 to put right what "has not been done in a workmanlike manner." They threatened to put his bond to suit and finally did so a year and a half later. The quality of construction continued in dispute. In the fall of 1815, the board sent James G. Cochran and John Dunn to inspect the courthouse and gaol in Marion District, then to inspect the Horry District buildings and report their findings.

Richard Singleton hosted commissioners Edward Conner, Robert Conway, Silvius Sweet, and John Dicks at his home on February 3, 1817. They accepted from Green a note for $165 in satisfaction of his contract originally negotiated in 1802. Green paid $35 down and agreed to pay costs of the suit. At the same meeting, they gave Richard Singleton a charge to maintain the public buildings. The first courthouse and the gaol were never satisfactory.

When the state appropriated ten thousand dollars for a new building in 1823, it reactivated the commission. Having agreed the first wooden building would no longer serve, the Commissioners of Public Buildings began to contract for the construction of a much larger, finer facility. Commissioners A. W. McRae, John Servis (Sarvis), William Johnston, Benjamin Gause Jr., and Sam Willson received four bids: "Thompson—$8000.00, Woodbery—9400.00, Tart—8400.00, [and] Warren—9500.00 acceptd." They let the contract to Russell Warren of Georgetown, contractor for the courthouse of Georgetown District. His was the highest bid. After their experience with the first courthouse, they evidently felt him to be the one most likely to meet his obligations. The accompanying jail was built later for eight thousand dollars.

Russell Warren signed the contract on April 24, 1824. Lot number 31, a prime site at the corner of Main Street and Third Avenue, became available from Joshua S. Norman and his much-respected wife, later universally called "Aunt Jane." Warren, as contractor, worked from sketches and gained specific permission to alter the staircases and portico. His construction follows a design by Robert Mills, commissioner of public buildings for South Carolina at the time of its construction. Documentary proof includes the specifications and correspondence with Mills. Specialists have included the design in a catalog of his works in this state.

A native of Charleston, Robert Mills had achieved success beyond the boundaries of South Carolina. Said to be the first American-trained architect, he studied under Thomas Jefferson at Monticello. Mills had many commissions before returning to South Carolina. Among his most famous are the Washington Monument and the old Treasury Building in the District of Columbia and the Fireproof Building in Charleston. He designed many courthouses and gaols for the state's ambitious program of public building. South Carolina is fortunate that many have survived. Mills specialists now generally recognize the Conway structure to be the finest historic building in Horry County.

Mills believed public buildings should be fireproof and designed the downstairs level of his courthouses accordingly. The walls in the Horry County courthouse, for example, are 30 inches thick. Records show instances of fires destroying the courtroom level of one of his buildings but failing to burn areas where documents were stored.

In contrast to the delay surrounding the construction of the first courthouse, Russell Warren delivered the second courthouse on time and apparently to an entirely satisfied board. The board made final payment to Warren's attorney when the building was turned over March 2, 1825, more than two months in advance of the May 15, 1825, deadline stipulated in the contract.

For the time and the place, the courthouse was imposing. Its two-story brick splendor dominated a river port village consisting of twenty-five or so wooden homes, a few store buildings, and about one hundred inhabitants. The outside stairs leading to the courtroom, the massive columns of the portico, the porch from which the court crier called the people to the spectacle of the law in action, the enormous arched hallway downstairs where the county officers worked—all bespoke the authority of law to a region still remote and rough. When the courthouse opened for use in April 1825, Horry's population was still sparse—just over 5,000 in 1820 and fewer than 25,000 in 1900—roughly that period served by this courthouse. County government was small. Most of the elected officers were able to run their offices by themselves, some of them part time.

Gaol construction went less auspiciously. The commissioners awarded the contract for eight thousand dollars to Capt. Henry Durant, who now included as partner his nephew John Wesley Durant. Determining just when the gaol was completed is difficult. The minutes of meetings in subsequent years disclose considerable bickering. At one point, the commissioners resolved that if Durant drew the whole sum, he must also construct a kitchen for the gaol. A kitchen, like the "necessary" (outdoor toilet), would at that time have been apart from the principal building.

By the turn of the twentieth century, it was clear that county government needed a new facility. Noisy log trains ran just outside along Main Street in downtown Conway. The noise disrupted court proceedings. Moreover, the old building apparently did not receive proper care. In a notable editorial in the *Horry Herald*, the editor wrote:

Cows on the Public Square

Officers at the court house [*sic*] have complained a good deal lately about stray cattle spending the night on the public square. It is stated as a fact that it is no uncommon thing for cows to sleep in the corridor at the courthouse. The county officers are obligated to have the corridor cleaned up quite often and sometimes it is no small job. We mention these facts here for a double purpose.

1st We wish those who allow their cattle to wander about at night to discontinue the practice.

2nd We wish to bring the matter to the attention of the proper authorities so that they may investigate and act accordingly. Our court house is not what it might be in size and elegance, but it is entirely possible to keep it clean and decent.

These buildings on Main Street served a growing population until 1908, when the present courthouse facing Third Avenue was occupied. The Hon. Jeremiah Smith, then mayor of Conway, arranged for the city to purchase the building for four thousand dollars. H. H. Woodward bought the gaol and "renovated" it into the Grace Hotel, named for his wife. Unfortunately, the old gaol no longer exists. The courthouse still serves as administrative headquarters for the city, and its courtroom still functions as city council's chambers as well as for court proceedings. The present role of the 1825 structure exemplifies adaptive use of historic buildings. The National Register of Historic Buildings recognizes this edifice, which is the keystone of Conway's historic district.

In 1906, after considerable discussion and negotiations, the county purchased from W. R. "Bill" Lewis a whole city square two blocks away. An editorial in the *Herald* at the time suggested that it might affect the business district adversely to divide it and put the courthouse "in the suburbs."

The third courthouse sits on a square surrounded by Third Avenue, Beaty Street, Second Avenue, and Elm Street. Col. D. A. Spivey introduced a bill in the General Assembly on February 17, 1906, which authorized its construction. Colonel C. P. Quattlebaum, John C. Spivey, and John P. Derham were named to the building committee, and the county commission sold the $40,000 bonds authorized for $40,706.60. H. P. Little of Conway won the contract for construction of the courthouse ($24,950.40). The Pauley Jail Company of Washington, D.C., won the contract for the jail ($9,400). Extra work on both buildings cost an additional $356, but in the end the county had more than $5,000 left over for bridges.

Construction, begun in October 1906, was completed about January 1, 1908. As described in the newspaper account of the dedication festivities, the courthouse was 81 by 70 feet with eleven large rooms besides the main courtroom, which was 43 by 70 feet. An all-day celebration on May 22, 1908, featured a parade and band concert, politicians (including Governor M. F. Ansel), a picnic, barbecue, reception, and baseball game.

The courthouse was renovated in 1927, in 1964, and in 1982-1983. The second renovation increased the available space by adding extensions on each side of the main building.

Longtime clerk of court W. L. Bryan did much of the early planting of the square, aided later by the garden clubs under the guidance of Mrs. J. T. Rutledge and still later by F. W. "Woody" Medlen when he was tax collector. Beautiful at any time of the year, the square is pretty as a picture when the dogwoods and azaleas bloom in the spring. The large magnolia on the Third Avenue side of the square is transformed in December into the community Christmas tree. County employees make ornaments out of "found" materials, such as plastic cups. Each year as the tree grows, it requires more ornaments as well as the replacements of those that wear out.

Just inside the front entrance of the building is a portrait of Brig. Gen. Peter Horry, for whom the county is named. John Szekes (pronounced *say-cash*) painted it from a miniature handed down in Horry's wife's family, the Guignards of Columbia. The Peter Horry Chapter, Daughters of the American Revolution, presented the portrait to the people of the county in 1976. A historic marker on the Third Avenue side of the square commemorates Horry and the foundation of the county.

Horry County has outgrown its third courthouse, which still houses the offices of judges, the sheriff, the solicitor, the probate court, and the master in equity, as well as the congressman of this district. Of necessity, many offices formerly located in the courthouse have been moved to other quarters. Even so, the courts are forced to use other space around Conway. County council is under pressure to build more courtroom space. A new facility has been in the planning stages for several years, but council still must face the question of what to do with this historic third courthouse.

THAT DAMNED INDEPENDENT REPUBLIC: A NICKNAME IS CONFERRED

Entirely separated from the rest of South Carolina (except Waccamaw Neck) by the Lumber, Little Pee Dee, and Great Pee Dee Rivers and their swamps, Horry County was left out of the mainstream of South Carolina political life until the coming of good roads, bridges, and modern communication systems in the twentieth century.

Its people developed a distinctive lifestyle and characteristic temperament. Citizens of Horry County tended to be independent in their views and their actions; fiercely devoted to their land, their community, and their churches. They were undereducated and poor. A man's word and a handshake were more binding than the most carefully drawn contract. Wary of the law and of officials, the people tended to settle their differences according to rough frontier principles.

As conflicts built which finally resulted in the Civil War, the people of Horry, most of whom owned no slaves, could not be counted on to support those who did have an economic stake in slavery. At some time before the Civil War, probably during the period of controversy over nullification, the county was derisively nicknamed "That Damned Independent Republic."

It is impossible to say just when the nickname was first applied, but by 1856 it was already in common usage. In that year Joseph Travis Walsh, who was to become one of the district's most distinguished citizens, came to Conway to practice law. Years later he said in his memoirs that Judge Munro advised him, "Go to Conway, Joseph. I lived with its people many years of my life, made a good living, and found them, though poor and primitive, as true as steel." Walsh married Mary Jane Congdon, whom he described as a great-niece of Col. James Beaty, "the King of Horry, which was called the Republic"—a contradictory title, to be sure.

Horry County provided three signatories to the Ordinance of Secession, passed in December 1860 though sentiment was divided about the impending conflict. Once the die was cast at Fort Sumter, however, the people of Horry were solidly behind their state in the defense of their land. They fought in Georgia, Mississippi, Tennessee, and Virginia.

Horry County was more isolated, more "independent," and more turned inward than ever after the war. Aside from work in the woods in the lumber and naval stores industries, there was little to do to earn a better living than the subsistence gained from their small farms. A few fortunes were eventually based on these industries, but the average worker was paid in tokens and almost never had money in the pocket of his overalls.

The financial tide did not turn until the introduction of tobacco culture in the last decade of the nineteenth century. The people of Horry had always practiced frugality, so however hard the Depression in the 1930s was, most of them had shelter and could provide themselves with food. They returned in large measure to the barter economy of earlier days. In these respects they fared better than people in many other places.

In 1941, the Writers Program of the Works Progress Administration published *South Carolina, a Guide to the Palmetto State*. Describing the county and its people, the writer said, "they developed a spirit of independence that is today a powerful factor in their success with new crops. Horryites are among the rare folk who deliberately live within their means.

A house may be built one room at a time, but the owner-occupants are happily secure because that one room is paid for."

We have come a long way from the mid-1890s, when our per capita income was said to be $2.50. Wealth made from the land and its products and the exploitation of the seashore have all but erased the memory of those days and the way the people of Horry lived until decades into this century. Changing economic fortunes have eventually eroded our characteristic independence—but slowly and far from completely. Despite all the conveniences of modern life and the improvements that have come with our changing fortunes, Horry County is still "the Independent Republic of Horry." The county seal proclaims it proudly.

NATURAL HISTORY

Originally this land of Horry was adjacent to the continent of Africa, 20 degrees below the equator. The Atlantic Ocean did not exist. Over time the land parted, and this portion drifted north. The ocean appeared. Our land is part of the bed of an ocean that reached as far as the Appalachians by some accounts. Usually the Fall Line through central South Carolina is considered to be the ancient shore. Bedrock, or basement rock, is 1,200 feet down.

The old barrier islands are the high ground in Horry County; behind and between them are ancient marshes. The Waccamaw River was probably formed from these marshes and the creeks that ran through them. The Pee Dee probably drained into the ocean at Murrells Inlet.

The Intracoastal Waterway, of course, did not exist. When it was cut through the high ground from Little River to Socastee Creek, fossils of ancient horses, sloths, and mammoths as well as those of marine creatures were found, enabling us to learn more about our geological history.

Communities often took their names from the nearest swamps: Maple, Brown, Playcard, Lake Swamp, Cartwheel, Pleasant Meadow, and Simpson Creek, for example. Old roads tended to run along the high ground on either side of waterways—swamps, rivers, etc. Where small branches ran across the roadway, travelers forded them or built small bridges.

In Horry County people traditionally have hedged their promises by saying, "The Good Lord willing and the crick don't rise," both being circumstances over which they had no control. Swamps were formidable barriers to commerce, agriculture, social, and cultural activities. During times of high water, or freshets, communities were isolated. People caught away from home by death were buried where they fell if the water was too high to transport the bodies to their family burial grounds.

Swamps provided shelter for the patriots during the Revolution. The guerrilla warfare perfected by Francis Marion depended upon the ability of his men to appear quickly from the swamps to ambush the enemy and then to disappear just as quickly into their shelter. Civil War deserters hid out in them until it was safe to return home. Gene Anderson, former president of the Horry County Historical Society, tells a story about the officer who went into a swamp after a man, found him, and then lost his way bringing the prisoner out. The arrested man offered to lead the officer safely out of the swamp in exchange for his freedom.

The Waccamaw is Horry County's own river, a black water stream that rises in Lake Waccamaw not far over the line in North Carolina. Almost its entire length lies within this county. Waccamaw swamp water is colored by the tannin in tree roots and other vegetation through which it flows. Although it looks black and visibility in it is very limited, if you hold up a glassful of it, it has the color of strong tea, or—if you prefer—of good bourbon. The Lumber and the Little Pee Dee Rivers are tributaries of the Great Pee Dee, which rises as the Yadkin in North Carolina. Bull Creek connects the Great Pee Dee to the Waccamaw across the southern boundary of Horry County.

Another distinctive feature of our landscape is the Carolina bay. These mysterious formations are depressions, rimmed with sand edges and filled with thickets of plants. They are home to the exotic Venus flytrap and any number of pitcher plants and other carnivorous species. They are also the home of many animals, including the black bear.

Many kinds of hardwoods, as well as pines and cypresses, grow in the forests. In certain seasons our woods are beautiful with flowers. Yellow jessamine (not jasmine) is a spring-flowering, climbing vine with bell-shaped yellow flowers. It is the state flower of South Carolina.

Several varieties of pines are native to the county. The longleaf pine's distinctive long needles and large cones are easily recognizable. In its early stages it looks more like a grass than a tree. This pine was almost destroyed in the pursuit of income from naval stores (products derived from its gum) in the nineteenth century. Quick growing varieties have supplanted it and are the staple of the pulpwood industry.

Cypress as a source of timber is pretty well played out here, but these trees still grace the deep swamps. Many visitors are intrigued with the "knees," that are associated with this tree. They appear to be part of the root system and may be a breathing mechanism for roots which remain underwater much of the time. Polished and carved knees are sometimes sold as curios.

The majestic live oak prefers high sandy land to swamps. It does shed its leaves but never all at once—hence its name. Many live oaks attain ages upward of 250 years. Those at Brookgreen, for example, were planted before the American Revolution. The fern that grows along the branches of this tree is resurrection fern. In dry weather it turns brown and curls up as though it were dead, but the slightest rain will bring it back to lush green life. The branches of these great oaks, although they are massive, can actually be moved with a little push.

Water, willow, and scrub oaks are common. In the fall the foliage of the scrub oak turns brilliant shades of red and gold, giving it the colloquial name "turkey" oak.

A magnificent flowering tree that grows wild in these woods is the *magnolia grandiflora*, celebrated in Southern romance. It has fragrant creamy white blooms the size of salad plates, and these give way to large seedpods. Leaves, blooms, and seedpods are frequently used in decorations. Its smaller cousin, the bay tree, *magnolia virginiana*, produces a much smaller, but still fragrant bloom. It flourishes in the Carolina bays from which it gets its name—or perhaps it is the bays which are named for it! Gordonia, *magnolia Gordonia*, which greatly resembles the bay tree and is often mistaken for it, blooms a little later and continues giving pleasure to the eye. The dogwood is also native to these woods. In the spring its display of white blooms turn the woods into gardens.

The gray Spanish moss which hangs from trees in this area is not a parasite. It is an epiphyte (air plant) and lives off rainwater, dust particles, and sunshine. Only if it becomes so heavy that it breaks branches does it pose a danger to the trees in which it lives. When the leaves are off the trees in the fall and winter, it is possible to see bunches of mistletoe high in their branches. This is a parasitic plant and does live off its host tree. Local youths harvest it for Christmas decorations by shooting it from the trees with rifles.

The tall cabbage palmetto, the state tree depicted on the state flag, is not really native to Horry County, its habitat being from Georgetown County south. Its use on the flag commemorates the victory of the colonists over the British at what later became Fort Moultrie, named for the colonial commander whose troops who were protected by a fort constructed of palmetto logs. The fiercest bombardment from the British ships could not penetrate the palmettos. Shells either bounced off or were absorbed by the spongy logs. The crescent on the deep blue South Carolina flag is not a moon, incidentally, but rather recalls the ornamental badge worn by the defending regiment. The low swamp palmetto has fan-shaped leaves which are sometimes used for weaving hats or rough shelters.

There are a number of native hollies, including yaupon (*ilex vomitoria*), which have beautiful berries of translucent red. This was prized by the Indians for its leaves and berries, which were brewed by the Indians to make a strong tea. This "black drink" was used as medicine, but, more importantly, as a ritual purifier for religious purposes.

The ocean waters yield excellent food fish such as drum and mullet, which are caught by surf fishing, and mackerel and swordfish, which are caught from deep-sea boats. Shrimp is caught from boats off the coast and in the saltwater creeks with circular hand nets. The rivers and swamps of this area are home to a number of wonderful food fish—bream, red-breast, crappie, etc.—as well as to the alligator and the water moccasin. Freshwater fishing is at least as popular as saltwater fishing and perhaps even more so among the natives.

Alligators are generally shy of man unless they have been fed by people who don't understand the danger of what they are doing. When a gator became a problem in the past, wildlife officers relocated it to a more remote area. That solution is becoming increasingly difficult as Horry County develops inland as well as along the beaches. The hapless troublemaker is apt to be disposed of now in a more permanent way.

There are many harmless snakes, as well as the moccasins, rattlers, copperheads, and coral snakes, which are poisonous. Horry winters are warm enough usually for walkers in the woods or swamps to encounter snakes lying in the sun along paths during months when they might be expected to be in hibernation.

Horry County still has a number of black bears. Nowadays they tend to be found in the swamps and bays, those being the areas least touched by man. These animals require a large area to roam about in and continuing development severely limits their habitat.

Beaver, raccoon, opossum, mink, otters, bobcats, red and gray foxes, and squirrels of several kinds abound in the woods. The slow-moving possum is frequently spotted as roadkill.

Mosquitoes are plentiful. Tall tales are told about the big ones that swoop down and carry their victims away. The efforts of man to control this pesky insect run from ineffective to feeble. As long as water stands in the swamps and ditches, there will be mosquitoes. They go with the territory. One helpful natural predator is the purple martin, a migratory swallow for which the locals put up gourd houses. Each spring the martin scouts come along early to find the homes for their friends and then go back along the migration route to lead them to their houses. Some houses are now made like miniature apartment buildings, but gourds please the birds just as much.

According to folk belief, the chinaberry tree and the mimosa help to discourage the mosquito. Whether true or not, most farmsteads had these trees close to the dwelling. There are other biting insects to encounter when enjoying the outdoors. Along the beach the peskiest is the "no-see-um," a minuscule biter which can turn a pleasant experience into a scratching torment. Deer flies, yellow flies, and red bugs, though annoying, are rarely dangerous, but the deer tick is responsible for the increasing incidence of Lyme disease.

Duck, quail, and dove are hunted for sport and food. In the past Horry County men hunted to put food on their tables. Most boys were taught to handle guns very early. A boat, a pickup truck, and a gun are still standard equipment in a culture with a strong bias toward hunting and fishing and the outdoor life generally.

The Carolina wren is the state bird. When it was depicted on the state automobile license plate in recent years, bird-watchers, instead of being gratified, screamed "foul." The most obvious identification feature of this bird is its uptilted tail, but the tail of the bird on the license plate drooped!

Songbirds abound. Mockingbirds, cardinals, and bluebirds, orioles, warblers, titmice, a world of sparrows, and other species give bird-watching a new meaning. The sales of bird feed indicate many people encourage feathered creatures in the neighborhood.

Along the beaches and around the marshes can be seen the busy sandpipers and gulls of various kinds, the herons, pelicans, ducks, and geese. Each season brings a different mix. The swamps also support a great variety of birds—wading birds, songbirds, birds of prey and vultures. (Locals call the vultures buzzards—an English word handed down from their British ancestors.) The fish hawk, or osprey, was nearly destroyed by DDT but has made a remarkable comeback since the insecticide was banned. Red-tailed and red-shouldered hawks may also be seen frequently, and several varieties of owls inhabit the region.

Even armchair watchers can put out feeders and watch the birds who come to dine. There are many places to get away to the outdoors and enjoy a great variety of plants and animals. Groups that try to promote and preserve nature's wonders welcome new members.

HORRY COUNTY HISTORICAL SOCIETY

To Edward Ernest Richardson (1915-1967), Horry County senator from 1948 to 1952, goes credit for initiating the Horry County Historical Society.

In 1966, working with friends and the Horry County Legislative Delegation, he pushed for the creation of the Horry County Historic Preservation Commission. In those days all local legislation came out of county legislative delegations. The two houses of the General Assembly usually adopted it without opposition.

Encouraged by Richardson, the commission turned its attention almost immediately to the creation of a society that would include anyone interested in the history of the county. When Richardson called a meeting of all those who might wish to become charter members, the small room in the courthouse could scarcely hold the people.

After a number of short speeches by Richardson and others, members of the audience gave a resounding response when they were asked to indicate whether they wished to undertake the formation of the Horry County Historical Society. The group moved quickly to the selection of a slate of officers and people to write bylaws and plan meetings. In short order 144 men and women signed the roster as charter members.

The first officers were C. B. Berry, president; Henry Woodward, Jr., vice president; Mrs. Russell Brown, secretary; and Miss Nelle Bryan, treasurer. Directors were Mrs. Manning Thomas, Miss Georgia Ellis, and Mrs. James Blanton. Mrs. Aleen Paul Harper became the historian of the society. Miss Florence Theodora Epps, Miss Laura Quattlebaum (later Mrs. E. E. Jordan), and Mrs. Catherine H. Lewis were responsible for publicity. Dr. Frank Sanders took the post of archaeologist.

Since 1967, the society has held four public meetings a year. At three of them members or guests present lectures, panels, films, or other programs. Each spring, the society sponsors a tour of some part of Horry County. On these occasions members share covered dish lunches before presentations by people from the area about their communities, families, churches, schools, and the like. In April 1991, on the bicentennial anniversary of the original event, the society sponsored a reenactment of the arrival of George Washington in Little River. Members and the public alike participated in remembering the first president's visit in 1791.

One of the first decisions of the new society was to begin a publication that not only would record the history of the organization but would provide a forum for sharing the history of Horry County. Florence Epps was named editor-in-chief. Although Catherine Lewis actually proposed the name of the magazine, there was never any doubt that it should be called *The Independent Republic Quarterly*. It is now informally *IRQ* and has published without interruption since 1967. Scholars and amateurs alike contribute information about the people, institutions, businesses, land, and folklore of the county. Hardly a topic comes to mind, but something about it can be found in *IRQ*, perhaps not enough to satisfy curiosity, but certainly enough to stimulate it. Miss Epps proved to be a magnet to contributors of articles, documents, maps, and pictures. As an editor, she tended to take a romantic view, and the *IRQ* issues she edited teem with references to the arts and heroes.

A publication committee was headed by the society's president, E. R. McIver, and John P. Cartrette succeeded her. Cartrette was not only a marvelous resource in himself, but he found pictures, maps, and other treasures that enriched the articles. Officers and other volunteers met regularly to prepare the material and to get the printed quarterlies ready to mail. The present editor is Christopher Boyle who succeeded Ben Burroughs. *IRQ* continues to solicit and publish articles provided by members and friends of the society. No author has ever received payment; still the *Quarterly* has never lacked material. Its back issues comprise a wonderful, rich, and varied archive of the land, lives and times, politics, families, institutions, and customs of Horry County.

2

In Order of Appearance

LITTLE RIVER: FIRST VILLAGE

A river, an unincorporated village, a community, and an area are all called Little River. This is a situation that is sometimes confusing to outsiders but not to those who are natives.

There may or may not have been permanent Native American villages in the vicinity of Little River, but long before Europeans came this way, the Indians made regular visits to the coast to enjoy the shellfish. Shell mounds provide clear evidence that the Indians had as great an appreciation of local oysters and clams as do the present inhabitants and visitors. Waties Island at the mouth of Little River has sizable mounds. Arrowheads and other artifacts are frequently found in the area.

William Waties, for whom the island was named, operated early in the European period as a trader with the Indians. The small bands, never very numerous, of Waccamaws, Winyahs, and Pee Dees along this coast had all but disappeared by the time the English began to settle here. Present-day Horry County has little trace of these peoples except for archaeological sites and a few place names.

The earliest written accounts of this area report fishing villages along the coast. These people may have come from ships wrecked along the coast, from coastal traders, or from pirate ships which sailed up and down the coast from bases in the West Indies. The villagers certainly had ties to the pirates and gave them shelter. Little River is said to have been visited by the likes of William Kidd, Edward ("Blackbeard") Teach, and Anne Bonney.

The coast, laced with islands and inlets, lent itself to the purposes of pirates and others who sought concealment and secrecy. It was easy to lose pursuers among the sounds and creeks. Little River itself is short, tidal, and flows north to the ocean. Off it are Dunn Sound and other tidal creeks that wind around and behind barrier islands.

In Order of Appearance

In the time of the Lords Proprietors, the Little River area was part of a very large political division known as Craven County. When there were royal governors, it was part of the Georgetown District, which covered the present counties of Georgetown, Williamsburg, Marion, and Horry and included parts of present-day Dillon and Florence. This huge area was divided into parishes that also served as the local voting precincts. All Saints Parish extended from Georgetown to the Cape Fear River originally, but later the province line was its upper boundary. All the land from the ocean to Waccamaw River fell within All Saints.

When a young Englishman traveled the coast in 1734, just a year before Kingston Township was opened to settlers, he reported that there was nothing between Murrells Inlet and Ashe's in Little River. He implied that Ashe operated a public house for the accommodation of the occasional traveler. While the name has disappeared from Little River itself, there is a community called Ash not far over the North Carolina line.

On New Year's Day, 1740, about six years later, preacher and missionary George Whitefield found the people of the village celebrating in traditional English fashion with music and dancing. Twenty-two years later, when the Rev. John McDowell preached at the boundary between North and South Carolina on May 9, 1762, he had the largest congregation he had seen since coming to America. Although the area was very remote, people found their way into it.

Those hardy souls had to learn to sustain themselves by wresting a living from the land by their own energy. Most lived a hardscrabble existence on small farms, growing a garden patch and small grains for their livestock and depending on what they could hunt and trap for much of their food and for skins to trade. The bounty of the sea provided variety in their diet. The forests supplied the materials for their homes and wood for their fires.

Some came to the Little River area, found it not to their liking and abandoned it. Members of the same families who became the rice barons of Waccamaw Neck at one time had holdings in the Little River area. William Alston had land in Little River Neck where General Francis Nash camped during the Revolution.

Josias Allston was a resident of the Little River area and a member of the Committee of Safety, which was established as the Revolution approached. He was considered a wealthy man. The appraisers of his personal estate in 1777 found among his belongings indigo hooks and seed, corn and peas, hogs, an oxcart, yokes and chains, horses, 70 head of black cattle, 24 working oxen, and 134 slaves. His farm was of considerable size, worthy of being called a plantation.

Most settlers were from the British Isles, but the Vaughts descended from a German, John Vaught, whose son Matthias was born at sea in 1750 on the way to the new world. Matthias fought in the Revolution and lost a leg at the Battle of Cowpens, January 17, 1781. The Vereens were French Huguenots who came to this continent in 1680 and were in the Winyah District by 1736.

The Bellamy family in the area is descended from John Bellamy, who had lands on the Waccamaw River as early as 1768 and in Little River Neck and Cherry Grove. His grandson Addleton Bellamy built a house near the Waccamaw River above present-day Highway 9 in 1775. It is shown in the *Mills' Atlas* as the only dwelling between the Little River Community and the area of the present-day town of Loris. Until the 1960s, when it was removed, it was a landmark along the road from Loris to Cherry Grove.

W. A. D. Bryan from North Carolina became a leading citizen of the area. He operated a gristmill on Cedar Creek and the store which held the post office a little way above it. Both are shown in the *Mills' Atlas*. Bryan served in the South Carolina Senate (1823-1826) and was the second postmaster of Little River, appointed in 1828.

Isaac Marion, descended from French Huguenots, lived in a house that sat directly on the line between the provinces of North and South Carolina. The boundary house is shown on a plat of land granted to Joseph Alston in 1814, but it may have been built by William Waties, the Indian trader. It was sometimes a public house, sometimes a private residence, sometimes both. In 1767 the Rev. John Barnett reported that he was preaching nine times a year at the Boundary House. While Isaac Marion lived there, he entertained his younger brother, Francis. He was there when news came of the Battle of Lexington, April 19, 1775, which touched off the American Revolution. The courier did not reach South Carolina until May 9, 1775, and Marion forwarded the message to the Committee of Safety in Little River, part of a defense and information network connected to Charleston. From Little River it was sent on to Georgetown and to Charleston. Empowered by the General Committee in Charleston, this committee constituted the only governing body of the area in the days before a state government could take hold. They could require local residents to show opposition to the English Crown by signing an oath of allegiance to the new government.

In Little River Neck, General Francis Nash encamped with his North Carolina troops in December 1776. They occupied and helped to clear land belonging to William Allston while they waited for the new American commanders to give them marching orders. Local men fought from time to time alongside Francis Marion and others.

In 1791, President Washington toured the southern states to cement their commitment to the new federal government. He entered South Carolina just north of Little River on April 17, 1791, and lunched with a Revolutionary War veteran named James Cochran. By day's end he had reached the home of Jeremiah Vereen just south of present-day North Myrtle Beach. On the next day he made his way to the domain of the rice planters of Waccamaw Neck.

The area was closely connected in many ways to the adjoining region of North Carolina, even after the establishment of the Horry District as a separate jurisdiction in 1801. Just on the South Carolina side of the Boundary House, out of reach of North Carolina law officials, Gen. Benjamin Smith fought a duel with his cousin, Capt. Maurice Moore of Old Brunswick Town, on June 28, 1805. The duel was actually begun in North Carolina, broken up by the law and reconvened just over the line. Smith was wounded but was rushed by ship to "Belvedere," his home on the Cape Fear River, where he recovered and later became governor of North Carolina. This was not the last duel the hotheaded Moore fought.

Robert Mills, the distinguished architect of the Washington Monument and many public buildings in South Carolina and other eastern seaboard states, compiled an atlas and statistics of his native state that he published in 1825. In it he described the area as follows: "There is another settlement made on Little river near the seaboard of about 25 persons, who carry on a considerable trade in lumber, pitch, tar, &c.... Little river admits vessels drawing 6 or 7 feet water up into the harbor, 4 miles from its mouth. There is a little difficulty at the entrance, but the harbor is perfectly safe from the effects of storms." The map of Horry District that Mills included in the atlas was drawn in 1820 by William Harlee. It shows not so much a village of Little River as a community, extending south and west from the state line.

The economy developed out of the forests and waters. The people depended heavily on the yield of the ocean and creeks and on lumber and naval stores derived from the great forests. Early in the nineteenth century commercial production of lumber and naval stores provided trading commodities which were highly valued in the outside world.

Colonel Daniel William Jordan typified the age of turpentine. He arrived from North Carolina, as did many others, in 1848 and during the next ten years accumulated 9,940 acres. He engaged chiefly in the production of naval stores and had several turpentine stills. He quickly became a leader in the community, served one term in the House of Representatives, and then, on June 9, 1851, became postmaster of Little River but served only a short time. For some reason he sold his Horry holdings to Nicholas F. Nixon, who had come from the New Bern (North Carolina) area, for twenty-five thousand dollars. Jordan acquired Laurel Hill, a large rice plantation in Waccamaw Neck (now part of Brookgreen Gardens), and moved his family there. It was a bad business decision, for he lost his slaves and much of his wealth during the Civil War. He moved permanently to Camden, where his family had been refugees during the war.

The big operators, those who owned the stills and built the commissary stores that supplied their neighbors with a place to barter whatever they produced for goods from the outside world, became wealthy in the naval stores industry. The men who worked in the woods exchanged what they brought in for wooden, paper, or metal "chits," or tokens, which gave them credit at the commissary store. These people got their living out of the streams, the woods, and the little cleared plots of land that produced grain and vegetables for their livestock and their families.

The commercial lumber industry of the district developed in the 1820s, and the timbers cut from Horry forests became famous and in demand worldwide. Giant pines and cypresses provided the long, heavy beams needed for construction in a day before there was structural steel. It was said that they could dress out cypress beams that measured 90 feet long and 15 inches square at the small end.

Little River became an active port, closely tied commercially to Wilmington. Ships put in here to load lumber and barrels of resin, pitch, and tar for shipment to the northern markets.

On March 16, 1840, trustees of a Methodist church were granted two acres of land by Anthony Brantly. Cedar Creek Cemetery is located on the Brantly land. This is the earliest documented church in the area, a century after George Whitefield baptized a child among the New Year revels. There may have been several others in existence at one time or another, but their records have not been found.

The Civil War temporarily disrupted both naval stores and lumber production and most of the able-bodied men went to serve in the Confederate forces. When the South needed salt, the traditional practice of evaporating ocean water was stepped up to supply the demand. Most of the military action in the Little River area involved either the defense or destruction of the saltworks along the coast. C. B. Berry, a local surveyor who is very knowledgeable about the history of the area, described the saltworks:

> The salt was manufactured by evaporating sea water and was a much needed commodity in the South at that time. To give you some idea of the size of the operation, the Yankee officer who commanded the forces that destroyed the factory, said there were about three thousand bushels of salt on hand and not knowing how to destroy it, had it mixed with sand so it could not be used. A salt water storage tank for this operation had water-lifting pumps operated by horses and had a capacity of 100,000 gallons. There were about fifty buildings that the officer reported he burned. The discovery of some ceramic grinding balls in that neighborhood recently, leads me to believe that this was not only a salt making operation, but might have been a gunpowder factory as well. (*IRQ* 5:3:18)

On Tilghman Point in Little River Neck, a place of spectacular beauty, are the remains of a Confederate battery that defended the entrance to Little River. It was called Fort Randall and was captured in 1863 by a Yankee naval landing party commanded by Lt. William B. Cushing (*LC*, pp. 143-44). The Confederates counterattacked and drove the invaders out.

During the Civil War period, Dr. William Kelland Cuckon practiced medicine in the area. His account book (1856-1869) has survived and contains the names of many area residents of the time. The difficulties and shortages of the period are revealed in its pages.

In 1868 an Horry correspondent for the *Marion Star* who signed himself "Waccamaw" wrote that Little River Village was

> a flourishing commercial place, that bids fair to become of great importance in the industrial interest of Horry and of the adjoining counties in North Carolina. [It contained] four stores, one steam saw mill, two gum stills, one academy, church, no jail (!) and a curiosity, in a new-fangled 'Pinder Picking machine.' ... Vessels of one hundred and fifty tons burden can come up to the village, and so make regular trips between this place and Northern cities, as well as to the West Indies. A large Schooner, commanded by Capt. Davis was taking on cargo for New York, during our visit....

> Prominent among the characteristics of the Little River people is their energy and hospitality, two traits often found among those who have commercial intercourses with other parts of the world.

The seductive nature of local foods was well established from the time of the Indians. "Waccamaw" testified, "These [mullet], with the oysters, that were abundant, and the ducks ... were luxuries that courted indulgence."

Captain T. C. Dunn, mentioned by "Waccamaw," was an enterprising northerner who had settled in Little River after having been part of the Yankee blockade of the coast. He was an energetic visionary who could see Little River as a major port. To that end he planned a canal to connect to the Waccamaw River, only five or six miles away at one point. This would have created a safe inland waterway for shipping from Little River to Georgetown on Winyah Bay. Inland, the Horry District had used Conwayborough as the riverport from which produce was sent first to Georgetown and then to its destination in northern ports or in Charleston. Since most of the commerce was with northern businesses, the development of this waterway and of the Little River port would have provided a shipping point much closer than either Georgetown or Charleston. Before the project came to pass, however, the age of canals was practically over, displaced by the age of railroads.

Dunn's next scheme was the construction of a railroad from Conwayborough to Little River. He was distracted from his purpose by an interest in politics. He was elected senator in 1872 and state comptroller general in 1875. In the election that ended the Reconstruction period in 1876, Dunn was soundly defeated in his home precinct and never again lived in this area. His political career ended under a cloud, and he left the state.

The last quarter of the nineteenth century saw little development in the area despite the promise seen by the *Star* correspondent. The people continued to grow peanuts, cotton, corn, and other small grains, to cut timber out of the forest and tap the trees for turpentine. During the last years of the century the naval stores industry began to fade as the great forests were tapped out. It moved on to Georgia, Florida, Alabama, and other Gulf states.

The lumber industry continued, but it became more difficult to get the logs to the mill as the cutting went deeper and deeper into remote places. A number of narrow gauge or tram railroad lines were built during this period. A quarter of a century after Thomas C. Dunn had left the state, his dream of a rail connection with the interior of Horry County was fulfilled. The Gardner and Lacey Lumber Company of Georgetown built one in 1905 that ran from Little River to Red Hill, across the Waccamaw from Conway. The logs were hauled to the Conway Coast and Western tracks at Red Hill and then on to the Dynamite Hole at the Conway Boat Landing on Highway 905, where they were dumped into the river, rafted, and taken by tugboat to the mills at Conway and Georgetown.

Shelley Point Plantation was the terminal for many miles of tram roads. Hammer Lumber Company, located "on the Little River Neck side just before you turn to go around Tilghman's Point," employed as many as fifty men in its operations. The company discontinued operations in the 1920s.

Around the turn of the century Tom Bessent operated a commercial oyster fishery at the spot where the Little River wharves are now. Oysters could be bought at the "factory" for ten cents a bushel.

The name of the Wilmington, Southport and Little River Steamboat Company pretty well describes the territory covered by the regular runs of the boats which served Little River. In 1902 the company built a steamboat in Little River and named it the *Sanders*. It was launched with a day of festivities, but the little steamer was ill fated. After five years in service it ran aground on the Little River bar and was later replaced by a larger boat, the *Atlantic*.

W. H. (Willie) Stone had a large general merchandise store located on southwest corner of the present main intersection of Little River, across from the Little River Methodist Church. The unpainted wooden building had a large porch on the front where customers used to sit. His brother, Dr. J. A. Stone, had an office to one side.

Willie Stone, who received his goods by boat from Wilmington and other places, needed to know when a boat was coming into port. About 1907 he hired Carl Bessent to install the first telephone which linked his store with a house on Battery (now Tilghman) Point in Little River Neck. A lookout called the store when a boat appeared at the mouth of the river, and Mr. Stone prepared to receive his merchandise.

Lucian Bryan built the Little River Hotel early in the century. He and his wife operated it and lived in it. He also had a fishery on Waties Island and operated a fish house in Little River, which packed salted fish for market.

The Bank of Little River, South Carolina, chartered November 4, 1910, was for many years the only bank in the village. On February 15, 1938, it was purchased by the Conway National Bank and liquidated.

Dr. R. G. Sloan was the resident physician in Little River for many years during the latter half of the nineteenth century. Dr. J. A. Stone cared for patients almost from the time he completed his education in 1905 until his death in 1950. Another practitioner who had patients in the area was Dr. S. P. Watson, who married a Little River girl. He lived at Round Swamp and treated patients from Loris to the Waccamaw River. These were all men who went to their patients, traveling by horseback, buggy, and, finally, by car.

Pig Pen Bay School, a very early school shown in the *Mills' Atlas*, was near Nixon Crossroads. When the site was used as a mustering ground for Confederate troops, it became known as the Mustershed School. The first schoolhouse in Little River Village was situated on the east side of the old Worthams Ferry Road and was in use before the Civil War. Later it was located north of the post office. A two-room school was built in the same location about 1910. A larger building constructed sometime before 1940 was used until consolidation created Wampee-Little River High School below the junction of Highways 90 and 57. With integration Chestnut High School joined Wampee-Little River to become North Myrtle Beach High School, which is now located on old Highway 9 east of Highway 90.

In 1930 Thomas C. Dunn's dream of an inland waterway became a reality. The U. S. Corps of Engineers began to acquire rights of way through the county for an intracoastal waterway. The people of Conway argued strongly for following the plan laid down by Dunn to connect Little River to the Waccamaw River by canal, but the corps opted to dig a new waterway 90 feet wide and 8 feet deep through high ground from Little River to Socastee Swamp. This section completed the project from New England to Florida, and there was a ceremonial opening at Socastee Bridge on April 11, 1936. Several travelers have described the section of the Intracoastal Waterway from Socastee to Winyah Bay as one of the most beautiful in its entire length. During Prohibition rumrunners found the islands and inlets of Little River as attractive as the earlier pirates and later drug runners had. Older citizens sometimes will talk of the big black cars and the strange city types who came to Little River in those days.

Except for its port, Little River was isolated until the 1930s. There were no good roads into the area. The sandy trails which led from home to home and community to community tested the hardiest motorist. Nicholas F. Nixon led a movement to get a good road from the interior to Cherry Grove. In the later 1930s the construction of Highway 9, from the mountains to the sea, gave Little River and its nearby beaches a sharp boost.

Little River suffered relatively little from the effects of Hurricane Hazel. The village had already acquired its deserved fame among sports fishing enthusiasts and had begun to cater to this group particularly. In 1955 it already had sixteen small craft ready for hire. It boasted three small hotels, several tourist homes and two "modern motor courts," including one located at the docks that cost ten thousand dollars to build. A reporter found that "customer satisfaction ... seems to be the motto around Little River." He found that "the captains have retained an ability to make each trip an adventure."

The last two decades have seen constant growth in the area, first along the Strand and more recently in the Little River area. In the early 1980s some residents started a movement to incorporate Little River, but that has not been achieved. An organization was established to bring water and sewer lines to the area. This infrastructure and the continued expansion of the road system encouraged development away from the Strand, all along U.S. 17 from the welcome center near Calabash to the intersection with Highway 9. Now the expansion is moving along the Sea-Mountain Highway toward Loris and down Highway 90 toward Conway. Little River retains the charm of a small place while rapidly creating all the amenities of a tourist Mecca.

CONWAY: RIVERPORT AND SEAT OF GOVERNMENT

Conway is located about fifteen miles from the coast at a bend in the Waccamaw River that is its farthest inland reach. The river's course is roughly east to west to this point, and then it takes a course almost directly south to Winyah Bay in Georgetown County.

Conway had its beginning when the English Crown decreed in 1730 that a township should be laid out on the Waccamaw River about a hundred miles from Charles Town. The site chosen featured a high bluff on the inland side of the river. A survey made by Alexander Skene and Justice William Wright in 1732 established the boundaries of Kingston Township and its village seat. The township was opened to settlers in 1735. Prior to that time there had been a few settlers, mostly Indian traders, but the remoteness of the area had discouraged Europeans from coming here.

When the township was opened for settlement, both speculators and settlers sought grants. The area turned out not to be suited to the rice plantation economy, already established along the seaboard of South Carolina. The land is threaded with waterways fed from extensive swamps. There were dense forests and thick Carolina bays. The settlers, mostly from the British Isles, who did come lived out of the woods and streams, hunting, trapping, fishing, and using the pine forest for building materials and for some primitive naval stores operations.

Few records have survived to help modern residents visualize what the town was like in the eighteenth century. When river travelers camped overnight on Kingston Bluff in 1734 and killed and barbecued a bear, there were no signs of settlers. A court record from 1768 describes a small frontier outpost of six or seven buildings, including a smithy, one or two public houses, and a few dwellings. Clearly the people who were moving into the township were moving onto homesteads instead of settling in a village.

What is now Horry County was part of the Georgetown District and was divided into parishes of All Saints and Prince George for the purpose of selecting representatives to the General Assembly. This huge district comprised present-day Horry, Georgetown, Williamsburg, and Marion Counties, plus parts of Florence and Dillon Counties. All matters which went through the courts, whether civil or criminal, required going to Charleston or, later, to Georgetown. These trips had their hazards, and shortly after the American Revolution a movement began to break up Georgetown Judicial District into smaller court districts.

In 1801 the inhabitants of All Saints and Prince George Parishes petitioned the General Assembly to establish the Horry District and to make the village of Kingston the county seat and rename it Hugerborough. The petitioners wished to honor Brig. Gen. Peter Horry, a Revolutionary War hero. The eventual name of the village was Conwayborough, honoring Col. Robert Conway, a Revolutionary War veteran and later brigadier general of the area militia.

Once it became a seat of government, the village began to grow slowly. Lots were sold in 1802-1803, and a small courthouse was built. Court convened in Conwayborough for the first time in 1803. That building, which stood on Fifth Avenue, has not survived, but the second one, built in 1824-1825, does. At present it is the seat of government of the city of Conway. The third, and present, courthouse was built in 1908.

Bishop Francis Asbury, who visited the area several times during the last decades of the eighteenth and first part of the nineteenth century, recorded that he preached to not more than one hundred persons in 1801. Robert Mills, who compiled district statistics in 1826, reported that Kingston contained about twenty or twenty-five houses and about one hundred inhabitants. By the time of the Civil War the village had grown to about three hundred persons. When it was finally incorporated in 1898, the official population was 705.

In the absence of road transport, the rivers were the chief highways until the twentieth century. When the naval stores and lumber industries began to ship products before the Civil War, most of it passed through the port at Conwayborough. The war years saw the first paddlewheel steamers on the Waccamaw. From that time until after the first World War, these little boats provided transportation for people and goods into and out of the county.

When the Civil War came, almost all the able-bodied men of the village went off to battle. The home front almost came to a standstill. Although Federal troops occupied Conwayborough at the end of the war, their stay was not long. The South's veterans returned to pick up the pieces of their lives, most of them earning their livelihoods from the woods in the naval stores and lumber industries or from small commercial enterprises that began to serve the surrounding countryside as well as the town.

The local economy was based in large part on a system of barter and tokens issued in lieu of cash by mills, stills, and other establishments who paid for services. Little cash passed hands, even among businesses, and certainly little of it came into the hands of the average citizen. Land was worth little and often it was difficult for owners to raise the money for taxes, although the amount assessed would seem ludicrous today. Firms engaged in naval stores and timber began to acquire cheap land, some of them acquiring vast acreage at little cost.

In 1883 the General Assembly officially shortened the old name of the village from Conwayborough to Conway.

The introduction of the railroad to Conway resulted from the need of lumbermen to get their product to the Waccamaw River for shipment to the outside world. The Chadbourn family built the line that terminated at the river, close to the steamboat wharves. The first train ran on December 5, 1887. The railroad also introduced the telegraph, the first instant communication with the outside world. The railroad and telegraph began to erode the isolation that had kept this area apart from the state and nation.

About the time that Conway received its charter of incorporation from the state, a colony of midwesterners arrived north of town and became the Homewood Colony. This group, though short-lived as an organization, helped introduce the farmers of the county to truck farming. In the same period the introduction of tobacco as a money crop gave farming a whole new cast.

Conway developed into a tobacco market. The first auction warehouse in town opened in 1899. For the first time, cash money began to replace barter and tokens in the lives of ordinary farmers. For nearly a century now the crop has dominated the agricultural economy of Horry and the culture of tobacco has been a way of life. Now, at the end of the twentieth century, as tobacco appears to have had its day, farmers must look elsewhere for their major income.

Just after the turn of the century the automobile appeared on the scene, bringing with it an increase in road transportation and the gradual decline of water transportation. Motorcars and trucks put an end to the importance of Conway as a riverport. The road system has never caught up with demand, nor is it likely to as long as the tourism industry along the Grand Strand continues to thrive.

Although the development of tourism can be dated from the period just after World War I, and there was a dramatic effort to establish a posh resort in the 1920s, the long depression years cut it off before it could get a good hold. Not until after World War II and the infusion of large amounts of capital did tourist development really take off. Conway people contributed their financial resources and physical energies to that development. Myrtle Beach gradually became the place where many Conway residents worked.

Conway has maintained its own character as the economy of the county changed. It has taken great pride in being different from the beaches. The town has taken steps to preserve its historic buildings and the great oaks which provide much of its beauty. Streets yield to the live oaks, and motorists take the hazards created by them as a price they are willing to pay. Nearly every yard has azaleas, camellias, and dogwoods. Tourists have come to the town beside the Waccamaw River in increasing numbers to enjoy a refreshing difference from the beaches. The city and private interests provide attractions such as the riverwalk, the marina, specialty stores, good restaurants, and tourist accommodations to bring visitors here.

Conway also has importance as the seat of Horry County government, probably the county's largest employer. Professionals associated with the courts and government departments live and have offices in the city.

As large organizations outgrow their old spaces, they tend to seek new space outside the city limits. Each time this happens, the offices of supporting services move also, resulting in the loss of tax revenues and money recycling through local businesses in the city. This has happened with the Conway Hospital, which is now located five miles out on the road to Myrtle Beach. Conway is working hard to offset these changes by revitalizing its downtown, redeveloping interest in the waterfront, and stimulating the growth of small business in the historic downtown area.

The lifestyle in Conway is that of a small town. It is relaxed, warm, conscious of neighborhoods and schools and churches. Its residents take advantage of all that a major beach resort has to offer, but live in an environment that is more personal and less stressful.

In Order of Appearance

CONWAY: AROUND CITY HALL

Artifacts around the City Hall reflect the history of the town. The town clock, which stands at the Main Street and Third Avenue corner near the courthouse, is as much as any landmark the symbol of the town. Back in 1938 the mayor, Dr. Carl L. Busbee, wanted to assure farmers who visited the town each fall to sell tobacco that the town appreciated their custom. Farmers' Day became an annual event. Council named a farmer-mayor and farmer-council for a day. Farmer-mayors included Tom Booth (1938), Ed Roberts (1939), Oliver Hardee (1940), and Jesse T. Smith (1941). World War II ended this annual festival.

All who failed to wear appropriate clothes ("overhauls") for the occasion or committed other "offenses" were hailed into court. "Fines" levied from these mock trials purchased the clock, a symbol of Conway merchants' dependence on the farmers of the surrounding areas. Master cabinetmaker W. H. Winborne designed the clock tower and built it of local cypress. William Taft Skipper, James Holloway Skipper, Colie Skipper, Norman E. Skipper, Newsome Harrelson, and Roy Martin assisted him. The clockwork itself came from Seth Thomas. Clock and tower took three months to complete and cost a little less than two thousand dollars.

When the clock was being put in place, excavation for the foundation unearthed a three-foot-long cannon barrel, believed to be the 1802 surveyor's mark. William Hemingway set it there as the reference point from which he laid out the streets. Earlier survey maps made in 1732 and 1783 are apparently lost, but Hemingway's map of the city plan is preserved in City Hall. The cannon barrel was reburied at the north side of the base of the clock.

A cross mark carved in the front steps of City Hall was also a surveyor's mark for measuring the Waccamaw River. Standing at that spot, a visitor today looks directly across to the mural of a riverboat painted on the wall beyond a parking lot. In 1983 James Frisino depicted a paddlewheel steamboat, one of those that regularly carried people and freight between Georgetown and Conway. The town relied on the river until well into the twentieth century. The city, Conway-Main Street U.S.A., Inc., Kingston Pointe Development Corporation, the Greater Conway Chamber of Commerce, the Horry Cultural Arts Council, and many private businesses, all focusing on downtown renewal, are restoring the historic riverfront area and drawing visitors once more to the waterfront.

The small courtyard garden beside the City Hall features a fountain purchased from the city of Charleston. At first it replaced a homemade trough that had stood at curbside and furnished refreshment "for man and beast." The fountain was removed to its present location when the city created the garden. Mayor Ike Long, well known as a practical joker, once stocked the fountain basin with fish.

In the downstairs corridor of the City Hall, portraits have been assembled of mayors who have served since the city's incorporation in 1898. Off this corridor is the mayor's office where the watch that belonged to Robert Conway is displayed.

LORIS: GATEWAY CITY

The upper reaches of Horry County were settled mostly by second- and third-generation Scots whose families had populated the Cape Fear region of North Carolina. Because there was no natural or geographical barrier between the provinces (later states), people moved back and forth without hindrance. The *Mills' Atlas* map drawn by Harlee in 1820 shows almost no settlement between Buck Creek and Lake Swamp but does show a road leading to Todd's Ferry on the Waccamaw River.

On July 4, 1881, a printer named J.W. Ogilvie arrived in Horry County. More than a quarter of a century later, he wrote a series of articles describing his impressions of his new home county as he traveled from the North Carolina line to Conwayborough. The railroad had not yet arrived. Of this vicinity he said, "Loris was unknown. The site of that coming city was but a worn out corn field that would not have brought at forced sale more than 25 cents an acre."

The livelihood of people in the area depended on what they could grow themselves and on timber and turpentine which came from the woods. Logging companies constructed their own narrow-gauge rail lines to facilitate getting logs from the woods and swamps to the nearest water to raft them to the mills. Chadbourn Lumber Company of Wilmington had logged timber and operated sawmills just over the line in North Carolina for a number of years. When the Chadbourns decided to extend their operations into Horry County, the firm persuaded townships along the proposed right of way (Green Sea, Simpson Creek, Bayboro, and Conwayborough) to issue bonds to finance it. Landowners hoped that the value of their acres would increase and that they would profit from the sale of timber rights and from better access to markets for their produce.

James Gould Patterson owned land in northern Horry County along Todd's Ferry Road. When the Chadbourn Lumber Company rails reached his neighborhood, Patterson, a canny Scot, struck a bargain with the

Chadbourn brothers. On December 7, 1887, he sold them land west of the right-of-way for a depot. The sale price was one dollar for a five-sided lot measuring 175 by 900 by 225 by 900 by 50 feet. The tracks were probably laid through the area in early to mid-1887 because the first train ran into Conway on December 15, 1887.

The depot was named Loris. Members of the Chadbourn family have offered different versions of how that choice came about. It is impossible to know the truth of either. One says that Loris was the name of a dog owned by the girlfriend of one of the Chadbourns and the other that Loris was a character in a popular novel of the time. The town probably will have to live with this uncertainty always. For such consolation as it may be, the name is at least unique among places in the United States.

The original depot had to be replaced in 1911 as the traffic in produce, merchandise, and passengers increased (*HH* 4 May 1911). A communication from Raymond Bullard, assistant vice president of SCL/LN, says: "The combination freight and passenger station at Loris was built in 1913 by the Atlantic Coast Line Railroad. We have no record of an earlier structure and assume this is the original building."

James G. Patterson's forebears had immigrated to the Cape Fear region of North Carolina, and his family was among those who gradually migrated south into the Waccamaw River area. Patterson (1816-1891), the son of John and Elizabeth Smith Patterson, married Martha Marlow. Their log house stood just in front of where the Loris Presbyterian Church is now located. Both are buried in Patterson Cemetery, a family graveyard which was later deeded to the town of Loris. Many descendants of the Pattersons still live in the Loris area. Many others moved along with the naval stores industry to Georgia, becoming prominent in the industry there.

A deed book at the courthouse in Conway shows that Patterson quickly sold a number of lots to merchants and others who wanted to locate near the depot. He became the first postmaster. Until recent years Main Street was named Patterson Street in honor of the city's founder. Now his name remains only in connection with the town cemetery.

By 1890 the community at this intersection of Todd's Ferry Road and the Wilmington, Chadbourn, and Conway Railroad had grown to four stores, operated by Y. P. McQueen, Patterson & Toon, B. R. King, and Boss Holt. When Loris was incorporated with a one-mile radius on July 26, 1902, the intendant (mayor) was D. J. Butler and the wardens (councilmen) were D. O. Boyd, J. C. Bryant, and H. H. Burroughs.

Little settlements near Loris in every direction had grown up around mills, gins, or turpentine stills. Each had a small general merchandise store, usually a commissary operated by one of the turpentine still or sawmill firms. Why Loris eventually developed as a town and others failed to do so is not altogether clear. Daisy, Bayboro, and Green Sea were among those which held as much promise as Loris in early days. Bayboro, for example, was on the railroad at that time and had five stores in 1899; Gurley, also on the railroad, had four stores, two turpentine stills, two churches, and a schoolhouse in 1900. In 1901 Daisy had three stores, a post office, a cotton gin, grits mills, and sawmills. Its newspaper correspondent bragged it had tri-weekly mail and telephone lines.

As early as 1900 Loris had a high school, and the school year opened in July! Hugh R. Todd, the first principal, later became president of the successful Draughan's Business Schools located in Columbia, Atlanta, and elsewhere. In 1908 Loris and two nearby school districts voted by a margin of 3-1 to fund a new building for the high school.

Meanwhile, tobacco began to replace turpentine as a source of income. The first $1,500.75 for a warehouse in Loris was raised at a picnic given for potential subscribers in August 1902, and the contract was let in February 1903. The officers of Loris Tobacco Warehouse Co., Inc. were J. C. Bryant, president; P. C. Prince, vice president; and Dan W. Hardwick, secretary-treasurer. Among the other stockholders were Doc D. Harrelson, Y. P. McQueen, D. A. Spivey, Jim King, N. E. Hardwick, and Sims Harrelson.

These men had no experience in operating a warehouse, so they brought in two Virginia men, John T. Edwards and Walter Tyree, to run it. The first year, a million pounds of tobacco sold for an average of less than six cents a pound.

In the next decade local men and outsiders invested in warehouses, sometimes losing heavily when mismanagement or lack of experience caused their ventures to fail. The short auction season tempted investors to find ways to make warehouses pay for themselves through the rest of the year. One, the Brick, burned while it was being used to store and cure sweet potatoes.

The cooperative movement also took its toll. The Farmers Warehouse, originally built by a group of farmers, was one cooperative that failed because of a lack of support by the farmers themselves and because of inadequate management.

Warehousemen played an important part in the economic life of the town. Their advertising and their reputations brought in the farmers with their golden leaf. The money paid by the tobacco companies provided the lifeblood of the town. In January 1909 a writer in the *Horry Herald* declared: "One visiting Loris now cannot help but note the difference in the busy little town—what it once was and what it is to-day and what she is to be in the future. Loris is one of the best cotton markets in the county and the largest tobacco market in this section of the State, having sold near[ly] one and one half million pounds the past season."

The Bank of Loris, established in 1907, occupied the town's first brick building on the northeast corner of the main intersection. Founded by Thomas Cooper of Mullins, its local officers were J. C. Bryant, E. L. Sanderson, W. A. Johnson, J. C. Prince, D. W. Hardwick, and J. D. Graham. In its first year it had deposits of "nearly $10,000."

The *Herald* noted that Loris also was making strides in government, revising and adding to its ordinances. The Town Council consisted of J. D. Bryant, intendant, D. J. Butler, A. F. Cannon, E. L. Sanderson, and Dan W. Hardwick, wardens.

The Conway Telephone Company installed a complete telephone system in Loris, connecting it to Conway and the outside world. Loris had had the telegraph from the beginning, for everywhere the railroad went, so did the wires. Every depot had its expert telegrapher.

In the early years Loris suffered many disastrous fires, not only of its warehouses, but of stores and homes. In 1911 the P. C. Prince Company and the J. C. Bryant Company burned. In 1914 fire destroyed the home of Y. P. McQueen. In January 1915, a number of stores burned, and the old wooden buildings were replaced by brick structures. When W. J. Hughes was mayor, the *Horry Herald* (February 27, 1913) reported: "Modern offices are just being completed at Loris by the Loris Supply Company, in the second story of their store building, these offices being the first to be offered for rent in the town. One of the largest of the lot is occupied by the Loris Telephone Co., which was recently purchased by O. E. Todd and his brother. The offices are lighted with ascetelane [sic] and in every way are convenient and well appointed."

By 1914 Loris was being called the Gate City, the first town on the railroad south of the North Carolina line. Its newspaper, the *Loris News*, had been established and, unfortunately, failed.

A number of medical men practiced for a while in Loris and the surrounding area and then moved on. Dr. Huger Richardson arrived in April 1912, and Dr. J. D. Thomas in 1915. They became the most popular medical practitioners in the northern end of the county until they died.

In 1915, Loris had a new board of trade and took a full page in a paper of countywide circulation (*Horry Herald,* August 19, 1915) to advertise its businesses and institutions.

While men from the area fought in the First World War, the people of Loris were active in home front activities. Toward the end in 1918, a War Savings Stamp rally in Loris drew a crowd "estimated at not less than 2,000," truly remarkable considering the population and the state of communications in that time. Both local doctors offered their skills to the Volunteer Medical Corps of South Carolina to deal with the influenza epidemic, but a local board decided that Dr. Thomas should go and that Dr. Richardson should stay to look after the home folk.

When the war was over, Loris celebrated with a general street parade. The newspaper correspondent (*Horry Herald,* November 14, 1918) reported that the citizens, teachers, and about one hundred schoolchildren marched in it. "Church bells were rung, guns were fired, and every boy had his horn, trumpet, bugle, or some old tin pan. Cow bells were swung on long poles and carried through the streets by the boys. The Kaiser was put into an oil barrel with a pound of powder and was blown high into the air. Parts of the barrel came back, but the Kaiser decided not to return this way."

On February 3, 1919, Dan W. Hardwick, Charles D. Prince, A. J. Mishoe, and O. E. Hickman secured a charter for a new bank and opened the books for subscription. The Farmers Bank opened for business on June 2, 1919.

Loris has always had its share of people interested in public office. In the early years of this century Doc D. Harrelson, William Armagy Prince, Montgomery J. Bullock, W. K. Holt, John L. Boyd, John Holt, and M. M. Stanley served in county and state offices. Others over the years have been Cornelius J. Prince, John Pickens Derham (Green Sea), John Robert Carter Sr., Edgar McGougan Derham, Walter Porter Gore, Clifford Hugh Hardwick, Forrest Brooks Whittington, Lloyd Berkley Bell, John Robert Carter Jr., Winston Wallace Vaught, John Wilson Jenrette Jr., James Paul Blanton, Charles Edward Hodges, and James Price Stevens, state senator for twenty years, 1955-1976.

In the 1920s and 1930s while Loris continued its slow growth, Conway, the county seat, with its stronger political position seemed to flourish. Fed up with what they considered the greed of Conway politicians who grabbed for the county seat every goody which political favor could secure, local men decided that northern Horry needed to be a separate county, with Loris as its county seat. Twice they mounted campaigns to secede. The first never got to the voting booth (*IRQ* 25:1: 9-16).

Leaders of the second campaign were Jefferson M. Long, a lawyer; William A. Prince, a member of the House of Representatives; Dan W. Hardwick; D. O. Heniford; and other business and civic leaders. They recruited a young newspaperman, Burroughs H. "Buck" Prince, and started a newspaper called the *Loris Observer* to give a voice to the "New County" movement. The group fielded a slate of candidates in the next election: William A. Prince for State Senate and Jefferson Long for the House of Representatives. They were soundly defeated, and the movement died, although this time it had made it to the ballot box.

By 1915 Loris had opened and closed one high school and opened a second. About 1920 the local high school was accredited by the state, and the eleventh grade was finally added (*IRQ* 2:4: 22-23). In 1921 Montgomery Jackson Bullock was named superintendent and his wife, Agnes Richardson Bullock, principal of the Loris schools. They set about persuading people to vote a bond issue for construction. In spite of some opposition, it passed, and a new two-story brick building was ready for students in January 1923. When a new high school building was completed in 1931, this earlier one housed the grammar school.

Home economics and vocational agriculture classes began about 1924. At Loris High every girl enrolled in home economic classes and every boy in vocational agriculture. Professionals associated with this movement and with the public health service began to make a marked difference in the quality of life in the Loris area. Beginning with the remarkable R. E. Naugher from Mississippi, the first vocational agriculture teacher, they led the slow process of helping farmers improve their land, their crops and livestock, and the quality of their lives. Public health services provided inoculations, instruction in simple hygiene, training for midwives, and referrals to help available from other agencies.

By the mid-1930s, Loris had a thousand residents. Jennings W. Hardwick, mayor, bragged in an address published in the *Horry Herald* (July 2, 1936) that fifty percent of South Carolina's tobacco crop grew within a twenty-five-mile radius of his town. Its four warehouses sold six million pounds a year. Strawberries, beans, Irish potatoes, sweet potatoes, lettuce, and poultry were grown for northern markets. Hardwick made a pitch on a Charleston radio station for canneries and manufacturing plants and named good labor, an up-to-date water system, good hunting, and State Highway 9 as inducements. The mayor pointed out that an extensive lumber and veneer industry had been built and that there was ample raw material for furniture plants.

Finally, Hardwick promised that one hundred paid members of the Loris Boosters Club, organized in 1936, would stand ready to assist prospects. He concluded on this ringing note:"For those who seek recreation, we bid you welcome; to those who have no home, we bid you cast your lot with us; and to those who have good homes, but desire better ones, we bid you to come and be a part of our community."

The Depression era is remembered for the closing of the bank, Hoover carts, and a community cannery. Nobody had much money, but most people lived well despite that. They grew their own food, wore their clothes to rags, and swapped produce for what they needed. Some local students went to colleges that accepted produce in lieu of tuition. The first civic club, the Civitans, organized in 1938 by Eldred E. Prince, continued the do-it-yourself tradition.

In 1940 young men began to sign up for the draft again, and in late 1941 the United States entered World War II. There were air wardens and aircraft spotters, ration books and shortages, and rumors of spies. Many men and women went from the town and surrounding farms to Wilmington and Charleston to work in defense plants, particularly the shipyards. Even with the wartime absences of people of this area, Loris continued to grow.

The leadership of the town worked to improve the local economy. In 1946 Needham Causey, Sam Hickman, and B. T. Ragan Sr. organized Loris Wood Products, the first real industry to locate in Loris.

The northern end of the county needed a hospital. The closest ones were in Conway, Mullins, and Florence. The Civitan Club secured enough signatures from the townships in the primary service area to persuade the Legislative Delegation to establish a special tax district to fund it. Loris Community Hospital opened for use on May 15, 1950, and has been in almost continuous expansion since that time. The members of the first hospital commission were S. F. Horton, C. A. Lupo, E. W. Prince Sr., Lundy Vaught, and Eldred E. Prince, chairman, who served in that capacity for thirty-six years.

The early Board of Trade and the old Boosters Club had included most of the business leaders of the town. In 1952 the Loris Merchants Association, forerunner of the Loris Chamber of Commerce, was organized. O. D. Freeman became the first president. An intensive effort to induce industries to locate in this area was needed, so a group consisting of Eldred E. Prince (president), George M. Lay, Rod Sparrow, B. K. Stabler, and Thomas W. Stanley formed the Loris Industrial Developers, Inc., for the express purpose of providing sites and buildings and negotiating with industrial prospects.

Local leadership never ignored the needs of the farming community that provided the base of the Loris economy. In 1958 the Legislative Delegation under the leadership of Sen. James P. Stevens created the farmers market in Loris, and Philip Cronkhite became the first manager. In the 1960s the Buck Creek and Simpson Creek watershed projects helped improve farms to the east of Loris through drainage.

The early 1960s were marked by a sharp upturn in the business of the town. There was construction along Main Street. When Loris Drug Store built a new and much larger store, its old quarters became the temporary location of Loris's second bank, Horry County National, which opened August 5, 1963. The Civitan Club sold house markers to prepare for the home delivery of mail, and service was instituted in the fall of 1963. The early 1960s also saw the passing of an era when Dan W. Hardwick died on November 30, 1963. Mr. Hardwick had been one of the earliest and most prominent among Loris leaders through his various business and banking interests.

Although in 1945–1946 Loris area representatives J. Robert Carter, W. P. Gore, and D. D. Harrelson had made up the House Delegation while Sen. Frank Thompson of Conway was in office, Loris reached in the 1960s and early 1970s a level of political dominance in Horry County it had never held before. James P. Stevens became senator and head of the Legislative Delegation in 1956 and Lloyd B. Bell, J. Robert Carter Jr., Winston Wallace Vaught, John W. Jenrette Jr., James P. Blanton, and Charles E. Hodges served under him. Bell and Hodges were particularly known for their fiscal savvy. Continuing representation in the House made the Loris area a consistent, strong political force.

The most significant governmental development in many decades came about in the mid-1970s with the passage of the Home Rule Act. This transferred local government away from the delegation to the hands of an elected county council. Senator Stevens played a critical role in developing public acceptance and in helping the voters of Horry County choose its form of self-government. The first county councilman from the Loris area, and the first black to serve, was Braxton Watson, who was appointed to a vacancy that occurred on the death of W. G. Sarvis.

Two Loris representatives had made attempts to change the system earlier. In 1962 Winston W. Vaught introduced a bill which would have provided eleven elected county commissioners instead of the five appointed by the Legislative Delegation. His bill failed passage. In 1968 James Blanton tried again to establish home rule with a bill that provided for proportionate election districts. His bill also failed, but the movement had by now become irresistible, and there was sufficient sentiment by the mid-1970s to get the Home Rule Act through both houses of the General Assembly.

Between 1960 and 1980 the population of the town grew by almost 29 percent, but in the early 1980s Loris experienced a significant economic depression. Industrial plant closings threw hundreds of workers out of jobs. National and international pressures on the tobacco industry caused doubts about the future of the growers and the market.

The people who live and work in the town and on the surrounding farms have great resilience and self-reliance. Loris celebrates itself each fall with a festival, the Bog-off, the centerpiece of which is a contest for the best cook of the local food specialty. Chicken bog is a tasty blend of rice, chicken, sausage, and spices. Each cook uses some spice or other ingredient to make it a signature dish. The basic recipe for chicken bog is to boil a hen until the meat falls from the bone, remove bones and cut up the meat, and cook rice in the broth (1 cup rice to 2 cups broth). Add to the rice and broth the meat of the chicken, sausage, and other seasonings.

In the 1930s the paving of Highway 9 put Loris on the state map by funneling beach traffic through Main Street. When a dual-lane bypass was constructed in 1984–1985, traffic to the beaches was routed around the town.

At the same time the phenomenal growth that has characterized the Grand Strand has begun to push outward along the Highway 9 corridor toward Loris, accelerated by the extension of water and sewer lines along the highway. Loris is set for another period of expansion.

LORIS: IT TAKES A WHOLE VILLAGE TO RAISE A CHILD

I have many happy memories of my childhood. Although I wasn't actually born in Loris, I lived there after I was born. The Loris of my childhood is peopled with some dear and memorable characters.

Miss Jennie

Mrs. R. Perry Hardee was known to everyone, young and old, as Miss Jennie. She and Mr. Perry, who was a partner in Loris Ford Company, lived across the street from my home, and I spent a lot of time in her bed-sitting-sewing room. Miss Jennie was the best seamstress I ever knew, bar none. She made clothes for me from my first memory until I finished college. I can't remember any dress or coat which came from the store as a finished product. She sewed for a large number of people in town, not just for my mother and me. This was full-time work, from early morning until well into the evening.

In addition, she was a demon for housekeeping and gardening and kept her pantry filled with canned and preserved foods. She rose each morning about four o'clock and did her housekeeping, fixed breakfast, worked in her garden in season, and then turned to the sewing. Miss Jennie also grew beautiful flowers and shared them. In a day when funeral flowers were mostly homemade offerings, she and my mother constructed many baskets and wreaths that celebrated their affection and friendship for a member of the community who had died. She was kindness itself.

Though she had no children of her own, she mothered a whole tribe of nieces and nephews—Kings and Henifords, for the most part, as well as all the neighborhood children. She was like a second mother to me. I remember and love Jennie Hardee, part of my happy childhood in Loris.

Hello, Central!

I remember when the telephone exchange, or Central, was located in a ramshackle building behind the building that now houses the Fashion Center. Grier H. Todd, who was a near down-the-street neighbor, operated it with the help of his family. In my mind's eye I can see him coming down the street on his way to take his place at the switchboard. He would relieve one or another of his family, his wife, his sister Gertrude, or Edith, Rudolph, Boyce, or Hazel. I don't recall that Carolyn was old enough, but perhaps she served after I went away to school.

As far as I can remember nobody had a private line. Everyone was on a party line and recognized his own combination of short and long rings. The telephones themselves were operated by crank. When you got Central's attention, you asked for the person you wanted to talk to by name. I am sure that there were numbers, perhaps even a little book of them, but I don't recall that people used them. If you had an emergency and the doctor wasn't in, Central could usually tell you where to find him.

Central could solve a lot of problems of locating people who were not at home. The exchange sat where there was a good view of the main street, and folks shared their comings and goings over the phone. Central was an essential service in the community. I think in the beginning the exchange was pretty self-contained, but eventually there were connections with the outside world.

Telephone communication was not something that people took for granted as we do now, a mechanical, impersonal, megasystem. In my childhood the telephone had the faces of Grier Todd and his family, friends, and neighbors.

Back to School

Going back to school in Loris in the 1930s meant going to Roy Hardee's store to buy your schoolbooks. Mr. Hardee had a wooden building in the vicinity of the grocery store now operated by his son and namesake but, as I remember it, closer to town. It was next door to the telephone exchange.

Most of the year he concentrated on groceries and a few sundries, but in the fall when schoolchildren were being outfitted, he was the vendor of textbooks. I have no idea how he got into it, but he had an exclusive "franchise" on this.

In those days, there were no free textbooks. All schoolbooks and supplies were purchased by the parents. On the first day of school, the teachers supplied each pupil with a list of what was required, and parents and children made a beeline to Hardee's Grocery to get them. Teachers expected them to be in hand within the first week of classes.

I doubt very much that there were as many different texts then as now. I certainly don't remember much more than a reader, an "arithmetic," a geography book, and a speller, more advanced each year. I remember using secondhand books. Changes were not made in textbooks every year, perhaps not even every five years. In the Depression years people had to "make do" in everything.

I am sure that Mr. Hardee didn't wait on all his customers himself, but in my memory he stands alone. His smile was always genial, his tone gentle. He worked hard and steadily. I am sure that many generations of Loris schoolchildren associate him with their school years.

Miss Katherine

When I entered the first grade, I was taught by Miss Katherine Richardson. So were hundreds and hundreds of other children who attended Loris Grammar School. In those days, it was Miss Katherine or no one. I started school in a small wooden building which had been the grammar school before the brick building was built. The brick building housed all other grades through high school until another high school was constructed in the mid-1930s.

Each high school had a superintendent, and in Loris he was Montgomery J. Bullock. The principal for many years was his wife, Agnes. Miss Katherine was her sister. Together they constituted a powerhouse of personality and drive and were altogether formidable.

I don't recall that people used Miss Katherine's last name except on the most formal occasions—and perhaps not then. Habit is too great. I have no idea how many years she was there, but she grew old in the service. I remember her as small, rather plain, and totally terrifying, so much so that I refused to learn! She was a founder and pillar of the Loris Presbyterian Church, so I am sure she must have been loved and respected by the adults she associated with.

Miss Katherine engaged in a tug-of-war with my father about the propriety of my wearing bibbed overalls to school. She did not consider them appropriate for a young lady in the first grade, although they were my preferred clothes at home, the winter was cold, and the classroom poorly heated. She sent me home, and Dad sent me back. As I recall it, he won, but again, the outcome was not as important to me at the time as the precarious position I occupied at the center of a struggle between two strong-willed people.

Cap'n Sid

In the 1930s there was a grocery store located on the southwest corner of Patterson (now Main) and Meeting Streets, in the same spot that the Fashion Center occupied until recently. The storekeeper was J. Sidney Bellamy, whose home was on Patterson at the corner of Mitchell Street (which is named for one of his daughters).

I remember Mr. Sid well and can see him now in my mind's eye. He had a mustache. I think of him as tall—whether he actually was or not, that was the way he appeared to me. Mr. Sid had come to Loris after spending a lot of his life on the Waccamaw River. He had operated Wortham's Ferry near Brooksville and had also operated a riverboat, the *Eva Mae*, named after his wife. The Bellamys named one of their daughters for her mother and another for a riverboat, the *Mitchelle C*, which came to the ferry from Conway. I have always thought them two of the most beautiful women in Loris.

I don't know how long Mr. Bellamy operated the grocery store at the main intersection in Loris. I remember being sent to the store by my mother early one morning to get a dozen eggs. In those days they didn't come in cartons. I was carrying the sack carefully in my hand as I trudged back home in the early light. I had a favorite great-uncle, Lewis Lafayette "Fate" Heniford, who was Loris's milkman and often let me make rounds with him. As I walked along, I could see his buggy pulled up in front of my home. I didn't want to miss this treat, so I began to run. There were no paved streets, no paved sidewalks. I stumbled, fell, and broke every egg. My memory has suppressed my mother's reaction when I got home—

and my punishment. It would have been sufficient just to forbid me to go with Uncle Fate on his rounds.

The Fair

The highlight of any year in my childhood was the coming of the fair in the fall. From my earliest recollection the Loris Fair Association put it on in October in the old Farmers Warehouse on Patterson (now Main) Street. Exhibits were inside, the carnival midway outside. The Fair Association collected a fee for entering the warehouse and grounds. I remember J. H. Yon and others acting as ticket sellers and takers at the front.

The tobacco warehouse disappeared amid the booths that were temporarily erected for all kinds of displays, both commercial ones sponsored by the merchants of the town and the community ones in which housewives displayed their crafts and homemade preserves and farmers their prize animals.

The big feature inside was always the food booth operated by the women of Loris Methodist Church, who had hereditary rights to a spot at the exit to the midway. In the Depression it was too expensive to eat out a lot and that wasn't the tradition anyway, but to eat at least one meal with the Methodist ladies was a civic obligation. No duty ever tasted so good. Good cooks to the last one of them, they worked hard and probably made a pretty good profit, since most of the food was donated.

For children the midway was fairyland. Rides, the penny pitch, ball throws, cotton candy, rides, freak shows, and girly shows (we only saw the free teasers on a little stage outside the tent before each performance), rides, gypsies and barkers, and the rides. Loris looked altogether different from the top of the Ferris wheel—if you could open your eyes.

On Friday white schools from the area paraded through town, their names carried proudly on banners by the biggest boys and girls—Sweet Home, Daisy, Green Sea, Oakdale, Red Bluff—they came for free admission tickets and one free ride each. Teachers strode beside their pupils. Saturday was the day for black schoolchildren.

Armistice Day

In my childhood THE war was still the Civil War and World War I was "the World War." My father and a good many of his friends were veterans of the Great War. It created a bond among them that was strong and special. The anniversary of the end of that war on the eleventh of November was a holiday, and we had a family celebration each year. The cease-fire came on the eleventh hour of the eleventh day of the eleventh month—magic numbers. We called it Armistice Day.

Our family and those of Dad's World War buddies usually went to Little River Neck for an oyster roast, fish fry, and fixings. There were no restaurants there, but the black creek fishermen provided the oysters and the fish. The men of our party were the cooks.

It must have been the role of the mothers to keep an eye on their offspring, but I don't remember being restrained by overly watchful adults. At the point where we picnicked, steep banks descending to the creek or marsh invited us to roll down them. Trees dared us to climb. A narrow boardwalk over the wide marsh and creek challenged us to cross to the ocean strand. I can still feel the terror of walking across that space with no railing to grab. Still I did it, again and again. If I had flinched or failed, I would have lost face with my two younger brothers.

My father loved oyster stew and prided himself on preparing it for the whole party. Everything else that had to be cooked was timed to be ready when Dad's stew reached the peak of perfection. I remember one year when the new minister of our church was a guest for the day and was requested to "ask the blessing." He did—at great length. So grateful was he that his conversation with the Lord went on until Dad's perfect stew curdled. And so did my father.

A Cup of Soup

When I went to grammar school, several recess periods a day allowed restless scholars to get outside for a few minutes to visit the outdoor privies and work off some of their pent-up energy playing games. Toward the middle of the day we had "big recess" during which we ate the lunches that we had brought to school from home. Swapping lunches was a popular way to socialize and to get some variety in the menu. The town children usually brought sandwiches made from store-bought bread, peanut butter, bananas mashed with peanut butter, or pimiento cheese. Country scholars brought sandwiches made of biscuits, ham, eggs, and the like. I remember my mouth watering for a taste of biscuit and ham, and I gladly swapped lunch with friends lucky enough to be from the country.

Our food was washed down with water from the pump in the yard. Each of us delighted in being the one to work the handle that brought water up from the well to the mouth of the pump. We drank from our cupped hands, from paper cups we folded from sheets of notebook paper, or from collapsible metal cups that we kept in our desks.

During the Depression, the federal government began the first school lunch program. R. E. Naugher, who had been the first vocational agriculture teacher in Loris, was the Washington official who planned that program. The menu was simple, every day the same. Cooks prepared huge vats of thick vegetable soup and served it, one large cup to a child. For those who had the money, the charge was a nickel. For parents short of cash, arrangements were made to accept produce—which went into the pot. The soup was probably more dependably nutritious than the lunches we brought from home, but it certainly lacked the socializing, sharing, and variety we got from swapping.

Going to the Post Office

Going to the post office was one of the daily rituals that marked my childhood. The postmaster and his assistants knew everyone, of course, and there was a daily exchange of opinion and information at the window.

Mail came on the train and the men at the post office got it into the boxes as soon as possible. There wasn't nearly as much of it in those days before junk mail. I can see the long rows of bronze boxes with their numbers and combination dials. When I was very small and couldn't work the dial that opened our box, I had to ask for the mail at the window. I never had to tell the person who served me my name—he knew all the children who came to his window. Later there were times when I still couldn't work the dial because the old mechanisms were loose and tricky to operate. No problem. The man at the window was willing to help.

The post office ranked right up there with school and church in my mind. I remember Mr. W. J. Hughes at the post office when it was located in the block between the main intersection and City Hall. The postmaster most familiar to me, however, was Thurman Boyd, who also was my Sunday school superintendent. Whether I met him at the window at the post office or in Sunday school assembly, Thurman Boyd symbolized all that was right with the Loris of my childhood. He was a friend of my father, a veteran of the First World War, a quiet man who held the respect of everyone who knew him.

Having his respect mattered to me, too. I wanted his approval as I did that of other older men and women who provided models for my growing up.

In Order of Appearance

Ladies Dressed to Go Downtown

Everyone I knew got up early in the Loris of my childhood. Anyone still under the covers at six o'clock was a lazy lie-abed. There were chores to do. Many of the stores in the downtown area were open by 7:00 or 7:30, and they stayed open later than they do now, particularly at the end of the week.

Not many of the married women of the town worked outside the home in those days. They kept their houses and raised their children. Their mornings were filled with laundry and cleaning and gardening and sewing, and all of those chores were done without the timesaving devices of today. Most homes had a washhouse out in the back yard, clotheslines in the yard, flatirons (later replaced with electric irons), pedal-operated Singer sewing machines, and gardens beside or behind the house.

Wives gathered and prepared the vegetables for the midday dinner, which was the chief meal of the day. Supper usually consisted of leftovers. When the men left their businesses to go home for dinner, there was a full spread of meat and vegetables, hot bread, and dessert. After lunch there was generally time for a short nap before going back to their stores.

The women cleared away the dinner and, if they had the chance, took a short nap themselves. Then they washed, dressed carefully and nearly as well as if they were going to church, put on their hats, and strolled uptown. Stores provided benches along the sidewalks where the ladies sat to visit and exchange news, views, and solutions to their common problems.

In my mind's eye I can see the baby carriages pulled up alongside the benches in front of the drugstores. Coca-Cola, called "dope" instead of "Coke," was a nickel a glass, and most of the ladies sooner or later sat at the spindly-legged tables or in the booths of the drugstores for their afternoon treat. After they had socialized, they did their errands at the grocery store, the shoe store, the dry goods store, or the post office.

Aunt Frances

When I was a child, the Hill was at the other end of a path that began at the back door of my home. It led down into some woods, across a foot log, and a short distance to the home of Frances and Isom Stevens. I was as familiar with their yard as I was with my own.

Frances Stevens worked for my mother as a domestic and was very much a part of our family life. She came in the early morning to help with the housekeeping, the washing, ironing, cleaning, and cooking. In the fashion of the times, she was my "Aunt Frances," and I loved her as a second mother.

Later Ella Jefferson, of the strong hands and warm, loving heart, moved from the farm to town and went to work for my family. She and her husband Tom were tenants on my uncle's place and were getting past the age when they could make a crop. In Loris they had a little house near the Bottom. Tom went first, but Ella lived to a venerable age.

For as long as I remember, the Hill was the section in which the black people lived. It was not a large community, but in it lived people who were very important in the life of the town. As a child, I knew that Charley Watson was an important man, for example. The black children with whom I played attended the school named for him. My family called on him to butcher cows when the need arose. I think the very first time I had a vivid awareness of death was the day he led an old milk cow down into the woods by the branch. She had had a vicious disposition and I wasn't sorry to see her go, but suddenly I was keenly aware that she wasn't coming back.

Golden Legette lived with and worked for my family for many years. He came from Georgetown County and had the lovely accent of those parts, but he didn't talk much. He just smiled, a wonderful smile that showed his gold tooth. He worked at the drugstore my father operated and later founded a funeral business on his own. I remember how glad I was to see him when he came to express his condolences at the time of my father's death.

Katie This and Katie That

One woman was called Kate, the other Katie, and both were outsiders. Mama was from Richmond, where her home was within blocks of Broad Street, the main shopping district. She loved the bright lights, beautiful store windows, crowds, and streetcars. She met my father at the Baptist church they both attended. He was a student at the Medical College of Virginia and boarded nearby. Katie Wolpert came to this country from Odessa, Russia. She had lived and worked in New York until she married Bernard Wolpert.

In the 1920s Loris was a far cry from the cities they had been used to. There were no sidewalks, no bright lights, no great stores. Plumbing tended to be primitive and often outdoors. I used to watch Katie Wolpert struggle to prime the pump in her yard. Why, she would wonder aloud, must you pour water in to get water out? Yet Loris was the place in which their husbands had decided to settle and make a living, my father in a drugstore and Mr. Wolpert in a clothing store.

Mama and Daddy and I lived on the second floor of the brick home of Edgar and Golda Stanley on the corner diagonally across from the Loris Baptist Church. The Wolperts lived in a small frame house across the street with their children, Robert, Bertie, and Raphael. Life in Loris in those days must have been difficult for them as the only permanent Jewish family in town. Katie Wolpert and Kate Heniford became true friends, sharing their daily lives and their occasional homesickness with each other. To the end of my mother's life, they visited and exchanged greetings on the great holidays of their two faiths. Long after my mother's death Mrs. Wolpert would tell me of her love for my mother and repeat the stories of the lonely young wives. She often told me that she and Mama would never have stayed in Loris "if we hadn't loved our husbands."

From time to time Loris had other Jewish merchants, but Joe Libbert was the only other one who remained for a long time. On Mr. Libbert's tombstone in Patterson Cemetery is a map of his long journey from England, through the great cities of the north, to Loris.

The Family Doctor

During my childhood we had two doctors in town, Dr. J. D. Thomas and Dr. Huger Richardson. Both were all-purpose general practitioners. My family had special ties to the Richardsons, who lived in a house just across and down the street from my home. Dr. Richardson had office space in the back of my father's drugstore.

Bald in my earliest memories, Dr. Richardson always seemed old to me. He came to Loris in 1912 from upstate after graduating from Wofford and the Medical College of South Carolina. Dr. Richardson practiced in Loris until his death in 1943 at age 59, not really old at all. About a year after setting up his practice here, he married a local girl, Margaret Butler. Dr. And Mrs. Richardson had two sons, Jack and George, both older than I, but I shared Latin classes in high school with Jack.

The family doctor of those days made house calls, often driving far into the country to tend patients. Dr. Richardson had a particular touch with pneumonia, and I heard many stories of his sitting with patients night and day until they passed the crisis. He delivered babies, some of whom were given his name. Count the number of Hugers around Loris. Most of them were named in his honor. He also enjoyed being asked to suggest names for babies, but his spelling was not reliable, and sometimes those children had oddly spelled names.

Doctors kept especially late hours on Saturday nights, when downtown Loris had a Dodge City atmosphere, except that the weapons of choice were more often knives than six-guns. Cutting victims were brought in to the doctor, held down by their comrades or anyone who happened to be standing by, and sewed up, often without benefit of additional anesthesia.

Dr. Richardson had few recreations that I remember, but he did enjoy playing bridge—auction, not contract, in those days—and often made one of a foursome at my home. A born kibitzer, I watched and learned. I can't remember when I didn't know how to play bridge, even if I wasn't allowed to speak, much less play. If Dr. Richardson arrived earlier than the others, he would indulge a little girl with a game of rummy.

Wholesale Tonsillectomies

A lot of people in and around Loris who were children in the 1930s have no tonsils. In those days before Loris had a hospital, surgeons came to town and offered mass removal of tonsils and adenoids that were causing trouble—and some, no doubt, that weren't.

The scene is fixed in my mind—the rows of cots that filled one of the large rooms upstairs at the new high school, anxious mothers nursing their young (sometimes more than one per mother), holding their heads as they threw up from the anesthesia, feeding them soup and ice cream to soothe their hurting throats. I visited my two little brothers who were patients, and I particularly remember the smell of the ether escaping from the makeshift operating room. (I had lost my tonsils and adenoids rather prematurely when I was still a baby, but it was done in the city in a proper hospital.)

In those days tonsils and adenoids were considered nuisance bodies that tended to become infected and adversely affect the health of children. Doctors felt that youngsters would be better off without them, so local physicians sponsored the teams of surgeons who came to offer the wholesale removal of tonsils and adenoids in towns without hospitals. Conway had similar clinics to the ones I remember in Loris.

Loris needed a hospital. When someone had an ailment that required hospitalization, the choices were McLeod Infirmary in Florence or Dr. Martin's little hospital in Mullins. I had had experiences in both by the time I was ten.

In 1943 Dr. Wilbert Kenneth Rogers, who grew up in Loris, returned to his hometown to practice. He had worked in the Loris Drug Store, my father's business, when he was in high school. Dr. Rogers established the Rogers Clinic in the old Bullock home near the high school, where he provided patient care until the Loris Community Hospital opened.

Loris was always a bootstrap community. After World War II the people of Loris felt that having a local hospital was essential and undertook to provide one. Town leaders saw a need and took direct action to meet it. The Civitan Club of Loris undertook to do the legwork. A committee, which included Civitans S. F. Horton and D. O. Heniford, obtained signatures from voters in the townships to form a special tax district to provide the money. The county's Legislative Delegation accepted the signatures without an official referendum and formed the Loris Community Hospital Tax District. The directors appointed by the delegation moved swiftly, and the hospital opened in 1950.

"The Revenooer"

Back in the days of my childhood it was a long, long trip between the home of my parents in Loris and the home of my maternal grandparents in Richmond. I remember making it by train in the company of a family friend who was going north. We left Loris in the afternoon and had to change trains in Elrod, North Carolina. There is no thrill for a child comparable to a train ride, as memorable for the smells as for the movement and the uniformed conductors and porters.

I also made the trip by car with my parents. I remember once Dad had a brand new car, a Pontiac, and he wanted to test its mileage. He filled the tank in Loris and was determined to make it to Richmond without a refill. He made it to Richmond, all right, but he gave out of gas going up Capitol Hill just about three blocks from my grandmother's house.

On other occasions my mother and I caught a ride with a local man who was an agent for the Alcohol and Tobacco Tax Unit—a "revenooer" whose duties included raiding liquor stills in the Virginia mountains. Victor Spivey's wife and sons lived about a mile south of Loris, but he was stationed in Richmond for much of his active career.

In those days federal agents of any kind shared the glamour of the FBI, and the G-men became heroes to every youngster in the land. Victor Spivey loomed bigger than life in my eyes. His work was dangerous and, I suspect, physically demanding and tedious, not glamorous at all, but I looked forward to trips with him as I would have to contact with a movie star. He told wonderful stories, and the long car trip went more quickly because of it.

He came home as often as he could to be with his family and managed to be active in such community activities as scouting, even though he had to spend much of his time away. Eventually, because of wartime rationing of gas, he was allowed to operate from his home in Loris during the last years of his active service.

Of Weather Men and Tobacco Men

There was a garden beside our house that my Dad tended with only negligible help from his children. Unable to give it as much time as he would like, he planted rows of gladioli parallel to the sidewalk to camouflage the untidy rows of vegetables.

Just at the edge of the sidewalk close to the house was a metal cylinder that housed a rain gauge. For a time Dad was the official weather observer and reported regularly to the U.S. Weather Bureau. This responsibility was sometimes delegated to me, and I fear the results suffered from my neglect. It was an easy chore to forget.

Later on, Edgar Stanley was weather observer for many years. Before they built their own house about 1929, my parents lived on the second floor of Golda and Edgar Stanley's home. The Stanleys' house was also home-away-from-home to tobacco buyers and other market people who came to Loris during the market season. Many of them returned year after year and were welcomed as old friends on their annual visit. Since hotel accommodations were limited, people in town frequently opened their homes and rented spare bedrooms to them.

I was three, four, and five years old during this time, but I vividly remember one tobacconist called Judge Avery. In the evening after supper he sat with me on the front steps of the Stanley home and told me stories about the stars in the early evening sky. I have no memory of him other than those pleasant "dusk dark" conversations, but those have lasted all my life.

Edgar Stanley was a very useful and industrious man. He rang the bell for services at the Baptist church across the street from his home. He sharpened knives and other blades. He was a coal dealer, delivered the freight that the trains brought in every day, and was mayor of Loris for two terms (1940-1941). A lover of flowers, his dahlias were famous. Most important to me, he and Miss Golda were among my best friends during my earliest years.

A Bird's Eye View

The first news reporter I remember was Buck Prince, who appeared from time to time when I was a child. His real name was Burroughs Prince, and he was Mrs. Edgar Stanley's son. I saw him when he came home to visit.

Buck ended his professional career as an executive producer for NBC news.

Then I remember the tall, lean Lem Winesett, who was in Loris when I was in high school. His sister Nell came to help him, married Nathan Hardwick, and stayed to raise her family. Winesett later was the owner of the *Marion Star*.

Fenton Miller came to Loris as a Presbyterian minister and was editor of the *Horry County News* and *Loris Sentinel* when I returned to Loris. Fenton went back into the ministry and met his death in a tidal creek near Pawley's Island.

Rod Sparrow was the newspaper's editor, reporter, and columnist when I returned to Loris to live in 1955. I can see him scurrying about Main Street with his pad, gathering the news that went into the weekly. Although he had people who helped him, he took on himself the rounds to secure advertisements, talk to people about what was happening, and write about what he found. Hard news went into the paper as articles. The rest became grist for his personal column, aptly called "A Bird's Eye View."

Rod was a night owl; late hours were his norm. I can remember being called anytime before midnight if there was something he wanted to talk about or ask questions about. He never knew when to quit. His job was also his recreation. There was once a remarkable issue of the paper in which the owner announced that Rod was exhausted and had been consigned to bed until he had rested. A lot of people have given a lot of themselves for the good of Loris, but few more unstintingly or selflessly than Rod Sparrow.

Going to the Movies

I grew up in the age of radio. The first one I remember had a headset for listening, one person at a time. Later listening to the radio in the evening was a family activity. The best-loved programs in our family were *Seth Parker, One Man's Family, I Love a Mystery, The Green Hornet, Let's Pretend, Lum and Abner, Fibber McGee and Molly, Fred Allen,* and *Jack Benny*.

There was no movie theater in Loris in those days. From time to time a tent show would set up in the vacant field behind the Farmers Warehouse, where the fair was usually held. I don't remember that my parents ever went, but, since we lived nearby, I was allowed to go if I took my two younger brothers. Since neither of them could read, it fell to me to read the subtitles of those old silent films. I vividly remember an old Grant Withers film which included a strip poker game in which shady ladies got down to their scanties. Imagine a little girl about seven or eight trying to explain that aloud to two little boys.

On occasions such as the arrival of a Bing Crosby movie, when my father thought the movie worth the trip, we would load up the car and go to Mullins, Conway, Tabor City, or even Whiteville. Fredric March was another favorite, and we went to Conway as a family to see *Anthony Adverse* in which he appeared. It sticks in my memory because my brother Davis persisted in calling it "Anthony Adverbs."

On my sixteenth birthday, a school group went to Columbia to take state examinations in various subjects. Loris High School regularly had students who won state recognition in English, algebra, history, and the like. The present-day equivalent would be the annual brain game competitions. As a reward when the examinations were over, our chaperones took us to see *Gone With the Wind*, which was playing in the capital.

Naturally there were many people who had never seen a movie when a theater was finally built in Loris. Mrs. P. D. Bell built the building in the late 1930s, and Henry Nelson came to manage it. The very first showing was on a Saturday afternoon. It was a western. At the height of the action, it began to appear to one man in the audience that the men in the black hats were getting the better of the good guys in the white hats. Armed with every Horry boy's best friend, a big knife, he went to their rescue. He succeeded only in slashing the screen and putting an end to the show.

AYNOR: THE LITTLE GOLDEN TOWN

The Burroughs railroad company, which had built the first tracks to Horry County's coast, changed its name from Conway and Seacoast Railroad to the Conway, Coast and Western Railroad in July 1904. This signaled a literal change of direction. It began to lay tracks toward the Little Pee Dee River with the intention of hooking up with the trading centers of Mullins and Marion and with the railroads that served them. Burroughs and Collins owned large tracts of timber in western Horry County from which the new rails would allow easier transport of logs to the mills in Conway and freight to country stores west of the county seat.

In July 1905, the CC&W was sold to James H. Chadbourn, of the family that had originally constructed the railroad from North Carolina to Conway. Chadbourn employed blacks on the construction gangs. When they passed Cool Spring, they were in an area beyond "the deadline." Though unofficial and, indeed, illegal in its intent, the deadline was meant to keep blacks out of western Horry County. Word had been passed that any black caught there who was not already a resident would be in severe danger to life and limb.

One night in the fall of 1905, the construction gang was sitting around the campfire when they were fired upon from the surrounding darkness. One man was killed. The incident was reported in the local newspaper in an article mentioning the deadline.

Construction stopped at that spot, the rails ending in the middle of land owned by the Burroughs and Collins Company that was known as the Aynor tract. In 1906 the company decided to lay out a little town there and sell lots. The town was named Aynor.

There is some mystery about the origin of the name. The newspaper at the time said that it was "named after Mrs. Aynor, a lady who resided in Horry county in years long gone. The station stands on land she once owned and the place has been named in her honor." The problem arises when historians try to research this lady and her family. No land transactions at the courthouse are recorded in that name, and there is no other official record that such a person ever existed.

Still, a body of legend has grown up about her. Local lore says she owned the land before the Civil War. Her husband disposed of it in the bad times after the war when he could not pay the taxes, trading it to a passing stranger for a one-eyed horse and a saddle. The stranger never paid the taxes and disappeared. Eventually Burroughs and Collins acquired it in a sale at the courthouse.

In a 1989 article in the *Independent Republic Quarterly*, Aynor native Carlisle Dawsey proposed another theory based on research in the records of Burroughs and Collins and in records at the courthouse. He believes the land belonged to a Jacob Eykner, whose name was sometimes spelled Eynner or Ikner. Eykner received a grant of 100 acres on November 1, 1790, and another on November 7 of the same year for 240 acres. Having traced the records carefully, Dawsey believes this is the land which was eventually known as the Aynor tract.

Burroughs and Collins sold lots around the railroad tracks in 1910. Stores and homes grew up around the terminus, and by 1913 enough people had located there to incorporate a town. Gabe Edwards was elected intendant (mayor) and the first wardens (councilmen) were Waterman Cook, Hugh Johnson, and John Shelley. Edwards owned a service station, Cook and Shelley operated a cotton gin, and Johnson was a farmer.

At the height of its early development, Aynor was a thriving tobacco market with warehouses and packing houses, a bank, a brickyard, a cotton gin, grist mills, and sawmills. It declined in the 1930s and only began to grow again in the 1980s.

It was during the late 1970s and early 1980s, also, that Horry's compass of political power seemed to swing from Loris toward Aynor. At one point the county superintendent of education, John Dawsey; acting county administrator, William J. Brown; the city manager of Conway, William Graham; and W. G. Hucks Jr. And Lacy K. Hucks, two of the most powerful and astute members of the Horry County Council, all claimed Aynor as their hometown.

In August 1984 Aynor citizens dedicated a mural celebrating the roles of the railroad and tobacco in their history (*IRQ* 19:1, cover). Although the tracks were taken up and the right of way abandoned by 1943, North and South Main Streets run parallel to each other, an indelible reminder that the railroad was there.

The people of Aynor call it the Little Golden Town. Each fall the citizens celebrate themselves in the annual Hoe Down, a community festival featuring local music and dancers, great food, and craft booths. Visitors are welcome.

MYRTLE BEACH: NEW TOWN

Along the coast around Withers Swash (earlier Eight Mile Swash) and the rock formations now known as Hurl Rocks, history is as interesting as anywhere in the county, but may be harder for visitors to find.

Settlers from the Waccamaw Neck tried to extend the plantation system to what they called Long Bay. Grace Wainwright obtained 600 acres in the area just south of Withers Swash in 1735, as soon as the colonial government began to issue grants. Others received grants in the pre-Revolutionary period, among them William Allston, Isaac Huger, Peter Belin, and members of the Withers family: John, Richard, William, and Mary.

At Prince George Winyah Episcopal Church, the gravestone of Mary Esther Withers (d. 1801) lies just outside the door that opens into the cemetery. "She gave up the pleasures of Society," it declares, "and retired to Long Bay, where she resided a great part of her life devoted to the welfare of her children," Francis, Richard, and Robert. The implication that the sons considered Long Bay not quite civilized is clear, in spite of the fact that together the Withers family owned almost 3,000 acres along the swamp that fed Eight Mile Swash. The swash itself came to be known by their name.

Small farmers and fishermen also settled in the area, living off the land and sea. The farms were usually small and self-contained. They were considered to be in the large area known as Socastee. Todd, Owens, Stalvey, King, Anderson, Simmons, and DuBois were families that farmed or fished in the area.

In Order of Appearance

In the nineteenth century, like other citizens of Horry County, they were engaged in the naval stores and timber industries. Land was cheap and productivity low. Taxes were low, but still many could not pay them. Many farmers offered their land to the timber and turpentine dealers for sale outright, instead of negotiating permission for their trees to be cut or tapped. In this way the dealers acquired large acreage along the coast. The firm of Burroughs and Collins was among them. The company had a camp for its workers located near what is now downtown Myrtle Beach.

Practically the only way that produce moved out of Horry in those days was by water on the little paddlewheel steamers that plied the Waccamaw and the Little Pee Dee. After railroads were introduced, produce from remote areas could be brought to the rivers more easily. Burroughs and Collins saw the benefit of building a line from the Waccamaw River opposite Conway to the coast to facilitate shipment of naval stores and timber. Franklin G. Burroughs, the founding partner in Burroughs and Collins, was the one who ordered the line surveyed.

His last surviving daughter, Mrs. S. G. Godfrey, related in her memoirs that he told her sister Ruth, "I won't live to see it, and you may not, but someday this whole strand will be a resort." Visionary or not, before he died Burroughs set in motion the building of a railroad from Conway to the coast. His sons carried out the project, and in 1900 the first streets were laid out in what they called simply New Town.

When the Burroughs and Collins families separated their interests in the firm around the turn of the century, much of their holdings in land along the coast went to the Burroughs heirs, as did the firm name. They continued in farming and timber, but naval stores was already pretty much played out.

The railroad made excursions to the seashore easier. A member of one party wrote a little ditty to commemorate such an outing: "The words we heard o'er and o'er / Was again to see the shore, / And what a pleasure it would be, / To once more visit the town by the sea."

In 1900, a little contest was held among the summer visitors to choose a more suitable name than New Town. Those present were allowed to submit their choices, and it was Mrs. F. G. Burroughs who carried the day with Myrtle Beach, honoring the native shrub that grows so abundantly along the coast.

The first tourist accommodation, completed in April 1901, was the Seaside Inn, a small, well-appointed hotel run in the style of a boarding house by the Burroughs family. According to the Conway newspaper, it "bore the magic touch of a refined woman's fingers." A stay there cost two dollars a day, meals included.

A few lots were sold for twenty-five dollars, mostly to Conway people. They were measured out along the beach with a thirty-foot cow chain. There was no rush to acquire this property, but gradually a few primitive beach houses were erected. Summer folk brought their own provisions or bought supplies from local farmers and fishermen. From the spring of 1901, there was a commissary store of the sort that timber and turpentine firms ran to supply their hands, but perhaps a touch more elaborate than the usual ones. It contained a "complete stock of general merchandise," according to the newspaper. Gradually Burroughs and Collins (the old firm name was retained) shifted its emphasis from timber and turpentine to farming. It had become so hard to generate income that they had decided to sell some of their land.

Through various intermediaries their offer finally reached Simeon B. Chapin, a Northern financier looking for investments in the south. In 1912 he came to Conway unannounced. He had decided not to invest because of the remoteness of the area, but decided to meet with the Burroughs brothers to tell them his decision in person. Their first meeting at the company office in Conway was cordial, but Chapin told them of his decision. As he left the office, according to his daughter, Elizabeth Chapin Patterson, he had second thoughts. He turned back and asked if they were prepared to enter into a partnership with him. So with a handshake, Myrtle Beach Farms was born. Chapin put in money for a half interest, and the Burroughs brothers put in nearly 70,000 acres of land along the coast.

Chapin visited the area from time to time to indulge his passion for hunting. The day-to-day operations, however, he left pretty much to Donald and Frank Burroughs. The Chapin Company, which operated a department store, was organized later and took the place of the old commissary store. This store in the heart of town is now considerably reduced from its heyday, but it has been a landmark institution since 1928.

On the south end of the beach below the holdings of the Burroughs and Collins firm, the Horry Land and Improvement Company, founded by Sen. D. Allen Spivey, owned a stretch of land which he developed into Spivey's Beach during the 1920s. This land included Withers Swash, the mouth and course of which wandered with storms and tides. In the 1940s heavy timbers were put in place to stabilize the swash to protect development, and a bridge was built to allow walkers to cross the swash whatever the tide.

Spivey's Beach included tourist accommodations. Among the first were small cabins which were rented by the day or week. These may have been the first tourist court along the Grand Strand. A pavilion at the south end provided competition for the one that Burroughs and Collins built near the downtown area.

In the early 1920s, a former Horry County newspaper editor invited the professional journalists of the state to come to Horry to see the wonders of this land by the ocean. James Henry Rice extolled the potential of the area as he led them in a caravan of automobiles from Myrtle Beach to Little River. He spoke to the Conway Chamber of Commerce and urged its members to promote tourism as an income-producing industry.

The area attracted the interest of John T., J. David, Robert I., and Edward F. Woodside, brothers from Greenville, South Carolina, who purchased from Myrtle Beach Farms some 65,000 acres in 1926. The Woodsides envisioned a plush resort that would rival the playgrounds of the rich in the north and soon set to work to build the first stages.

Until 1928, when a road between Socastee and Myrtle Beach was paved, there were no good roads. People came over dirt roads from Conway by way of Socastee. Trains still brought visitors from the outside over the little line from Conway to the beach. There were no airlines to bring them in, nor was there a harbor in which the yachts of the wealthy could find berths. How, exactly, were the visitors to get to the waiting accommodations?

The construction of the first golf course and clubhouse began almost at once and attracted visitors who were entertained with hunting, fishing, and golf. Their second phase was a "million dollar" hotel on the beachfront. The crash of 1929 occurred before the Ocean Forest opened for business on January 15, 1930. Nonetheless, there was a formal opening gala on February 21.

The Woodsides, like many other investors of the time, could not meet the payments on their debt. The land reverted to the Myrtle Beach Farms. The company was short of cash, so some of the land had to be sold to satisfy taxes, but thousands of acres were left, land which would become more valuable as the beach developed. The Myrtle Beach Farms became the chief engine for the continuing development of the town.

The completion of the Intracoastal Waterway in 1936 effectively created a coastal island. It separated a rapidly developing area from the rural part of Horry County. People from the western part contributed their financial resources for the first wave of development at Myrtle Beach, and, even more important, were the workers who made it go.

In 1935 Myrtle Beach got a newspaper, the *Myrtle Beach News*, and the next year a telephone exchange. A new bridge over the Waccamaw and a road from there to the coast meant that travelers did not have to go by

Socastee to reach the resort. It was not until March 12, 1938, however, that the town received its official charter and elected W. L. Harrelson the first mayor. A fire and police department followed. The city hall was built in 1941.

The city opened a small municipal airport in 1940 which was, in effect, commandeered for the war effort after Pearl Harbor in 1941. The Army Air Force also seized land for a bombing and firing range, and many aviators were trained in Myrtle Beach during the war years. German prisoners of war were confined in local camps.

When World War II was over, Myrtle Beach began another building phase. Most of the new accommodations would be called "mom and pop" operations now, but the resort was enjoying an increasing popularity, particularly in the Carolinas. The Sun Fun Festival was initiated in the spring of 1954.

Hurricane Hazel struck with deadly force on October 15, 1954. Until 1989, when Hurricane Hugo ended a lucky streak, time along the coast was divided into before and after Hazel. Many of the small tourist operators did not have the resources to rebuild, but those who did have the financial strength were able to buy land on which to put up larger hotels.

The fame of Myrtle Beach has been vigorously and imaginatively promoted by public and private interests alike. Its success can be measured to some extent by the discomfort suffered by the locals. In the early years, the people who lived along the Grand Strand gained some respite during the winter months when tourist activity was minimal. Then the season began to lengthen and promoters created "shoulder seasons" for golf and senior travelers. Locals grumped but coped as the tourist traffic continued from early spring to Thanksgiving and after.

Then the area began to attract retirees for year-round living and "snowbirds" escaping the cold of their northern homes during the winter months. Golfers came to enjoy the snow-free courses that were being built as fast as they could be designed. To all intents and purposes, winter respite is gone. The inability of road building to keep up with the pressures of increased population and visitor traffic has become the standard fare of complainers, locals and visitors alike.

The closing of the Myrtle Beach Air Force Base in 1993 was devastating to those who depended on it for employment or for the services it provided to military retirees. It was only a temporary blip on the economic growth of the area, however. Although the big decisions about the utilization of the base land still are pending, it is clear that the closing did not long stay local economic development.

Myrtle Beach appeared as New Town as the twentieth century began. Even those who may have foreseen a thriving resort "someday" would doubtless be astonished that it has developed at the end of the century into a place visited by people from all over the world.

BRIARCLIFFE ACRES: A VERY PRIVATE TOWN

The little town of Briarcliffe Acres may not be unique among towns in South Carolina, but it certainly is unusual. On June 1, 1946, Kenneth C. Ellsworth and his associates in Yaupon Acres, Inc., acquired 600 acres from Pauline K. Springs and Louise W. Springs for $150,000. The property lay on each side of Highway 17, had about 3,500 feet along the ocean, two freshwater lakes, and two swashes. The rest was wooded.

The next year Ellsworth engaged a landscape architect to design the layout of a private residential community, which he named Briarcliffe Acres; Ellsworth said that the name referred to the native briars and the high banks of the Intracoastal Waterway, which marked the western edge of the property. These reminded him of Briarcliff, a community in New York state. The "e" was added to "make it fancy."

The area to the east was laid out for single-family dwellings and the portion to the west for more diversified uses, including a marina. The western portion came to be called Briarcliffe West; the area to the east later became the town. In the latter privacy and seclusion were hallmarks of the design. Lots were an acre each, arranged along three main entrance roads, several cross streets and numerous cul-de-sacs.

The first lots were sold November 12, 1946. The Ellsworth group used the income from them to continue the landscaping of the tract. The first homes, when they were built, were anything but pretentious. They were meant to be vacation hideaways. Air conditioning was nonexistent and other amenities few.

Gradually, of course, the residences became more substantial and more numerous. By 1954 there were enough people living there or owning lots in the development that they formed an eleemosynary corporation named Briarcliffe Acres (later Briarcliffe Acres Association) "to promote and improve the community ... To promote good neighborly feeling and brotherhood, to promote a governing body of the community to better formulate and carry our policies and programs of the community...." On the heels of this development, the Briarcliffe Realty Company, successor to Yaupon, gave this association the right to control and manage all the public areas of the community—that is, the beachfront, parks, easements, lakes, and roads.

This set the stage for almost continuous litigation until the town was incorporated on February 25, 1976—and after. Ellsworth's successors in the realty company challenged the association's control of the common areas, and dissident residents even challenged the incorporation of the town. The first election was held on November 16, 1976, in a ham radio shack owned by a member of the community. A. L. "Roy" Emptage was elected mayor.

At the swearing-in ceremony the new council was served with an injunction immediately after the members had taken their oaths. The injunction was soon lifted, but it only signaled the difficulties to come. Because by deed only residential buildings were allowed in the town (except the cabana on the beach), there was no place to hold the meetings of the new town council. At first they met in a vacant house belonging to a nonresident member of the association, but there were immediate protests of the use of a private home from some members of the community.

The council arranged to meet at the Lutheran Church of the Risen Christ across Highway 17. Dissident residents got a court order to prohibit the council from meeting outside the city limits! In time the problem was solved when the town annexed the property of the church. The church and its school are the only nonresidential buildings in the town to this day.

The town had, in effect, a dual government. While the town council exercised all the powers of government usual to cities, rights of control over the public areas, including the roads, rested in the Briarcliffe Acres Association. Council had to secure its acquiescence in decisions regarding anything but the private residential lots. On almost every question that was raised or action taken the community "chose up sides," and one group brought suit against the other.

Consider the problem of the roads. They were not county roads, nor state roads, nor city streets. Laid out by the developers of the residential community, they were therefore private. The town lacked the authority—to say nothing of the funds—to keep up the roads, much less pave them. Council could not even request help from the Horry County or state authorities because those governments are prohibited by law from doing work on private property. Eventually it was necessary for the town to bring condemnation proceedings to acquire the roads from the Briarcliffe Acres Association.

Several times successors to the original firm established by Ellsworth and his associates have tried to exert ownership over valuable property along or near the beach. For more than ten years the association fought back these incursions. The question was finally resolved in its favor. The development of anything but single-family residences has been forbidden.

Nonetheless, outside development has impinged on the seclusion and privacy of the people in Briarcliffe Acres. On its southern boundary, it is protected by the Meher Spiritual Center's quiet woods and lakes, but across the highway Briarcliffe Mall brought heavy traffic to the area and stimulated business development along the Highway 17 corridor. Considerable commercial, entertainment, and residential development both north and west of the town adds to the tourist and local traffic, which grows greater every year. A planned highway route that bypasses Conway will exit in the neighborhood of the town. The bridge that will span the Intracoastal Waterway and connect this route to Highway 17 is already in place.

The town was organized on the eve of home rule, which would have prohibited areas within five miles of an established city or town from becoming incorporated. It can, therefore, resist the efforts of either of its larger neighbors to annex the town. Given its history over the better part of a half century, Briarcliffe Acres is likely to continue the fight to be a very private town.

SURFSIDE BEACH: OUT OF THE ARK

John M. Tillman, who was born about 1800, owned land totaling 3,194 acres on the Atlantic Ocean. The Horry County land records do not indicate how he came by this property, which was known as the Ark (Arke) Plantation. He may have inherited it, because he had it resurveyed in 1838. The property included a mile and a half of beachfront and extended some three miles inland from the ocean.

Tillman lived in a four-room, two-story house—two rooms up and two down. The Tillman home is noted on the Harlee map of 1820 (*Mills' Atlas*) on the "Shore Road from Georgetown to North Carolina" (King's Highway). Tillman's house was generally known as "The Ark," after the name of the plantation.

Before the Civil War John Tillman was a prosperous planter. The records show that in 1850 he owned fifty-seven slaves. They produced sweet potatoes and rice, both staples of the local diet, as well as valuable exports. The same census listed the worth of his property as five thousand dollars. As far as can be determined, Tillman never married. His will, which he signed in 1854, devised all his property to friends and relatives, as the estate administration recorded after his death in 1865. Eventually it became the property of the Roach family and during that time was known as Roach's Beach.

It was still known to most of the local people who visited it as "The Ark." People from the southern part of Horry County went there in the fall to fish and enjoy the ocean at the end of a year's hard work. The old Tillman house survived the great Tidal Wave of 1893 and was a local landmark. Louise Chestnut Squires, who came to the area as a little girl, related the story of how the Ark, which stood atop a dune some distance from the oceanfront, survived: "There were places chopped out of the floor of the lobby to let water run out. This was done by fishermen who were on the beach and saw the tidal wave coming. It swept over the beach. They escaped by running to the hotel."

In time the property passed into the possession of George J. Holliday of Galivants Ferry. He changed the name to Floral Beach, honoring his wife, Flora. He moved a sawmill onto the property and used it to prepare timber cut from the woods for building. Holliday built a pavilion for the recreation of visitors and increased the size of the old Tillman house to accommodate them overnight. The Ark thus became the first hotel.

Holliday also built a commissary store with living quarters behind it for his year-round overseer, James Chestnut, whose children lived there with him. For his own family, he built a five-bedroom house so that his wife and children could spend the summer months at the beach. Holliday also built three bedroom cottages for the use of summer visitors.

There is little evidence that there was any significant promotion of Floral Beach during the 1920s and 1930s when it was in the hands of the Hollidays. It may have been that his other interests demanded too much of George J. Holliday's attention. In any event, he sold the land to the Caldwell Company of Columbia, South Carolina. This firm sold a few lots for thirty-five dollars each and ended up in bankruptcy.

In 1952 a mostly Horry County group consisting of G. W. ("Buster") Bryan, James A. Calhoun Jr., Craig Wall Sr., Ervin E. Dargan, James Nettles (of Columbia), and Collins Spivey purchased 1,700 acres for $150,000. According to James Calhoun, it was Collins Spivey of Conway who initiated the project. They got 800 acres on the ocean side of Highway 17 and 900 acres on the other side. By selling those 900 acres to V. F. Platt, they were able to afford to purchase another 337 acres on the ocean front for $55,000 from the Burroughs family of Conway.

James Calhoun described how the beach received its present name: "Buster said his wife had been down in Florida and she had picked out a name. I said, 'What is it?' and he said it was Surfside. I said, 'That sounds good to me. Just add Beach to it and we will have it.' I was president of the company, so that is what we did. We named it Surfside Beach."

They divided the parcel into individual homesites, except for a section for business along the highway. Among the home lots, especially on the south end of town, on land purchased and developed by J. A. Fuller, were some multifamily lots. It was the intention of the founders and apparently those who came after them that this beach should be primarily residential.

The population grew to the point that it needed city services such as garbage pickup, water, and sewers, so Surfside Beach, roughly two miles square, was incorporated on March 14, 1964. T. J. Harrison was the first mayor. Among the six who have served to date were two men who had experience in the office in other cities. Cecil Ratcliffe had been mayor of Hemingway before moving to Surfside Beach, and Blue Huckabee had been mayor of Conway.

In spite of some controversy in the early administrations, the mayors and councils have clung to the concept of a family-oriented town and early adopted zoning regulations which have helped to keep the town clear of intrusive commercialism. Surfside Beach was sufficiently foresighted to pass a beach protection ordinance in the early years and to control density of housing—that is, buildings per acre. Along the beachfront are two hotels of several stories which required special consideration by the town council.

Careful planning and generous gifts have enabled the town to have parks and other amenities which contribute to the attractiveness of the area. A town ordinance protects its trees from careless destruction. Land for churches and for a public library branch was provided by interested owners. Surfside Beach has been attractive to retirees. About 60 percent of its present population consists of older citizens. There is no school in town. Children go to Socastee and St. James schools.

Across Highway 17 from Surfside Beach is a large golf course and housing complex known as Deerfield. To the north is the Ocean Lakes Campground developed from land which V. F. Platt acquired. It is now owned by Platt's daughter, Mary Emily Platt Jackson (Mrs. Nelson Jackson III) and her family.

Like other Grand Strand beaches, Surfside Beach suffered mightily from Hurricane Hugo. It was on the northwestern, the dangerous, side of the eye of the storm, which came over land in the vicinity of McClellanville. The mayor, Dick M. Johnson, helped to direct emergency efforts from the city hall. As soon as the storm had passed, he contacted the Myrtle Beach Air Force Base commander to ask for help in the cleanup. Airmen and their equipment pitched in to help clean up the town.

Surfside Beach faces the problems of infrastructure and provision of city services like other Horry municipalities, but it is likely to continue a distinctive community of homes and small business.

ATLANTIC BEACH: BLACK PEARL

Atlantic Beach is singular among the municipalities of Horry County. It is situated on the beachfront within the city limits of North Myrtle Beach, a small enclave surrounded on three sides by its bigger neighbor. Less than 100 acres, all told, it is the only town in the county which has a completely black government. Most, if not all, of the property in town is black owned and controlled.

Writers have given different stories about how Atlantic Beach came to be. Early in this century the few people, white and black, who lived in the area were small farmers and fishermen. As the nearby white beaches developed, black people found employment in the tourist industry. Blacks were excluded from the use of white beaches, so Atlantic Beach became known as a black resort. A few local entrepreneurs and some from the outside invested in small visitor accommodations and eating establishments which operated during the summer.

As long as segregation continued, Atlantic Beach, which came to be called the "Black Pearl," flourished. It was the only place where black visitors to the coast could find accommodations, giving it a virtual monopoly on that trade. During World War II a group of black professionals from Horry and nearby counties formed an investment company to develop property in the town. J. W. Seabrook, president; Dr. Robert K. Gordon, vice president and treasurer; S. W. Thaggard, secretary; and Dr. Peter C. Kelly incorporated the Atlantic Beach Company, Inc., on March 29, 1943.

Their effort was to be one of a number which failed to bestow the prosperity for which Atlantic Beach has a clear potential. The people of the town have competing values which have tended to thwart every effort to develop it. On the one hand, Atlantic Beach landowners need and want the thriving tourist economy they see their neighbors enjoying. On the other, they have not had the resources to accomplish that development themselves. Reluctant to sell to white developers for fear of losing control and thereby losing their heritage, they continue to resist investment which would threaten the unique black character of the town. The price of this impasse has been lagging development. Atlantic Beach is the only municipality along the coast which has not thrived on the tourist industry.

Atlantic Beach was incorporated in 1966 to avoid what its citizens perceived as a threat to their control. The four municipalities which were its closest neighbors agreed to merge to form a more efficient government. Atlantic Beach declined the option to join for fear of being swallowed up in the larger town.

The first mayor of Atlantic Beach was Emory Gore, and the councilmen were Millard Rucker, Daniel Gore, Le Grant Gore, and John Mark Simmons. The city government has always been entirely black. What the new government soon found out was that, as a separate municipality, it did not have the resources to be a viable town. It has required assistance from its neighbors and the county government to maintain its police and fire services. Although it has received state and federal grants for the improvement of services, it still has not succeeded in developing a stable governmental structure.

NORTH MYRTLE BEACH: ONE OUT OF FOUR

One of the earliest visitors to the area which is now called North Myrtle Beach was a young English gentleman traveling from Charleston to Cape Fear along "the only road to South Carolina from the northern part of the continent" (*CGHS,* rpt. *IRQ* 23:1:8-20). He declared it a poor excuse of a road, "nothing but a sandy bank," which every traveler from New England or New York had to traverse on his way to Charleston.

It was 1734, the year before the area was formally opened for settlement by the colonial government, and the young gentleman encountered nothing from Muenly's, where he spent the night, 25 miles from where he crossed into Waccamaw Neck, to Ash's or Little River. The trip along the strand took a full day from five in the morning until dark. The Englishman and three other members of the party lost their horses. The poor beasts gave out from the difficulty of traveling in the deep sand and had to be left behind.

The great stretches of white sand and the rolling breakers along the Horry County coast, however, have generally beguiled visitors. From the time of George Whitefield, who visited the area in 1740, men, women, and children—especially children—have enjoyed the beach. Whitefield found the residents of Little River celebrating the New Year. He rebuked the revelers but had to listen to the fiddles and dancing after he retired. After his night in Little River, he rose and, after reproving them again, wiped the dust of that place off his shoes. After several miles his path along the coast road opened onto the strand. His disgruntled frame of mind dissolved amidst its charms.

Gradually settlers moved into the Long Bay area. Some like the Vereens and Vaughts came from the south, through Charleston and Georgetown, but many came from the north, from Virginia and North Carolina. For a time the wealthy families of the Waccamaw Neck also held land in Little River and the nearby coastal areas. Through the Revolution there were Allstons and Marions entrenched in the area. Land in the Cherry Grove area, for example, was granted by King George III to John Alston in 1767. William Allston owned a tract in Little River Neck.

Daniel Morrall, for whose son present-day Murrells Inlet is named, owned an estate there, and the old Cherry Grove Inlet was once known as Morrall's Inlet. It is distinctly disorienting to the modern reader to look at an old map which locates Murrells Inlet on the northern coast of Horry. Futch Island, bounded on the north by Hog Inlet and on the south by Cherry Grove Inlet, was joined to the mainland by a developer in this century.

Among the early settlers were the Gause family. William Gause Sr. from Bertie Precinct, North Carolina, settled on a large swash that became known as Gause's Swash but has changed names over the years and now is best known as White Point Swash.

The plantation system did not take hold here as it did in Georgetown County, though there were some exceptions. Typically, the large original grants were divided gradually by sale or among heirs, and most families held small farms which supplied their needs but not much for sale. There were fisheries, too, along the strand.

Beginning with the Indians, the earliest seasonal migrations to this region from the interior were people looking for seafood to vary their diets. After the whites settled on their small farms they came from beyond the Waccamaw to fish in the fall after they had gathered their crops. These visitors came by covered or uncovered wagon and camped for days or weeks on the land of the farmers and fishermen along the coast. Families, sometimes related, sometimes not, joined forces to seine for mullet, which came in great schools. They salted these down to be eaten during the winter. This activity was at once work and recreation.

During the Civil War, the South needed salt. Along the ocean strand the people traditionally derived salt from ocean water by evaporation. Production was stepped up to supply the demand. Most of the military action in Horry County involved either the defense or destruction of the saltworks which were operated at several places along the coast.

Those who returned from the war settled back into the old work of farming and fishing. The land along the coast was valued primarily for fisheries. In the area that is now Tilghman Beach, for example, William and Abraham Bessent operated a fishery before the Civil War. The pleasures of the beach were enjoyed only by the locals and those few hardy visitors who came to fish.

Before the time of the automobile, visitors came by covered or uncovered wagons, crossing at Wortham's Ferry or at Star Bluff. They camped for days or weeks on the land of the farmers and fishermen along the coast. Gradually the landowners discovered that this traffic could be a source of income. They built or improved facilities for the visitors.

During Prohibition the sparsely populated coast provided access to rumrunners. One story tells about a large ship anchored offshore at White Point, south of Windy Hill Beach, in deep water. Small boats brought the cargo to the strand. Boards were laid down for the truck wheels to run on. After the transfer, the strand and the ground in the woods were swept to blot out the evidence. Federal agents arrested the man on whose land the ship was unloading and picked up other ordinary folk, mostly local, who were involved, but did not snare any of the big operators. When these local men were brought before a federal jury consisting of other locals they were turned loose out of a sense of fundamental fairness.

Eventually local men, including Nicholas F. Nixon Sr. (1862–1942), blazed the trail for a road from Loris to Cherry Grove across the Waccamaw River at Bellamy's Landing. It was constructed by the county. "Constructed" did not mean paved. For a number of years it remained a rough road, which nonetheless made it possible for Loris residents to spend an afternoon under the fishing shelters (pine boughs on a head-high frame) at Cherry Grove Beach and take a swim in the ocean.

The children in these family parties looked forward to reaching Nixon's Crossroads. Not only did sight of it promise that the beach was close, but there was a "monkey stand" at the Leland Bellamy store at the intersection of U.S. 17 and Highway 9. The monkeys in a cage and a bear tethered nearby provided youngsters and parents with an entertaining break in their trip.

For many years Nicholas F. Nixon, with his white beard and black hat, was as much a landmark in the area as his family home, which overlooked the marsh. In 1924, the Nixon family prepared for the subdivision of Cherry Grove, which took its name from an early plantation in the area and for a native tree.

In 1950 C. D. Nixon closed Cherry Grove Inlet to join Cherry Grove Beach to Futch Beach. He had to blast open a new outlet to Hog Inlet so that the tide would continue to flow into the marsh and keep the oyster beds healthy. Hurricane Hazel cut a new inlet on October 15, 1954, which was quickly closed with the use of federal emergency assistance funds.

Cherry Grove Beach was incorporated on March 26, 1959. The first mayor was C. D. Nixon and the councilmen were R. Marvin Edge, Nicholas F. Nixon, J. L. Vereen, and K. V. McLeod.

Tilghman Estates lies between Cherry Grove and Ocean Drive. Charles T. Tilghman and members of his family and began this development in 1948.

A group of professional men from Florence bought land in 1926 to form Ocean Drive Estates and subdivided Ocean Drive in 1927. On June 8, 1948, Ocean Drive Beach became the first of the area towns to be incorporated. The citizens elected Luther W. Fenegan mayor and Hardy S. Bennett, James B. Harris, A. M. Rush, and J. Blakeney Jackson councilmen. In the early years automobile races were held on its broad strand, billed as the "widest beach in the world."

Of the northern Horry beaches, Ocean Drive was probably the most famous. The Roberts family of Green Sea and Loris built a pavilion there which was a favorite hangout of young visitors. There was music and dancing and the chance for boys to meet girls. The locals came from miles around to mingle with the summer people. The kids named the beach "O.D." and spread word of it wherever they went. The pavilion was destroyed by Hurricane Hazel and "The Pad" at the main intersection became the favorite hangout.

Crescent Beach, earlier known as the Ward Estate, was purchased by a Whiteville, North Carolina, group and prepared for subdivision in 1937. Among the North Carolinians who came to stay were A. Elbert Jordan and Carl Pridgen. Other early developers were J. W. Perrin of Florence and Charles N. Ingram. Their development was known as Ingram Beach. Perrin became the first mayor when Crescent Beach was incorporated in 1953. The first council consisted of J. O. Baldwin, C. B. Berry, Richard K. Cartrette, and Harry Livingston.

Windy Hill was owned mostly by the heirs of W. R. Lewis of Conway. In 1947 a group of businessmen formed Windy Hill Beach Corporation and began developing the property between the Lewis tracts and the Bell Tract (later Atlantic Beach). The great dune which had attracted George Washington's attention was a landmark and a favorite picnic ground for many years. Windy Hill was incorporated October 19, 1964. Its first mayor was John T. Harrell and the councilmen were Charles W. Byers, P. K. Fleming, W. Leamon Todd, and David Witherspoon Jr.

A. Elbert Jordan is generally credited with beginning and promoting a discussion of combining the northern beaches into a larger, stronger municipal government. A steering committee with membership from each of the towns was formed to work out the details of consolidation, which took effect in 1968. It was agreed that the new town would have a new name, and North Myrtle Beach was chosen. Clearly the name is meant to associate the city with the larger resort down the coast, but there has always been a certain amount of rivalry between them. For many years the northern beaches featured beach houses and a few inns, but a skyline is gradually developing as the high-rise movement spreads up the beach.

The first mayor of North Myrtle Beach was Robert L. Edge. Council consisted of six men, one from each of the former towns and two at large. This tends to keep the identity of the former towns intact. The first councilmen were Mance Watkins for Cherry Grove, Jennings Livingston for Ocean Drive, M. A. Thompson for Crescent Beach, David B. Witherspoon Jr. for Windy Hill Beach, and Eli T. Goodman and J. Bryan Floyd, at-large. The consolidated government was housed in the Crescent Beach municipal building. Merlin Bellamy was named police chief. Douglas P. Wendel became the first city manager.

In the first years of real development most of the beaches had houses along the front two rows and small commercial districts. Progress was fairly slow and steady. Then came the great storm which everyone who lived in the area in 1954 remembers. On October 15, 1954, Hurricane Hazel swept ashore at high tide, just after full moon. The eye came in directly over the state line, devastating beaches to the north and the south. One eyewitness said that the storm surge, the great wave driven by wind and tide, topped eighteen and a half feet. Other accounts put it at thirty feet or more. The memories of the locals are full of stories about the destruction and the freakish nature of some things that happened. Some structures were left in matchstick pieces. Others were moved and gently set down in another place. A post office was destroyed totally. Nothing was found, not even the iron safe. The beaches were strewn with litter.

Many people sold their land rather than rebuilding, and it became possible to acquire the necessary land for larger commercial units. Capital from the outside became available for construction. Although the northern beaches still elected to rebuild many single dwellings and small public accommodations, larger beachfront developments became possible, courtesy of Hurricane Hazel.

Increasing tourist activity is bringing major changes to North Myrtle Beach. Although the perceived character of the city is still fairly "small town," the influx of visitors and permanent residents has set change in motion. The area has become attractive to retirees, who have a compelling effect on government and commerce. Golf courses, each with its residential community, are located both within the town and nearby.

Growth has resulted in critical overcrowding on Highway 17, the only north-south artery. Solutions are restricted by the physical location of the town. North Myrtle Beach is long and narrow, bound on the one side by the ocean and on the other by the Intracoastal Waterway. Both are inflexible. The town is dependent on one thoroughfare—Highway 17, the only uninterrupted north-south corridor. The long-planned bypass (Carolina Bays Parkway) on the inland side of the waterway will give some relief at some time in the future but at the same time will open new development possibilities along Highway 9, Highway 90, and Little River Neck Road, which presently feed traffic into Highway 17.

Some breakout possibilities lie in the city's power to annex territories contiguous to it. If it is able to move its boundaries outward to incorporate Little River Neck, Little River, and nearby areas adjacent to Highway 9, it has the potential of becoming equal in size to Myrtle Beach. The two cities have begun to cooperate in the provision of some services, which raises the intriguing question of whether there might someday be one metropolis from Little River to the Georgetown County line and beyond. Even now it is hardly possible to tell where one municipality begins and the next ends along the whole Grand Strand.

3

Ladies and Gentlemen

PETER HORRY: "NO MAN MORE EAGERLY SOUGHT THE FOE"

Peter Horry was born March 13, 1743. His father, John Horry, had become wealthy in slaves and rice. John's father, Elias, came to the Santee as a Huguenot refugee from France. He "worked many days with a negro man at the Whip saw" to clear the land for rice planting. Elias Horry married a Miss Huger. They had four sons, Daniel, Elias, Peter, and John, and two daughters, Margaret and Magdaline. John's sons Peter and Hugh grew up in Georgetown District and both served under Gen. Francis Marion during the American Revolution. Peter Horry never actually lived in the area later to become Horry District and subsequently Horry County.

When John Horry died in 1770, he left Peter a plantation near Winyah Bay. Over his lifetime Peter added additional lands, and at the time of his death on February 28, 1815, he owned Belle Isle, Prospect Hill, and Dover plantations.

On June 12, 1775, South Carolina's Provincial Congress named him captain and assigned him to the Second Regiment, South Carolina Line. He was among twenty distinguished men raised to that rank at one time and was listed fifth in order of precedence among them. On September 16, 1776, he was promoted to major, then in 1779 to lieutenant colonel. At that time he was transferred to the Fifth Regiment. In February 1780 several regiments were combined into three new ones, and Horry was not at that time assigned a command. He hoped to be named soon to the Continental Line. When he was ordered to report to General Horatio Gate's headquarters at Hillsboro, North Carolina, in July of that year, his hope renewed.

Gates, however, because Horry had no command at the time, assigned him to the South Carolina militia. In December 1780, Francis Marion, like Horry a lieutenant colonel, was named by Gov. John Rutledge to command the lower brigade of the South Carolina militia and given the rank of brigadier general. Horry became one of his most trusted officers. Under Marion he organized a regiment of light dragoons for the state service. It was only toward the end of the war that his regiment was consolidated with that of Col. Hezekiah Maham and placed in the Continental Establishment.

After the war Horry, who kept a record of his service, wrote a biography of General Marion, whom he greatly admired. Finding no publisher on his own, he gave the manuscript to a traveling parson, Mason L. Weems, who had had enormous success with his biography of George Washington. Weems, who had greater regard for a good story than for the truth, is responsible for such Washington myths as the cherry tree and the dollar across the Potomac. He took the same liberties with the life of Francis Marion. The result so offended Peter Horry that he refused to associate his name with the book.

The soldiers of the Revolution from this area who served under Horry called him "Stuttering Pete" but used the nickname with affection and respect. *American Military Biography* (1830) records this story: "Colonel Horry was once ordered to await the approach of a British detachment in ambuscade, a service which he performed with such skill that he had them completely within his power; when, from a dreadful impediment in his speech, by which he was afflicted, he could not articulate the word 'fire.' In vain he made the attempt—it was fi-fi-fi-fi, but he could get no further. At length, irritated almost to madness, he exclaimed, 'Shoot, damn you, shoot— you know very well what I would say—shoot, shoot, and be damned to you!'"

This biographer also said of him: "Never were his principles shaken; never, even for a moment, did the thought of submission enter his bosom. No man more eagerly sought the foe; none braved danger with greater intrepidity, or more strenuously endeavoured to sustain the military reputation of his country."

Men from this area who had served under him admired him so much that, when Horry District was formed on December 19, 1801, the General Assembly honored their wishes to name their new judicial district in his honor. Shortly after the Revolution Horry became brigadier general of the Sixth Brigade of the militia and served in that place until 1806.

On February 9, 1793, he married Margaret Guignard and built for her a house located on Senate Street in Columbia, just across from the present campus of the University of South Carolina. He called it "Mrs. Horry's house," suggesting a certain lack of closeness in the marriage, and maintained for himself a place in the countryside outside the city.

Although he is listed in the 1810 census of Georgetown County (with property including one hundred slaves), he died in Columbia in 1815.

Even in death Peter and Margaret Horry are not together. He rests in Trinity Episcopal churchyard across from the capitol, where he served from 1784-1787. She lies buried at Prince George Winyah in Georgetown. The stone marking her grave, which refers to her as his "relict," is tangled in the roots of the beautiful live oak at the back of the church.

His stone reads: "Sacred To the Memory of / General Peter Horry / who left this mortal life on the / 28th day of February A.D. 1815 / aged about 68 years. / He displayed conspicuous / Character as an Officer / in the American / Revolutionary War." The epitaph does not mention the county which bears his name.

ROBERT CONWAY

In the original design of the Carolina colony, very large landholders were to be titled landgraves and their holdings baronies. Robert Daniell was the first landgrave of Winyah Barony. He acquired the grant on June 18, 1711, and the next day sold it to Thomas Smith. It was a quick and no doubt profitable turnover. When the northern part of the Carolina colony had grown to the point that it became necessary to send an administrator there to carry out the policies of the government in Charleston, Robert Daniell was given that position. Later still, he became governor of South Carolina.

Governor Daniell's daughter Ann married Alexander Goodbee of Charleston. After Goodbee's death the young widow married Daniel Conway, son of John Conway. They became the parents of Robert Conway about 1753. The date of his birth must be inferred from his obituary (*Charleston City Gazette and Commercial Advertiser*, December 8, 1823), which reported his age as seventy years. The young man became a cabinetmaker in Charleston. His marriage at about eighteen to Juliana Easton was registered at St. Philips Parish on November 16, 1771. The deaths of two sons (John Bennet, d. September 13, 1780, and William Hopkins, d. October 21, 1780) are also in records at St. Philips. The third child was Amelia, born about 1785, when Conway was about thirty-two years of age.

Robert Conway served during the Revolution. Thereafter public records and the press always mention him with respect and by military title. Judge Joseph Travis Walsh, who arrived in Conwayborough in the decade prior to the War between the States, mentions in his autobiography that Robert Conway was a captain under Marion. Gregg's *History of the Old Cheraws* speaks of him as "a colonel of the Sixth Brigade" (572). In spite of the lack of official records of his service, one must accept that high regard for his military service led to his later commissions in the militia.

In 1785 the village and area on the Waccamaw River known as Kingston, though it was only 100 miles from Charleston, was still undeveloped except for a few hardy settlers. Why Robert and Juliana Conway decided to migrate to the Waccamaw region is unknown. They may have known others who had preceded them or may have heard family tales about land speculation by her grandfather, Landgrave Daniell. Perhaps Robert saw an opportunity to build an estate through land granted for his Revolutionary service. Perhaps his business in Charleston wasn't doing well, and he hoped for a new start on the "frontier."

The Conways—Robert, Juliana, and Amelia—arrived in the Waccamaw region without land sometime in 1785-1786. Among their closest friends were John and Mary Baxter, their neighbors on the Waccamaw riverfront, for whom they named the twins born to them in 1786. The boy was named John Baxter Conway and the girl, Mary Baxter Conway.

Colonel Conway began to acquire grants of land. Over the next fifteen years, he received more than 3,000 acres in eleven different grants ranging in size from 100 to 1,000 acres. On July 2, 1787, he received 223 acres on the northwest side of Kings Town Lake, site of the old township village of Kingston. Since this was a place where others were already in residence, it is not clear how or why this land was granted to Conway. Fifteen years later, when the village was designated the seat of the new judicial district, he transferred this property to the new district commissioners for a nominal price, reserving to himself his own homesite and one other lot.

Robert Conway built a house for Juliana, the three children, and himself alongside the Waccamaw River. The two-story dwelling stood on lot 135 on the Hemingway plan for Conwayborough made after the village became the district seat. It was just downriver from the confluence of Kingston Lake and Waccamaw River, just below the ferry house. This dwelling stood until the railroad came to Conway in 1887, when it was demolished to make way for a station at the end of the line. The site is just beneath the Waccamaw River bridge at the end of Main Street.

On Sunday, February 8, 1801, about fourteen years after Robert Conway had arrived, Bishop Francis Asbury, the famous Methodist missionary, spoke in the village of Kingston. In spite of his renown and the lovely weather reported that day in his *Journal*, his audience consisted of not more than one hundred persons, "including the colored folks." His comment provides a rare glimpse of the town, revealing how few people lived in the vicinity.

Toward the end of that year, Kingston was renamed Conwayborough and became the seat of the new Horry District, formed from substantial parts of All Saints and Prince George parishes.

As a large landholder and leading citizen, it was natural for Robert Conway to become politically active. In 1791, when he was about thirty-eight years old, he was elected to the South Carolina House of Representatives for Horry District (at the time still part of the larger Georgetown District). He served through 1807, save for 1798-1799 and 1802-1803 (Thirteenth and Fifteenth General Assemblies).

Conway was in the legislature when local men petitioned in 1801 to have a court established in the village of Kingston. They hoped that they would no longer have to undertake the rough trip to Georgetown to attend trials and transact legal business which had to be entered in the public records. The petition spoke plaintively of the lawlessness that was growing because of the difficulty of bringing wrongdoers to proper trial. Furthermore, approximately 550 qualified petitioners (i.e., free, adult, male property owners) wanted the new district named Horry and the name of the village seat changed from Kingston to Hugerborough.

These people were serious about disassociating their village from the monarchy. They chose the name of a prominent Huguenot family of Georgetown District. Benjamin Huger, patriarch of the family, had entertained the Marquis de Lafayette on his arrival in Georgetown District to participate in the Revolution. Lafayette visited the Huger family again when he returned to the new United States. Francis Kinloch Huger was reported to have rescued Lafayette from an Austrian prison later. An exploit such as this might well have captured the imagination of the patriotic men of the area.

The General Assembly named a committee composed of Robert Conway, John Nesmith of Williamsburg, and Erasmus Rothmaler of Prince George Winyah to determine whether the request of the people merited favorable action. The committee in due time asked and received permission to present a bill. It reached the House late in the session, passed on December 17, and went to the Senate. It became law on December 19, 1801, as Robert Conway was ending his fifth term in Columbia.

Some people were not happy to discover that the name of the village was not to be Hugerborough. The next year they petitioned the General Assembly to undo the action which was "disagreeable to their wish" and make the name of the village Hugerborough. Although Robert Conway was not a member of the House when it arrived, the petition was ignored.

The new commissioners named in the act to oversee the construction of a courthouse and jail soon discovered that Robert Conway owned 223 acres of the village land! On August 6, 1802, after negotiations, he conveyed to them for five pounds "all that plantation or Tract of Two Hundred and Twenty three acres of Land (more or less excepting one Lott known by lott No. 135 and also one other lot No. ___ [sic] formerly occupied by John Tamplat which land was granted unto me July 2nd 1787 bounded NE and SE by Kingstown Lake and John Baxter's (now Thomas Mitchell's) land NW by John Cross land and SW by vacant Land and hath such shape and marks as a plat annexed to original Grant will fully Shew" *(Horry County Deed Book* UU, p.1).

Robert Conway continued a preeminent public figure during the first decade of the nineteenth century. What his primary business was is not clear. Papers related to a court case referred to him as a shopkeeper, but he may also have been a planter and contractor. He held both elective and appointed offices at the local and state level, served as justice of the peace and justice of the quorum, coroner, and commissioner of buildings for the erection of the courthouse and jail. He served again in the House from 1804 until 1808, two more terms.

In instruments dated April 1, 1802, Conway provided for a three-way split of his property among his three children, dividing his land and livestock, household goods, even personal effects *(Horry County Deed Book* A1, pp. 328-30). The older daughter is referred to as his "beloved daughter" Amelia Porter. The 1800 census shows that she must have been married at about age fifteen. Her husband may have been Benjamin Porter, who owned a lot next door to Conway and who witnessed the deed by which Conway sold Jane Cawsway 1,000 acres on September 20, 1799. The documents name John Rogers Sr. guardian of the twins, Mary and John, who were about fourteen or fifteen when these interesting documents were signed.

Colonel Conway was probably considered a well-to-do, if not wealthy, man by the standards of the time and place. The lists of household goods in these documents show that he owned considerable furniture, goods, and five slaves. He retained lifetime rights in his property for himself but did not mention his wife Juliana and made no provision for her. Perhaps he provided for Mrs. Conway in another document which has not come to light. On August 7, later in the same year, she signed away her dower rights in the land conveyed to the commissioners.

Robert Conway had been named lieutenant colonel of the Twenty-fifth Regiment about 1794 and served in that capacity until he succeeded Peter

Horry as brigadier general of the Sixth Brigade of militia in 1803. He served in the post until 1812. These appointments tend to confirm his Revolutionary service.

The death of Juliana Easton Conway occurred on November 28, 1811 (*CT*, 14 February 1812), forty years to the month after she and Robert Conway married. There is no record of where she was buried, but it may well have been close to her home on the Waccamaw in the community cemetery, which is now the churchyard of Kingston Presbyterian Church in Conway.

Robert Conway had persistent financial difficulties. Although he held considerable land, he seemed to be short of cash much of the time. He is listed as defendant between 1807 and 1813 in nine suits recorded in the *Judgment Book for Horry County Court of Common Pleas 1804-1829*. All but one concerned promissory notes or bonds. In every case, the result went against General Conway. In a suit brought by the assignee for Origen Dwight, who had become bankrupt, Conway was accused of "contriving and fraudilently contending craftily and subtilly to deceive and Defraud." The fact that several plaintiffs were from Charleston and Georgetown suggests that Conway may have tried to protect his reputation in Conwayborough by borrowing money out of town. It may, however, given the economy of Horry District at the time, simply have been that money was available in those two centers and not in Horry.

In spite of his lengthy career of public service, the record is curiously silent about the personality of Robert Conway. No letters, journals, or personal papers have been found. In 1802, when he was not in the House of Representatives, but was a member of the governing commission of the district, he was accused of stealing "Eight weight of sugar out of Mr. Fleming's store" in Georgetown. Thomas Dawsey claimed "He is a Damned old Sugar Thief" and "I can prove him a thief." Conway brought suit on July 14, 1802, against Dawsey for "speaking, uttering and publishing certain false, scandalous and malicious words of him" and asked five thousand dollars in damages. Through his attorney, Erasmus Rothmaler, with whom Conway had served in the legislature, he claimed that he had been "a good, true, honest, worthy and faithful citizen ... from the time of his nativity ... held, considered and respected among all his neighbors and other worthy citizens to be a man of good name, Fame, Credit, Character and Reputation [who] has always during his lifetime hitherto lived and continued, free, clear, and unspotted."

The case was heard in the court of common pleas, where on November 1, 1802, a jury found in Conway's favor and allowed him one hundred dollars and costs. Clearly Conway was not seriously injured by this slander, for he was later named brigadier general of the Sixth Brigade. During this period also he served in local and state offices, returning to the House of Representatives in 1804 and serving until 1808.

The minute book of the building commissioners provides some record of Conway's career until he left this area permanently. Conway was present on February 3, 1817, for example, when the commissioners agreed on a settlement with Richard Green on his contract of March 23, 1802, for the construction of the first courthouse and gaol.

In 1819, when he was about sixty-six years old, after nearly seven years as a widower, General Conway married again. Susannah Beaty Crowson, widow of Thomas Crowson, was a member of the prominent Beaty family. She was about forty-one years old. The bond for this marriage was executed March 16, 1819. The *Charleston City Gazette* for April 7, 1819, took notice of this union:"Married at Conwayborough (the capitol of Horry District, South Carolina) Robert Conway, Esq., late Brigadier General, and a meritorious soldier of the Revolution, to the amiable Miss [sic!] Susannah Crowson."

The record of the offices General Conway held during this period reflect a gradual move to Georgetown. Amelia Conway Porter and her family may already have been residing there. Conway was coroner for Horry District from 1820-1823, was listed in the 1820 census as a resident of Conwayborough, and in 1821 a justice of the peace for Prince George Winyah Parish. In 1823 he was manager of elections for Georgetown.

General Conway's death was recorded in the register of the Methodist Church of Georgetown, but the December 8, 1823, issue of the *Charleston City Gazette and Commercial Advertiser* gives the only information available about his funeral: "Died at Georgetown, Gen. Robert Conway, formerly of this city [i.e., Charleston] a soldier of the Revolution aged seventy interred with military honors."

The obituary does not state that he was buried in Georgetown, and there is no known record of his burial there. In his manuscript "A Narrative of Horry County History," Dr. James A. Norton records local (i.e., Conway) tradition:"Some say he was buried in the old Kingston burying ground...." It was close to his former home on the Waccamaw waterfront and became Kingston Presbyterian Church Cemetery. This view is consistent with traditions among his descendants and with the probability that his first wife, Juliana Easton Conway, also was buried there.

The widow of General Conway appears as Susannah Conway in the 1830 census of Georgetown. She does not appear in the Georgetown census under any name which can be identified in 1840 or 1850. *The Pee Dee Times* of October 18, 1854, carried her obituary: "Died on the 10th inst., Mrs. Susannah Ferari, formerly the widow of the Gen. Robert Conway, in memory of whom as a revolutionary officer, the capital of Horry District took the name of Conwayboro. After the death of her second husband, she kept a tavern in this town—and sustained a good reputation. She was about 76 years of age."

Susannah Beaty Crowson Conway Ferari is buried in the old Methodist cemetery at the corner of Orange and Highmarket Streets in Georgetown. Apparently no stone survives now, but church records mention her burial there.

Robert Conway has many descendants, though none of his surname. John Baxter Conway, the son who survived to adulthood, married first Ann Causey, but this marriage ended about January 23, 1807. Conway gave up all claim to the property which Ann had brought to the marriage. There is no record of children. About 1810 he married Rebecca Beaty, daughter of John Beaty and Elizabeth Mary Prince, but this union produced only daughters: Juliana (b. 1815), Elizabeth (b. 1816), and Margaret (May 18, 1822–July 14, 1888). The 1830 census of Horry County no longer recorded John Baxter Conway, so he may have died (or moved elsewhere) before it was taken. The name died with him.

No portrait of Robert Conway is known to exist, but his silver watch, made in London and carrying the letters of his name rather than numerals on its face, was handed down through descendants in the Bailey family. On November 15, 1981, the watch was presented to the people of Conway in formal ceremonies at City Hall. It has remained on display in the office of the mayor ever since.

GEORGE WASHINGTON SLEPT HERE

The first two years of George Washington's presidency were productive but hard on him. Now in his late fifties, he had endured much physical suffering and emotional stress in his life. He delivered his inaugural address on April 30, 1789, and set about stabilizing his new country. During that summer he was operated on for a tumor on his thigh and nearly died. That fall his mother, aged 81, died. At the close of the first session of Congress, President Washington traveled from his residence in New York through New England.

In 1790 he had to act as referee between two factions headed respectively by Jefferson and Hamilton. The compromise of the conflict between them resulted in moving the capital from New York to Philadelphia for about ten years while a capital city on the Potomac was being prepared. So it was Philadelphia from which he prepared to depart for his journey through the southern states in early 1791.

Jefferson opposed the trip, fearing the hardship of travel would affect the president's health. Washington had never visited the states south of his native Virginia, however, and wished to assess the security of the union among the people to the south and to evaluate their development agriculturally, economically, and socially.

The hard trip through New England had taught him something about the perils of presidential travel. Having experienced too much advance publicity on that tour, he was determined not to release the details of his itinerary through the South. He also determined that he would not accept private invitations except in the case of close connections with his hosts. He had no desire to inconvenience anyone nor to be obligated to anyone for entertaining him and his retinue.

He intended to move south along the coast and return along the fall line. Realizing that he would be virtually out of contact with the government for which he was responsible while he was on the road, he worked out every detail in advance. He left with his cabinet in Philadelphia an itinerary with dates so that dispatches could reach him if necessary.

He chose as his chariot his old carriage, a concession to his experience of bad New England roads, then had it completely refurbished. Scenes depicting the four seasons as well as his own coat of arms were displayed against a white and gilt background. The chariot was drawn by four horses. There were two extra coach horses and four saddle horses besides his own. He was accompanied by his aide, Major William Jackson, who doubled as his speechwriter, his *valet de chambre*, a coachman, a postilion, and two footmen. Baggage for himself and his retinue was aboard a second vehicle.

It was not entirely possible for the first president to avoid advance word of his progress from reaching cities and towns along the way. He was greeted with adulation at each stop, wined and dined and feted with such extravagance as each community could muster. Some of the ceremony he enjoyed, but much of it was tiring, if not boring. People created special ceremonies to celebrate him. At Belvedere Plantation outside Wilmington, for instance, he was met at the wharf by thirteen young women in white, representing the thirteen states (Rhode Island, which he had avoided on the New England trip because it had not ratified the Constitution, had finally come into the union). His passage was particularly gratifying to Masonic Lodges whose members greeted him as a brother and considered it their particular right to entertain him.

Washington enjoyed the ladies and frequently recorded in his diary his impressions of the beauties he encountered. In Charleston, for example, he records that one afternoon he "was visited about 1 o'clock, by a great number of the most respectable ladies of Charleston—the first honor of the kind I had ever experienced and it was as flattering as it was singular." One evening in the same place he attended a dinner given for him by the Members of the Cincinnati "at which were 256 elegantly dressed and handsome ladies." The father of his country had counted them! The next evening he attended a concert at the Exchange "at wch. There were at least 400 ladies the number & appearance of wch. exceeded any thing of the kind I had ever seen."

Departing from Philadelphia on March 21, 1791, Washington went first to Mt. Vernon, reaching his home on the Potomac on the March 30. A little more than a week later, he left. In Virginia he progressed through Fredericksburg, Richmond, and Petersburg and passed across the state line to Halifax on April 16.

Little complaints begin to find their way into his diary. He found it particularly uncomfortable to ride behind his honorary escorts from each town because of the dust their horses raised. At Petersburg, when he learned of the intention of a large group to see him out of town, he let it be known that he would depart about eight the next morning, but got up early and was on his way about five. Many of the taverns and other accommodations along the way the Potomac squire found uncomfortable and mean. He described many towns as "trifling places." Along the way through North Carolina, Washington was surprised by the scant population and how little development he could see along his route. He visited Greenville, New Bern, and Wilmington, not tarrying long anywhere.

On April 27 Washington ate breakfast at the home of William Gause and crossed into South Carolina about 12:30 P.M. Two miles farther along he dined at the home of James Cochran, a veteran of the Revolution. He was following the old King's Highway, portions of which may still be seen at the Vereen and Brookgreen Gardens.

The little party traveled fourteen miles more before it reached what Washington thought to be a public house to spend the night. His host, Jeremiah Vereen, in Washington's words, "either did not keep one [i.e., public house], or would not acknowledge it—we therefore were entertained (& very kindly) without being able to make compensation."

Both Cochran and Vereen, veterans of Revolutionary War service, must have felt honored by a visit from General Washington. Beyond naming him, Washington had nothing to say in his diary about his host at the midday meal. It is difficult to discover much about Cochran. Land transactions and some court actions recorded in the office of the Horry County Register of Mesne Conveyance are of little help. Two 1804 deeds speak of him as James Cochran of Brunswick County, North Carolina, but he was a large landholder along the border in South Carolina. Alas, apparently he was not always solvent, and men he owed sometimes sued him for debt.

Jeremiah Vereen received more attention in the diary. He was descended from a family that was among the first settlers of the region and was the holder of considerable lands. Jeremiah was the son of Jeremiah Vereen and Mary Coachman, who settled on Singleton Swash; grandson of Jeremie Vereen and Jane Evans, who came from Charleston to St. Thomas and St. Denis Parish; great-grandson of Jacques (James) Varin and Susanne Horry, who came to the new world from their native France. Thus Washington's host belonged to the fourth generation of the family in America. Descendants of this family are numerous, particularly in the coastal areas. Jackson Vereen, born April 9, 1882, gave 100 acres of Vereen land to Horry County for a memorial park.

Washington did not tarry on Horry soil. Following his night at Jeremiah Vereen's home, he struck out for Georgetown. Vereen guided him safely across treacherous Singleton's Swash, bade him farewell, and saw him off on his journey south. The president rode along the beach for a distance he estimated at sixteen miles before he turned inland to follow the King's Highway another five miles through the woods. He got food for himself, his party, and his horses at the home of George Pawley. The Pawleys were conspicuous in the early days of both Horry and Georgetown Counties.

Along the road down Waccamaw Neck he ran into Dr. Henry Collins Flagg, who invited him to spend the night at his home. Dr. Flagg was from Rhode Island and had served as chief surgeon under Gen. Nathanael Green during the Revolution. After the war he had settled in Waccamaw Neck and married Rachel, widow of Capt. William Allston (two "ls"). Washington was now among people who could furnish the kind of accommodations the Potomac squire would appreciate. The Flaggs were his hosts on the night of April 28 at Brookgreen. According to his reckoning, he was thirty-three miles from the home of Jeremiah Vereen, where he had spent the previous night.

The next morning, the party moved on to Clifton, home of Col. William Alston (one "l," the Colonel having dropped one letter to distinguish himself from his kinsman of the same name), a "large, new, and elegantly furnished house overlooking extensive rice fields which Washington, a farmer, greatly admired. A distinguished group met him at Clifton. It included Gen. William Moultrie, Col. William Washington, and John Rutledge Jr., representing Gov. Charles Pinckney.

The enlarged party was rowed in an "elegant painted boat" down the "Waggamau" to Georgetown early on the morning of Saturday, April 30, 1791, the second anniversary of his inauguration. The oarsmen, decked out in their finest uniforms, were captains of the vessels docked in the harbor. The water route was three miles down the river and then across Winyah Bay and up the Sampit to the city. He was welcomed by cannon and entertained at tea by fifty ladies.

Somewhat peevishly he recalled in his diary that "The inhabitants of this place (either unwilling or unable) could give no account of the number of Souls in it, but I should not compute them at more than 5 or 600."

Two days in Georgetown was sufficient. On Saturday, May 1, he departed for Charleston. He rode some 15 miles before breakfast, which he ate with Mrs. Daniel Horry (Harriott Pinckney) at Hampton. He found her company so delightful he stayed for midday dinner as well before setting off again.

Nineteen miles farther down the Charleston road, he spent the night at the home of Joseph Manigault, whose country home was unpretentious and would not have given Washington an inkling of the splendors which awaited him in the "Holy City," where both Joseph and his brother Gabriel had homes designed by Gabriel. Joseph's home is now a house museum near the Charleston Museum.

Washington arrived in Charleston on May 2 and spent May 2–8 in a constant round of breakfasts, dinners, teas, and balls. He stayed in quarters supplied by Thomas Heyward Jr. General Moultrie and Sen. (Major) Pierce Butler accompanied him on his way to Savannah. At Purrysburg when Washington reached the Savannah River, General Moultrie said goodbye. The president was in Georgia from May 12 to May 20, progressing from Savannah to Waynesboro to Augusta.

Colonel Wade Hampton was a member of the party of notables who met Washington in Augusta to accompany him to Columbia. Colonel Thomas Taylor, who had sold his family plantation to the state of South Carolina as the site of its new capital city, and Robert Lythgoe and a Mr. Jameson were the others. The first day the travelers covered 40 miles and lodged at the Pine House near present-day Ridge Spring. The following night (May 23) he was in Columbia. Along the way he had been joined by other riders.

No contemporary accounts say where he lodged in Columbia. On May 23 he was feted at a public dinner in the state house attended by 150 persons. He noted that 50 or 60 of them were ladies. The state house had been occupied in 1790, just in time for his visit. The General Assembly had held its first session in it in January 1791. Otherwise, he found Columbia a very primitive place.

On the way to Columbia through country he described as "a pine barren of the worst sort, being hilly as well as poor," one of his horses had foundered. This compelled him to stay in the new capital of South Carolina longer than he intended. He left on Wednesday and reached Camden (36 miles by his reckoning) by two o'clock. This road also lay through pine barrens and sand.

The next morning General Washington viewed the British works at Camden before heading for Charlotte. Along the way he visited the sites of several Revolutionary War engagements and commented on the strategy of the various battles in his diary. He spent the night of May 27 at the home of James Ingram. Twenty miles from that place he reached the road that for some miles formed the line between North and South Carolina.

Along the road he was met by a party of Catawbas who told him of their apprehension that a move might be on foot to take away lands ceded by the colonists in a treaty made at Augusta, Georgia, in 1763. (This dispute was resolved 230 years later in a settlement with the remnants of the Catawba in York County.) The site of their meeting with Washington was the home of Major Robert Crawford. It was the president's last stop in South Carolina.

His way now lay through Charlotte, Salisbury, and Salem on his journey back to Mt. Vernon, which he reached June 12. Home must have been a welcome sight to the president, now in his sixtieth year, after two and a half months on the road.

When Washington returned to Philadelphia he noted that he had traveled 1,887 miles. He was proud that "the same horses performed the whole tour and, although much reduced in flesh, kept up their full spirits to the last day." He himself had "rather gained flesh."

The next year was an election year. Washington wanted to retire. Counselors on all sides begged him to reconsider. While he deliberated, war in Europe between Britain and France threatened the well-being of the young

America. The Electoral College, not having had an absolute refusal from the first president, unanimously elected him to a second term on February 13, 1793. Washington thus was coerced to continue what he described as "the extreme wretchedness of his existence." On December 7, 1796, he was finally able to give his farewell address. He retired to Mt. Vernon, where he died three years later on the night of December 14, 1799.

WHERE ALL THE WOMEN ARE STRONG

Imagine the first small parties coming up the dark waters of the Waccamaw River on a raft or in a small boat. What dismay the women must have experienced at first sight of these forests and streams, swamps and bluffs! How would you choose a place to unload your few provisions and face the prospect of the first night in the wilderness? How long did it take to fell enough trees for a shelter? How was the first meal gathered and prepared?

Those women bore and tended children, planted and harvested, spun and wove, created homes and eventually created communities where there had been only wilderness. They instructed their daughters in the skills which they brought from their homes to the new world. Although many of them lived and died leaving no records, not even tombstones, to mark their passing, we do have a few records which help us to imagine the lives of women in the nineteenth century.

The Beaty family is said to have been here before the township of Kingston was established in 1732. The first John Beaty was an immigrant from Ireland, and by the time of his grandson, John Beaty III, the family was one of the most influential in the area. John Beaty III served in turn as justice of the quorum, clerk of court, and sheriff. Other men of the family dominated these and other public offices for generations. It used to be said that no young man could expect to succeed in Horry District without connections with the Beaty clan.

Beaty wives and daughters and other women like them cemented the growing town together. They supported and encouraged their menfolk, nurtured their children, kept their houses, and went about doing good in the community. They had no laborsaving devices to help with the daily chores and no medical help for serious illness and childbirth.

Sarah Jane Beaty (1791-1881) was the daughter of John Beaty III, an early sheriff, and Elizabeth Mary Prince Beaty, daughter of Nicholas Prince. Jane was the second of their eight children, the eldest daughter. In 1811, at age twenty, she married Joshua S. Norman, said to be the son of Sir Joshua

Norman, a sea captain who fought the pirates. He must have been a charmer. Jane met him when she was employed as a weaver by Col. William Alston of Waccamaw Neck. The young man and the maid flirted when he stopped by the plantation home to inquire directions, but she did not learn his name until he showed up later at her home in Conwayborough.

Jane Beaty Norman bore Joshua eight children. He proved an inadequate provider and put the family in financial jeopardy again and again. Conwayborough, though only a village of perhaps 150-200 inhabitants, was a riverport and courthouse town. It had enough visitors to provide Jane Norman the opportunity to support the family by operating a small hotel. In those days Conway had few professional people in residence in the town. When court was in session, the lawyers and judges who came to conduct the business of the court stayed with "Aunt Jane" or "Aunt Norman," as she was called. She was a gracious hostess and set a fine table. She was also a sympathetic chaperone to the young people of the town who gathered in her parlor. Many a match flourished under her watchful eye. She and Joshua Norman sold Horry District the lot on which the second county courthouse (now the Conway City Hall) was built in 1824-1825. The lot cost fifty dollars.

About 1828 Jane Norman led a group of women gathered in her home for worship to begin collecting money for a church building. A storm at the turn of the century had destroyed the only church building known to exist in the village before 1800. Although there was a camp meeting ground on the Georgetown road, there was no sanctuary set aside for worship in the town until Mrs. Norman and her friends were successful in erecting a Methodist church in 1844. The present-day First United Methodist Church treasures the little bowl which she circulated among her friends to collect their offerings. When the Presbyterians formed a congregation in 1855 and in 1858 decided to build a church, Mrs. Norman provided the land for that purpose.

Jane Norman died September 12, 1881, at ninety years of age. The funeral party took her remains to Georgetown, a forty-mile journey, for burial. They traversed sandy roads and ferried rivers to get there. No one seems to know why they chose Georgetown, nor why burial was refused when the cortege arrived at its destination. The party had no alternative but to return to Conway.

The heat of September was unbearable. Mrs. Norman had been dead a week, the body unembalmed. Small wonder, then, that the mourners decided to commit it to the earth as soon as they arrived at Kingston churchyard about midnight. They buried Aunt Jane by the light of lanterns and lightwood torches. Her grave was marked by an urn with the one word "GRANDMA." The repainted urn no longer bears that title, but a small stone with their names and dates memorializes Jane and Joshua Norman.

Frances Norton Norman, born in 1817, was Aunt Jane Norman's third child. She received from her mother excellent religious training as well as practical training in the running of a large establishment. A good thing, too, for she was to marry Henry Buck from Maine, who had come south in the 1820s to establish sawmills along the lower Waccamaw River.

Buck courted and married Frances in 1838, more than a decade after he had settled in Horry. Fanny assumed responsibility for managing his large plantation household at Upper Mill. A newspaper reporter who visited them just as the Civil War was beginning described a remarkable woman, "a kind and considerate mistress, who [was] the physician" (*AP*: repr.*IRQ* 17:1:16) to three hundred slaves in addition to managing her home, providing its food, entertaining its guests, and bearing seven children. A biographical sketch of her husband (*Cyclopedia of Eminent and Representative Men of the Carolinas of the Nineteenth Century*) describes her in this way: "She was a woman of great worth. The needy poor never applied to her bounteous purse and tender heart in vain. Her carriage was found at the door of the destitute and sick at all times of the day and night, and the deathbed of many poor wretches was sweetened by her godly, loving presence, and their last moments comforted by her touching faith in the power of her Master to redeem. A mother to the community in which she lived, she was long known by the sweet title of 'Aunt' Fanny, and her death was sincerely mourned by all."

Two of her sons served the Confederacy. One died, one survived. She and her husband established a large family connection to which belong many prominent Horry County names. Given her mother's great age, Fanny Buck died young, only sixty-eight.

Jane Beaty Norman's youngest sister, Mary Harriet Beaty, married a young businessman, Timothy Cooper, who, unlike Joshua Norman, became very successful. Their ninth child and youngest daughter was Adeline. This young woman had an education which was remarkable for her time in Conway. She and her older sister, Margaret Ellen, completed the schooling available at Conwayborough Academy and went on to the Spartanburg Female Academy during the early years of the Civil War. Ellen later wrote of their preparations for entering the school in Spartanburg:

My mother had two nice dresses bought before the war, these she gave to us, telling us that we could remodel them and they could be our best dresses. The plaid silk she gave to Addie, and the brown serge, to me. Now we must have at least three nice homespun dresses. The warp and filling for these must be of fine cotton to make pretty cloth, so father bought this from the wagons from Fayetteville, N. C., who came through the county selling black cotton for weaving. We did not know how to put it in the loom, but Mother knew. She set up the looms for us, and Addie and I wove the cloth to make our dresses. Each one was woven in different colors. It took eight yards for each dress. It did not take us long to weave this cloth—we could do two yards a day, but this was according to the number of threads. Some ladies could weave as much as five or six yards a day. When the cloth was woven, we made our dresses! These were made with a blouse waist and plain skirts, with trimmed collar and cuffs. Now we must have hats and a cloak, or cape. Both were worn then, but it would take more cloth for a long cape than a cloak, so we chose the latter. These were made from a piece of nice gray cloth which my mother had purchased before the war. Now we must have buttons! We had no button molds, so we cut pasteboard molds and covered them with black silk, then sewed on black jet beads, for we had learned to do many things during the war.

My father had Mr. Bill Abrahams make our shoes—two pairs for each of us. These were high-top shoes and very nice. Now that our dresses were finished, we must have hats. These were made of strips of palmetto. We had learned to make these. Palmetto braids were made by stripping the palmetto into small strips, and braiding them into hats. The braids were very smooth and white. We could buy palmettos in Conway at ten cents a bunch. Two bunches would make each of us a sailor hat. We also made a small toque each. They were much in style in those days. We made these from pieces of silk and ribbon left over from other days. We had our little black silk mitts of better times, and my little jacket of last summer could not be forgotten. A few more things, and our small wardrobe would be complete.

Both young women became teachers and worked until their marriages. Adeline married young Franklin Gorham Burroughs, who had migrated to Conwayborough from Martin County, North Carolina, before the Civil War. He entered service early, became a prisoner of war in Tennessee, and spent the rest of the war in a Federal prison near Chicago. After the war he came back to Conwayborough, re-entered business, and courted and won Adeline Cooper. They married in 1866. He was thirty-two, she eighteen.

Within a year Burroughs had bought Snow Hill, a property on Kingston Lake. During the Civil War the house on the property had been home to the Weston family, who had fled from Hagley Plantation to Conwayborough, fearing Yankee attacks on their home and other rice plantations along the lower Waccamaw River. As their family grew, the young Burroughses moved this little house to another site and built a larger one in its place in 1881.

Snow Hill was a full farm operation with a gristmill, a cotton gin, stables, and a dairy. The family lumber mill was across the lake. Miss Addie's hands were no doubt busy. She and Franklin had eleven children, three of whom died young. Since he was building an extensive business, the management of farm and family fell almost exclusively on her shoulders. Her decisions were law in both. One of her daughters later wrote: "I don't know how my mother ever managed, for there was never a meal or a night that she knew how many guests we would have. Papa's business friends and commission merchants from the North and the outlying communities were always there, and they brought their families."

The Burroughses also annually gave a big barbecue for the town, but entertaining was the least of it. A granddaughter wrote: "Aside from the daily routine at Snow Hill there were the yearly events: hog killing in the cold winter weather with its sausage and liver-pudding making; rendering lard and soap; preparing hams and side meat for the smokehouse; the yearly trip to the ocean, Singleton's Swash being the selected place for the ten day or two weeks campout to which everyone in the Conway area was invited." F. G. Burroughs planned this trip and furnished the location, but Miss Addie carried it out.

Five of the children were under twenty-one when F. G. Burroughs died of pneumonia on February 25, 1897. Only two were married. Four were still to be sent to college. Miss Addie then had the responsibility of managing his extensive enterprises with the help of her son Frank, who at twenty-five had married and was captain of a steamboat.

Though he himself had little education, F. G. Burroughs had insisted on higher education for the children. He valued his wife's education, feeling that it contributed to the fine moral and cultural atmosphere of his home and provided stimulation of the minds of the children. He insisted that his daughters be sent to college.

In 1898 Addie Burroughs leased a large area around Grantsville north of Conway to a group which established the Homewood Colony there. Her agent in this and on other occasions was D. M. McNeill. Her sons constructed the railroad from Conway to the coast which her late husband had planned. The first train ran on the Conway and Seashore Railroad in 1900, and Mrs. Burroughs was the one who suggested in 1901 that the New Town be renamed Myrtle Beach after the wax myrtle.

When the downtown cemeteries at the Baptist, Methodist and Presbyterian churches were full and had to be closed, Mayor Hal L. Buck asked Mrs. Burroughs to give the city land for a cemetery. In November 1903 she gave Conway six acres of her farm along Kingston Lake, including the family's graveyard. She asked only that a road be constructed from Main Street directly to Lakeside Cemetery. It was lined with oaks and ended at the entrance.

Miss Addie was visiting her eldest daughter, Effie Egerton, in Hendersonville, North Carolina, when she died at seventy-one in July 1919. The family had spent summers there where the climate was beneficial to her asthma. She had been active in community affairs and the management of the farm at Snow Hill until less than a year before her death. Her family returned her body to Snow Hill and buried it in the family plot at Lakeside Cemetery. She is remembered as a figure of authority, but quiet, pleasant, serene. Her skills as a wife, mother, and manager were evident throughout her long life.

Her family continued to operate the various businesses established by F. G. Burroughs. In 1912 they formed a business partnership with Simeon B. Chapin which was called Myrtle Beach Farms. All these interests and others were combined into the present-day Burroughs and Chapin.

Adeline Burroughs and her sisters, the daughters of Timothy and Mary Harriet Beaty Cooper, were among the most prominent women of their time in this county. They, like their first cousin, Frances Norman Buck, formed through their marriages and children a family connection which is remarkable. The youngest, Laura Jane, married B. G. Collins, business partner of F. G. Burroughs and one of Horry's most prominent businessmen. Laura Collins's daughter Mary Essie married Doc Allen Spivey, and Emma married Austin Charles Thompson.

Warren Johnson, a talented photographer, was the son of Adeline's sister Margaret Ellen, who married Charles Johnson. Shortly before Ellen Cooper Johnson's death, she wrote her memoirs, an engaging and remarkably informative account of life in Horry County before, during, and after the Civil War.

James P. Stevens, longtime Horry County senator, is descended from Adeline's sister Frances Elizabeth, whose second marriage was to William Currie. Their daughter Frances married Y. P. McQueen, early settler and businessman of Loris, Senator Stevens's grandfather.

HENRY BUCK FROM BUCKSPORT, MAINE

Both Bucksport and Bucksville were named for Henry Buck, who arrived in South Carolina from Bucksport, Maine, in the 1820s. Bucksville became a thriving town with a lumber mill, stores, a Masonic lodge, an inn, and a number of professional people, as well as laborers. Although now only a ghost village, it once rivaled Conway in importance in the county.

Bucksport was a smaller place but survives today as the home of a largely black community. It, too, had a lumber mill. There was a third, Upper Mill, at the home which Buck built beside the Waccamaw. Chimneys of the old mills at Upper Mill and Bucksville recall the glory days.

Buck's family, which had founded the New England town, was engaged in shipbuilding and lumbering. He was looking for the kinds of timber which would be suitable for establishing a mill in the South. He found what he was looking for along the lower Waccamaw River in Horry County. Eventually the three mills he and his sons owned along the river became world famous for their production of pine and cypress lumber.

Buck is reputed to have been the wealthiest man in Horry County before the Civil War. A northern reporter who visited Upper Mill plantation above Bucksville early in the Civil War period recorded his impressions of a comfortable life in *Among the Pines* (published by J. R. Gilmore, 1862). Gilmore, who used the pseudonym Edmund Kirke, also used fictitious names for the people he encountered, but evidence favors Henry Buck and his family as the subject of comments about this area.

When Kirke stumbled on the lane leading to their Upper Mill home in the late afternoon as he traveled to Conwayborough (which he described as a one-horse town), the Bucks invited him to stay the night. He was delighted with the hospitality he received at the hands of the lumberman and his wife. The evening's conversation at the dinner table and later over fine Havana cigars dealt with world and national affairs. Although himself opposed to slavery, the reporter was impressed favorably by the management and care of the three hundred slaves Buck owned. Mrs. Buck (born Frances Norton Norman, a native of Conwayborough), as chatelaine of the plantation, was responsible for their health and well being.

By Kirke's account Buck's mills shipped lumber to "nearly every quarter of the globe, to the Northern and eastern ports, Cadiz, the West Indies, South America ... And California." As a native of New England doing business in his home state and with other Northern businesses, Buck opposed the impending war. Once South Carolina seceded, however, he cast his lot with his adopted state and gave large amounts of money to the Southern cause. Kirke describes this money, which he estimated as high as forty thousand dollars, as penalties for his unionism. Kirke also claimed that five Buck vessels were seized in northern ports. Two of Buck's sons entered the Confederate forces. One died of disease contracted in military camp.

After the war the Buck mills began again to ship lumber all over the world. On the ways at Bucksville, Buck built his own ships in competition with the Maine shipyards. He brought from New England the skilled designers and carpenters he needed to do the work. The shipyards also produced sailing ships for the China trade, vessels too large to return to their home port once they traveled down the winding Waccamaw to where their masts could be raised. The most famous of them was the *Henrietta*, two hundred feet in length, which was lost in a typhoon off Japan.

Following the adoption of a new constitution for South Carolina in 1868, local leaders prevailed upon Henry Buck to offer for the State Senate as a Democrat. His Republican opposition was the Rev. Henry Wallace Jones, a black Methodist. Buck won the election, served two years, and died in office. His death occurred in 1870 at Saratoga, New York. His body was returned to Horry County and buried in the family cemetery across the road from Hebron United Methodist Church, which is listed on the National Register of Historic Buildings, near Bucksville.

William L. Buck (1828-1880), born in Bucksport, Maine, son of Henry Buck's first marriage, also served as senator from Horry County from 1876-1880. Henry Lee Buck (1872-1947), a grandson, served in the South Carolina Senate, 1912-1920.

His great-grandson, yet another Henry Buck, lives with his family in the house the first Henry built beside the river at Upper Mill plantation, which is also listed on the National Register. The home, built in 1828, has been restored. The oak and pine allée which led from the road to the house as described by Kirke in 1862 is gone, but on its spacious grounds the old chimney of the steam mill that his great-grandfather built still stands sentinel beside the Waccamaw.

Bucksville is also gone. After the war the lumber mills continued to operate successfully for a time, but gradually, as cutting depleted the giant cypress, they became less productive, and the operations at Bucksville ceased. The once thriving port was reduced to a public landing area from which fishermen and pleasure boat operators gained access to the Waccamaw. The landing has now been relocated.

LORENZO DOW: ECCENTRIC MISSIONARY

Lorenzo Dow Suggs (1867–1962) planted fields of amaryllis at his Cedar Lane Farm between Pleasant Meadow and Live Oak, not far from Loris. He was known well beyond his home community, for he liked to experiment with new crops and new methods of farming. When he was well past ninety, he was still tearing about the countryside, driving himself on errands and visits to his friends. Dow Suggs had a twinkle in his eye that belied his years. His Methodist faith was not a sober-sided religion.

Like other businessmen of the time, Suggs made his own money—literally. A full series of coins or tokens, from penny to dollar, bore his name and with them he paid the "hands" in his various enterprises. Cedar Lane was a substantial farm operation, but in addition he engaged in the timber business and owned a gristmill. The millpond was a favorite swimming hole, and the nearby Live Oak Baptist Church used it for baptizing new members.

His given name was a common one among Methodist families in Horry County. There were dozens of men named Lorenzo Dow, or L. D., or Dow, for an eccentric itinerant, a sometime licensed Methodist preacher who passed through Horry County in 1804.

Lorenzo Dow was born in Coventry, Connecticut, on October 16, 1777. He came under religious conviction when he was seventeen years old and began preaching. Time and again he tried to get the Methodists of New England to license him to preach, but he was not exactly the sort they wanted to sponsor. Once they did accept him conditionally, but three months later they dismissed him from the circuit. Lorenzo Dow struck out on his own and achieved his unique reputation in an era of famous itinerant missionaries.

Dow was described as thin, sallow, and consumptive and was given to antics that made him memorable to his contemporaries. He himself said that they called him "Crazy Dow." Apparently he never was robust, and he certainly dealt carelessly with his health. Always poor, frequently to the point of near starvation, Dow depended entirely on the kindness of people along his way to feed and clothe him. Some accounts describe him as barefoot in the dead of winter, without a coat to keep him warm in the snow.

In 1802 Dow struck out on an evangelistic journey through the south. He preached to the Indians in Alabama, said to have been the first to do so. On his return trip he came to Charleston, where his reception from local Methodist clergy was not cordial or enthusiastic. Continuing up the coast in January of 1804, he came to Georgetown. His journal for January 14 says: "Hence we went to Georgetown, where I held a few meetings, and then rode forty-three miles to Kingston. I put up at a tavern though a Methodist preacher lived near, hired a room for a meeting, and called in the neighbors. Next day I fell in with brother Russell, who was going to his station, so we crossed a ferry together and continued on upwards of eighty miles [to Wilmington]."

Though he was here three years after the name of the village was changed from Kingston to Conwayborough, he referred to it by its old name. Bishop Asbury had been guilty of the same lapse. No matter. What is significant is the lasting impression Dow's brief visit evidently made on his hearers. Naming male children for this eccentric preacher probably came about initially because the parents experienced his powerful preaching or heard about it from others. Even though Dow was not generally approved by the Methodist establishment and never enjoyed the prestige of Asbury, he is certainly a runner-up in the naming game. Many Horry County families gave their sons Asbury's name spelled in a variety of ways and sometimes shortened to Berry. Dow's appears in combination with almost all the well-known surnames.

Dow says nothing in his journal about his reception by the Conwayborough neighbors who came to hear him, nor indeed how many came. He apparently was more popular with his impromptu congregations than with the clergy, who turned a cold shoulder to him all along the way. At the end of this journey through the South, he dined with a New England cleric and met young Peggy Holcomb. On the day he met her, he inquired how she would answer if God should direct her to marry an itinerant preacher. When she showed some interest, he explained that she would have to agree never to stand in the way of his traveling to preach. Undaunted by the conditions of his proposal, Peggy agreed. They were married in 1804. On the day after the wedding, he departed on another missionary journey!

In 1805 he went to Ireland to evangelize the Irish and took Peggy with him. She was his staunch supporter, his companion when he suffered her to be, and his defender. A modern woman has to wonder!

From time to time, his health would entirely give out, and he would

Ladies and Gentlemen

have to retire temporarily from the fray. Never giving his poor body the consideration it needed, he would force himself up and again on the road. He met death unexpectedly on February 2, 1834. That he reached his mid-fifties is amazing!

Dow is sometimes credited with originating the camp meetings for which frontier religion was noted. Although he didn't preach there, worshippers in Conwayborough were using a campground south of town along the Georgetown highway. No record of a church edifice in Conwayborough between 1798, when a church was destroyed by a storm, and the building of the first Methodist Church in the town about 1844, has been found.

THOMAS DAGGETT SANK THE YANKEE ADMIRAL

Horry County has had a continuing New England connection. Men and women from that area have come to this county since its earliest days for a variety of reasons and have left their marks on its history.

One of the most remarkable was Thomas West Daggett, born in New Bedford, Massachusetts, on October 24, 1828. When he was sixteen years old, he left home to seek his fortune. In Charleston, Daggett found work in a machine shop as an apprentice. The skills he learned qualified him as an engineer, and he followed this line of work most of his life. It led him for a time to Darien, Georgia, where he ran a large sawmill. Daggett returned to South Carolina when the opportunity came to manage a rice mill for Francis Marion Weston at Laurel Hill in the Waccamaw Neck.

On July 4, 1856, because of his engineering skills, he was appointed captain of Company 4, First Battalion, Thirty-third Regiment, South Carolina Militia. By the time the Civil War began, Daggett had become fairly affluent. He entered Confederate service as an ordnance officer and was eventually made responsible for all the coastal defenses from Little River to Georgetown.

As the commander of the Waccamaw Light Artillery, he built the blockhouse and magazine at Fort Randall and armed it with two six-pounders. The fort was situated on a high bluff overlooking the mouth of Little River and commanded one of the most beautiful views in Horry County. It fell to the Yankees in 1863, but its defenders immediately regained it (*LC*, pp. 143–44). The Waccamaw Light Artillery was also responsible for Fort Ward.

As the end of the war neared, U.S. Navy gunboats entered Winyah Bay on February 23, 1865, to take over the city of Georgetown. The city surrendered on February 25. The next day Rear Admiral John A. Dahlgren arrived in his flagship, the *Harvest Moon*. He freed the slaves, ordered their former owners to provide them with provisions for sixty days, and placed the town under martial law under a naval officer. A garrison of white and black soldiers under an army officer arrived March 1 and took control of the town.

Admiral Dahlgren turned the *Harvest Moon* back down the bay. At about 7:45 in the morning, March 1, 1865, the admiral was in his cabin waiting for his breakfast when his ship hit a crude floating mine or torpedo. It blew a hole through the starboard quarter, tearing away the main deck over it. The ship sank in five minutes. There was only one casualty. Another boat picked up the admiral and his crew. The wreck of the *Harvest Moon* may still be seen from the Confederate gun emplacements of Battery White at Belle Isle.

The torpedo was the work of Captain Daggett, fashioned, it is said, on "the second floor of the oldest store in Georgetown, occupied at the time by S.W. Rouquie, and later by H. Kaminski." According to one newspaper, a northern relative who recognized Daggett offered a reward of one thousand dollars for his head delivered on the point of a bayonet to Georgetown.

Financially ruined at the end of the war, Daggett returned to the mill business on Waccamaw Neck, but rice milling was diminishing with the gradual destruction of the rice culture. In 1875 or thereabouts Daggett, who had been responsible for the sinking of the Yankee admiral's flagship, became the captain of the government dredge boat on the Waccamaw and Little Pee Dee Rivers and moved to Conwayborough.

In those days all goods and travelers moved to and from Horry County by paddlewheel steamers which depended upon rivers clear of obstructions. The writer of his obituary credited Captain Daggett with securing federal appropriations to remove snags or obstructions from the Waccamaw and the Little Pee Dee Rivers. It is impossible to overestimate the importance of his work to the commerce of the area in the period that followed.

Daggett's family may have lived in Conwayborough earlier. One of his daughters, buried in Kingston Presbyterian Church cemetery, died in 1863. Perhaps, like the Plowden C. J. Weston family, they were refugees during the Civil War. The captain quickly became an integral part of the local political and social scene after the family made the permanent relocation in 1875. He played an active role in the 1876 campaign to elect Gen. Wade Hampton governor. The community called upon him when engineering skills were needed. For instance, it was Captain Daggett who designed and built a "scientific" gallows, last used in 1906, for the jail and who designed and installed the earthquake rods in the present city hall.

In 1880 Captain Daggett served in the South Carolina Senate, succeed-

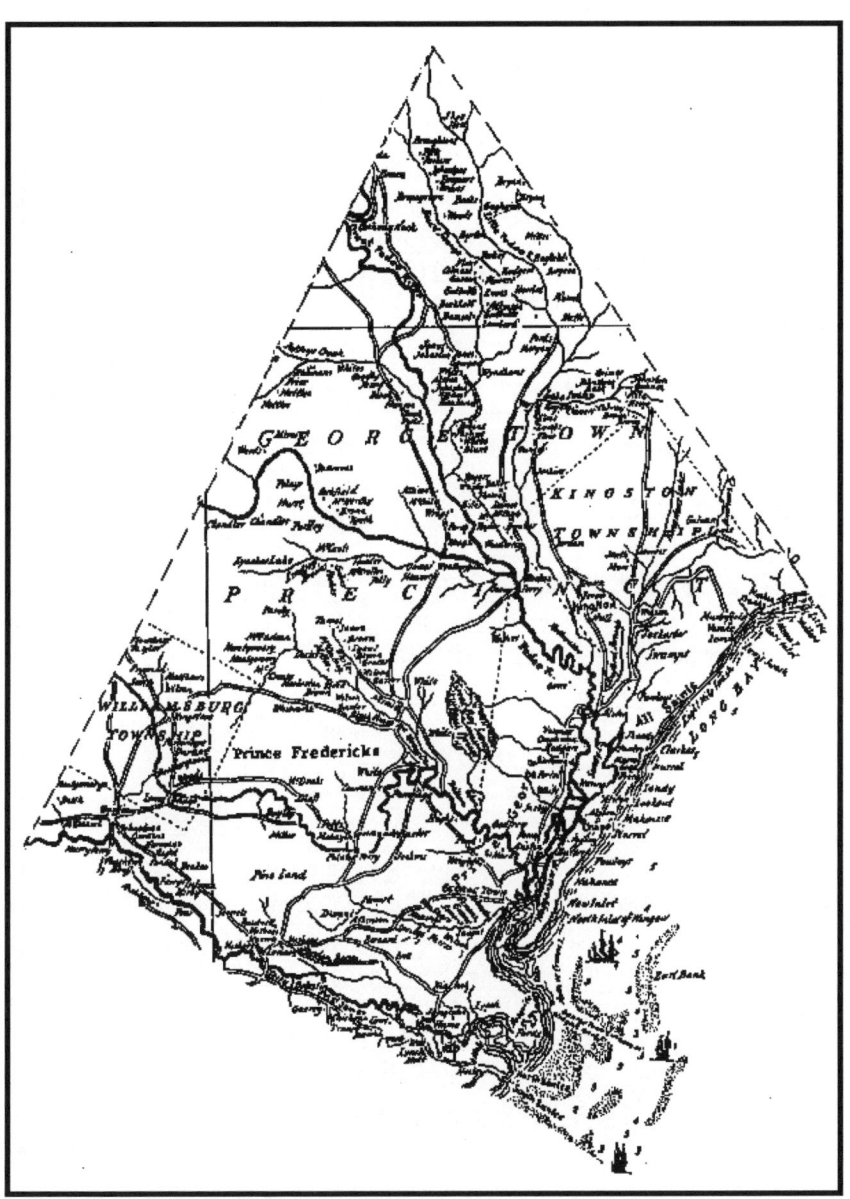

Map of Georgetown District, 1775, drawn by Henry Mouzon and other surveyors. It shows Kingston Township on the Waccamaw River.

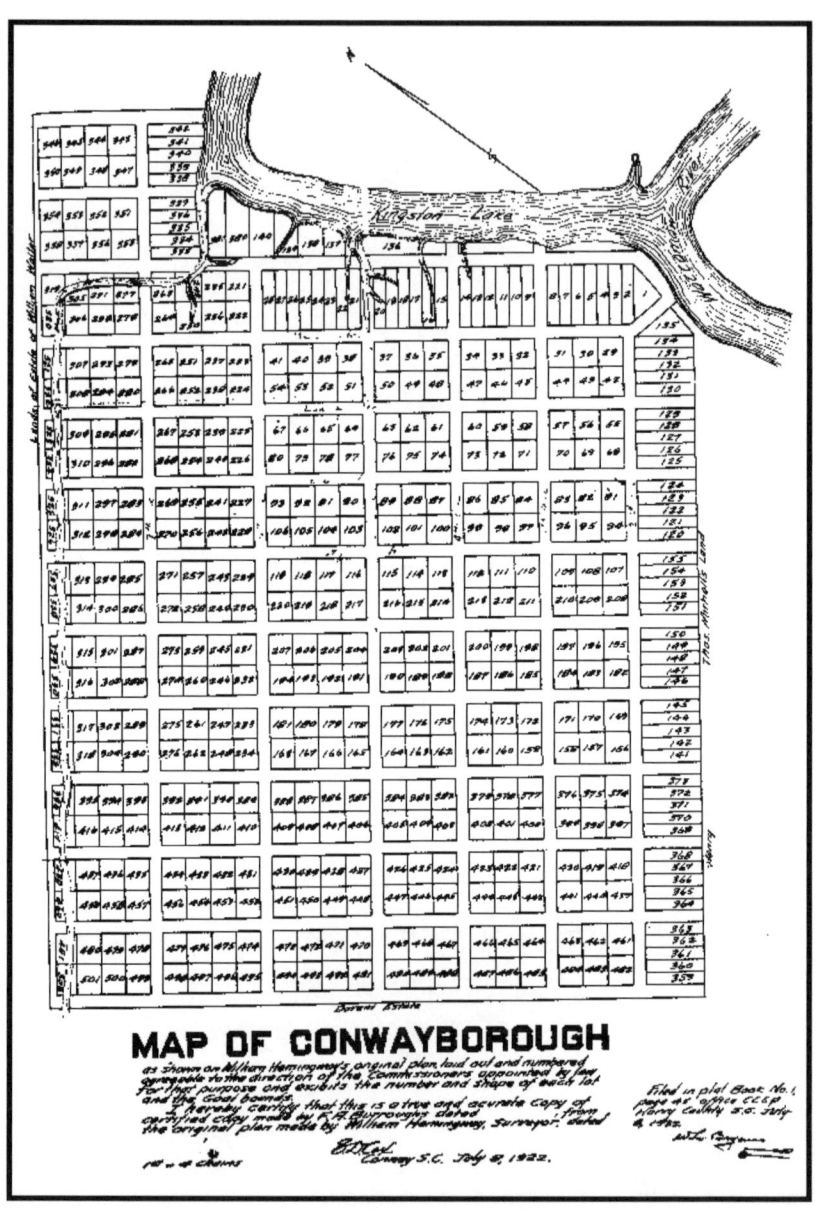

William Hemingway's map of Conwayborough, 1802, as copied by S. D. Cox, surveyor, in 1922. The original is located in Conway City Hall.

Harlee's map of Horry District, 1820, published in Mills, *Atlas*, 1825

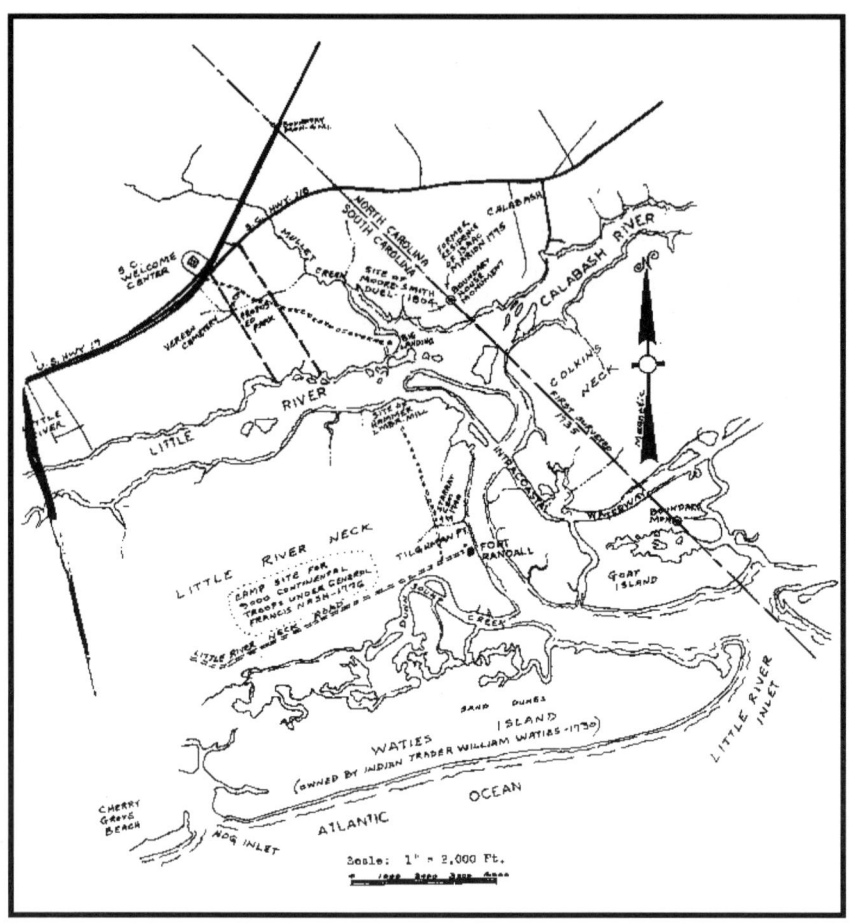

Little River area, showing sites of historical interest, drawn by C. B. Berry. Used with his permission.

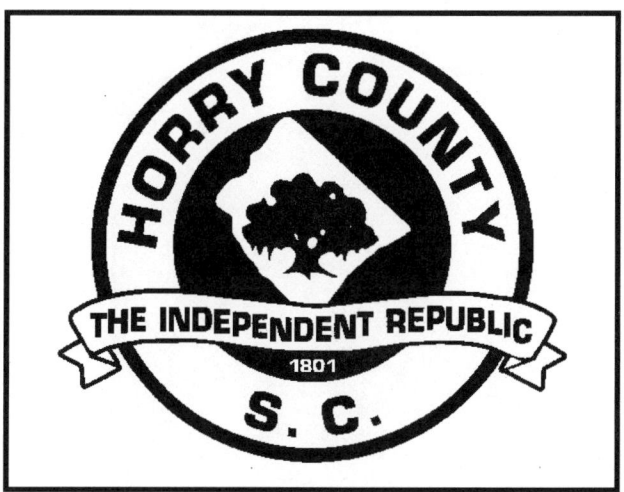

Horry County seal shows the "rough diamond" outline of the county, a live oak, the county's nickname, and the year the county was created from old Georgetown District.

The *F. G. Burroughs* and the *Ruth,* steamboats of the Waccamaw Line, at Bucksport.

Peter Horry, Huguenot planter who fought under General Francis Marion. Petitioners of this area asked that this district be named for him.

The second Horry County Courthouse, 1825–1908, now the Conway City Hall. Shown in the late nineteenth century.

Tokens used to pay workers were made from paper or metal and bore the name of the issuing firm. They could be spent only in that firm's commissary.

Tobacco farming occupied the whole family. This picture was made by William Van Auken Greene, an itinerant photographer who worked in the Aynor area in the 1930s.

The third Horry County Courthouse, built in 1908, shown just as construction was being completed. The jail is in the left background.

Loris, about 1895

Downtown Myrtle Beach

Ocean Forest Hotel, Myrtle Beach

Franklin Gorham Burroughs and Adeline Cooper Burroughs

Henry Buck

Confederate memorial near the corner of Sixth Avenue and Elm Street is sheltered by a great oak which is in the middle of Sixth Avenue.

John P. Derham house at Green Sea

Lieutenant Governor Robert Scarborough

> **FUNERAL NOTICE.**
>
> The friends and acquaintences of Mr. and Mrs. T. W. BEATY, are respectfully invited to attend the funeral of H. Brookman, their only son, and the last of their children, from their residence, to-morrow at 9 o'clock, A. M.
>
> All Sunday School Scholars, are especially invited, to attend the remains of their little class-mate to its last resting place.
>
> *SATURDAY, SEPT.* 16, 1870.

Beaty funeral notice. The date at the bottom of the invitation should read 1871, not 1870.

Colonel Doc Allen Spivey

Burroughs School, opened in 1906

Conwayborough Academy

The Gully Store was located at Ninth Avenue and Elm Street in Conway. It later became in turn the Burroughs Hospital, an apartment building, the first home of Waccamaw Academy, and now a private home.

Edmund Bigham on his way to court, 1926. This photo was made by local photographer Warren Johnson and sold as a postcard.

The sailing ship *Henrietta* was launched at Bucksville in 1875

The *Henrietta* being built at Bucksville. Drawing made April 1, 1875, by S. S. Stevens of Cherryville, Maine, who helped build her. The original is in the Penobscot (Maine) Marine Museum.

HOMEWOOD

The Garden Spot of the South.

IN THE OLD CAROLINAS.

Healthful, Delightful, All-the-Year Climate. Fertile Soil and Abundant Rainfall equally distributed throughout the year. Pure, Soft Water from flowing wells. Rail and Water Transportation. Rapid Transit to all the great Seaboard Cities where the largest and best Markets are found.

CHEAP LANDS ON EASY TERMS

With unsurpassed opportunities for gaining a livelihood and a competence. Land cleared and put into cultivation for non-residents on the

PROFIT-SHARING PLAN.

WRITE FOR TERMS AND ROUTE.   SEND FOR MAPS AND DESCRIPTIVE CIRCULARS

FARM, FIELD AND FIRESIDE.

Advertisement for the Homewood Colony (*Farm, Field, and Fireside,* July 9, 1898)

ing William L. Buck, who had died January 4 that year. Daggett qualified on February 14 and served until Thomas W. Beaty was elected later that year. In spite of failing health, he served in the House of Representatives in 1890-1891.

Daggett married three times, two of his wives having died before he left Charleston. We have no record of children by these early marriages, but several sons and daughters blessed his union with Mary A. Tillman (b. ca. 1840), daughter of Benjamin A. Tillman of Waccamaw Neck. Six children and his widow survived him.

His obituary called him "generous, brilliant and influential." He had suffered a long illness, it said, and "he wrestled with death, who could accomplish its victory only by slow degree," on January 10, 1893. He is buried at the rear of Kingston Presbyterian Church in Conway.

THE IRISH DERHAMS OF GREEN SEA

Surrounded by many of its original outbuildings, the handsome old home of John Pickens Derham stands beside Highway 410 in the center of the little community of Green Sea in northwest Horry County. One of Horry's most distinguished men built it and maintained his home there until his death.

Michael Derham and his son Joseph Henry were born in Loughre, County Galway, Ireland, the father in 1779, the son in 1838. They migrated to the United States in 1845. Michael's wife, Mary Hoban, died and was buried in Brooklyn, New York, in 1870 before he moved south to join his son, who had already come to Horry County. Joseph was settled in business and already married to Sallie Enzor of the Spring Branch area of the county by the time the 1860 census was taken.

Because he had lost an arm as a child, Joseph was ineligible for service during the Civil War. During that period, he worked as an overseer on a plantation near Winnsboro. When Sherman marched through, Joseph was able to save some of the owner's horses by hiding them in the woods, but not his son's pet pig, which the Yankees butchered, cooked, and ate in view of the horrified little John.

After the war Joseph returned to the area in which his wife's family lived. He borrowed money from his relatives in New York and opened a store at Green Sea. Before the time of the railroad and the establishment of Loris as a trading center, Green Sea was the commercial center of much of the country for ten or twelve miles around. There is a local tradition that the Derhams named the area Green Sea because it reminded them of Ireland. Green Sea Bay, however, is mentioned in old grants in the area long before the Derhams arrived on the scene. The community name likely came from it. Derham's commercial enterprises at Green Sea were successful. His father, Michael, helped him. As a dealer in turpentine, he acquired enormous acreage of pine forest at Green Sea, Little River, and Fair Bluff, North Carolina.

Michael Derham died in 1876, just three years short of a century old. Joseph H. Derham, like his father, was born and died a Catholic, but he married into a staunch Baptist family. His mixed religious heritage caused objections from both families when his son, John P. Derham, wished to marry Lula Jackson McGougan, a well-educated young woman from a prominent family. Her family thought she ought not to marry a Catholic—and his that he should not marry a Baptist. They were married on January 30, 1884, and John Pickens eventually adopted his mother's faith. He became a deacon of the Green Sea Baptist Church and a member of the anti-Catholic Masonic Order. This did not keep his opponents in one election from trying to enlist the Masons against him.

Joseph and Sallie Derham had four children, three boys and one girl. One son died in infancy while the family was in Winnsboro. Sallie died with a newborn son in April 1869, and the baby was buried in her arms. Emily Frances, their daughter, married the Rev. Samuel Daniel Page, but had no children. Six months after Sallie's death, Joseph married Sarah Amanda Bryan of Little River. He was almost thirty-two, and she not quite seventeen. They had a son and a daughter, William Patrick and Ida Bryan. The little girl died when she was just four and a half.

Republican (i.e., carpetbagger, in that era) governors Robert F. Scott, Franklin J. Moses Jr., and Daniel H. Chamberlain named Joseph H. Derham county treasurer from 1868–1876. Their administrations were generally regarded with great disdain by local people, but staunch Democrats declared, "It was generally regarded as fortunate that we had the services of an honest man and good official. [Derham] made an excellent officer and turned over a clean sheet on his retiring."

After the home he had built in Green Sea burned, Derham lived in a house in Fair Bluff, the first town he had lived in after he came south from New York. Derham suffered the same losses as other turpentine operators when the industry played out in Horry County and moved on to Georgia. He made plans to follow it but died in 1882, leaving large land holdings, though little money.

J. H. Derham's son, John Pickens Derham, was born April 10, 1861, at the Enzor home at Spring Branch. He attended local schools in Green Sea and Fair Bluff, where his family had moved, and to Bingham Military School in North Carolina. His mother, Sallie Enzor Derham, died when her son was only eight. By age nineteen he was in Green Sea helping to manage the family enterprises.

His interest in politics began early. As a mere stripling of fifteen, he was among the Horry men who welcomed Gen. Wade Hampton to Conway during the gubernatorial campaign of 1876. He joined the Horry Hussars, the local militia, and became a lieutenant. Voters elected him county education commissioner, his first public office, when he was only twenty-five years old. Two years later he became auditor for a four-year term. At age thirty-one (1892) he was elected Horry County senator and served with distinction in that office.

James Norton, then comptroller general of South Carolina, named Derham his chief clerk in 1894. He was a delegate to the State Constitutional Convention of 1895 that devised the constitution under which South Carolina still operates. In 1897 the legislature named him to succeed Norton as comptroller general.

In the election of 1900, the shadow of his father's appointment by a Republican governor fell over the son. An opponent named N.W. Brooker circulated a scurrilous attack on him, claiming that he was no Democrat at all, but a closet Republican. This disinformation was printed on stationery that bore the emblems of the Masons, an obvious ploy to enlist Masons against Derham, though Derham himself was a member of the order.

For six years Derham had served as the chairman of the Democratic Party in Horry County, on the state executive committee of the party, and as delegate to state conventions. Men who knew him rose to his defense. They said, "No one has ever been known to question his loyalty to the Democratic party." They described Brooker as a "notorious slanderer" and his charges were branded "reckless" (*HH*, 23 August 1900). The Masons declared that "these insinuations will be resented and the style of campaigning inaugurated by this political sore-head will be severely condemned at the polls."

Brooker also charged that Derham neglected his office by spending too much time at home in Green Sea. J. C. Bryant, a near neighbor, gave the lie to that. He said that except for the time of the illness and death of Derham's little daughter in 1899, his visits home were short and not as often as the community would have wished.

When election time came, Horry gave Derham 95 percent of its votes. (The other race that year in which Horry had a real interest was for the Sixth Congressional District, in which favorite son Robert Bethea

Scarborough received 88 percent of the Horry vote for that office.) Derham also carried the next election in 1902. In 1906 he returned to the legislature, this time to the House of Representatives for one term. When the South Carolina State Tax Commission was formed in 1915, Governor Richard I. Manning named him a member, acknowledging his expertise in tax matters. He served until his death, which occurred at Green Sea May 30, 1947, ending a career that spanned six decades. He was eighty-six. His death opened the door to statewide office for another Horry County man. James A. Calhoun Jr., then Horry County treasurer, was named by Gov. J. Strom Thurmond to Derham's seat on the South Carolina Tax Commission.

Lula Jackson McGougan Derham died on September 5, 1956. She and her husband are buried in the family plot in Green Sea Community Cemetery. They had ten children, eight of whom lived to maturity.

ROBERT BETHEA SCARBOROUGH, LAWYER-STATESMAN

A deal had been struck. Only the formal ratification on the floor of the South Carolina Senate remained. The power brokers nominated their choice for comptroller general of South Carolina and expected unanimous approval. The handsome freshman senator from Horry County, Robert Bethea Scarborough, arose. He thought J. P. Derham of Green Sea more worthy for the post than the nominee whose name had been put forward. His eloquence moved the body, the first and last time (according to one witness) a nomination speech has ever changed the mind of that body.

Physically imposing, Scarborough had a vocal gift to match, and he used body and voice to great effect, becoming one of the most eloquent orators of his time, both in the courtroom and in the political arena. Community leaders called upon him to speak whenever a ceremonial occasion demanded moving words. His eulogy of his first and only law partner, Judge Joseph T. Walsh, has survived as an example.

He was born on October 29, 1861, on a farm in Chesterfield County into the family of Lewis Scarborough, an itinerant Methodist preacher. The Reverend Scarborough had a number of pastorates, including Conway, before they settled in Marion County. Robert finished his formal education at Mullins Academy. After farming and working in timber, he became a teacher. When he was twenty, he married Mary J. Jones, and they went together to Little River, where he had been engaged to run the school.

Seeing the possibility of a professional career, Scarborough read for the law under the tutelage of various lawyers and was admitted to the bar in October 1884. Although Judge Joseph Travis Walsh had moved to Marion, he had retained his office in Conway. Walsh accepted Scarborough as a full partner, and he began his practice in the Conway office. He was successful from the first. In 1888, after ill health had forced Walsh to abandon the law, Scarborough opened his own office so that he could be independent. He also became active in Conway's rapidly developing banking enterprises.

Perhaps even that early he considered a political career. Scarborough was a conservative Democrat, opposed to Benjamin T. Tillman and all his adherents. He won his first race in 1896 for the State Senate and immediately made his mark. In his second term he was president pro tempore. Then, before Scarborough's second term ended, Governor Ellerbe died in office. When M. B. McSweeney moved up to the governorship, Scarborough became lieutenant governor of South Carolina and president of the Senate on June 3, 1899.

Excitement in Horry, his home county, was high in the fall of 1900. Two favorite sons were in races for important offices: Scarborough for the U.S. House of Representatives from the Sixth District and John Pickens Derham for state comptroller general. Derham's race turned ugly and was bitterly fought. Horry voters were fighting for both but were especially intent upon the House race. Not often had Horry put candidates into the field for statewide and national offices. Imagine the satisfaction felt in every precinct when Scarborough and Derham both won. Scarborough served in the U.S. House from 1901-1905. Although no one was in the field against him, he declined to run for another term. He returned to Conway to his practice, his family, and friends.

Scarborough held many posts in his church and community apart from his law practice and elective offices. His interests and commitment to the welfare of his county may be seen in their variety. He was a member of the Knights of Pythias, a Mason, chairman of the board of trustees of the Methodists' Horry Industrial School, member of the governing board of the State Hospital for the Insane, and member of the Pee Dee Historical Society. When the First World War came, he became chairman of the eastern district Selective Service Board.

He was not afraid to take firm stands on controversial issues, none more so than free range. The custom of allowing livestock to roam free in the woods (and elsewhere) was slowly going out of style as agricultural acreage increased, but there was still a lot of popular feeling about it. Indeed, exemptions for parts of Horry County remained on law books until the last gasp in 1922.

About 1926 Scarborough gave up active practice because of ill health. He enjoyed sitting on the porch of his Conway home, where friends called to him as they passed, and going to his little place at Murrells Inlet. He died on Thanksgiving Day, November 23, 1927, survived by his widow and two sons, Charles R. And Dr. Henry L. Scarborough. He is buried at Lakeside Cemetery, Conway.

MARY BEATY: A NORTHERN LADY WITH SOME PECULIARITIES

Before the Civil War education in Horry County was haphazard at best, dependent largely upon itinerant schoolmasters who were not always well qualified. Most children were lucky to get any education at all. For them to be able to read, write, and cipher a little was to be counted fortunate. Few communities could provide more than a few weeks of instruction.

A few families, among them the Bucks of Bucksville and Bucksport, could provide privately for the education of their children. They sought young women of good families and good education in the North to come to Horry and provide instruction in their homes. Frequently children from the neighborhood would be included in their classes. Eligible Horry County men found these accomplished young ladies attractive.

Mary Brookman, a first cousin to Henry Buck, was born in Bucksport, Maine, on April 5, 1825. She came south in 1849 and for two years was tutor and governess to the Buck children. Fannie Buck's first cousin, young Tom Beaty, an up-and-coming member of a prominent family, courted her; but at the end of her two years, she returned to Maine. Beaty followed and persuaded her to accept him. They married September 21, 1851, and returned to Conwayborough. Thomas Wilson Beaty became successful as a newspaper publisher, businessman, lawyer, politician, and community leader. He and Mary gained the lasting respect and admiration of the community.

Thomas W. And Mary Brookman Beaty lived in a house on Kingston Street in Conway. It was built for them by carpenters and mechanics who came from Maine to work for the Bucks. The grounds around the home stretched from Kingston Lake to Main Street and included the property on which the Horry County Museum now stands at Fifth and Main. The house, which was purchased by D. A. Spivey after Mrs. Beaty's death, is still standing. At one time, it was occupied by the Conway Chamber of Commerce and is now the home of one of Spivey's descendants.

Thomas Beaty, born October 11, 1825, went as a delegate to the Secession Convention and signed the Ordinance of Secession. He served in the Civil War, but ill health cut short his service in 1862. He busied himself working on the home front to recruit men and gather supplies for the armed forces. He served in the South Carolina House of Representatives in 1864-1865.

A young newsman from Sumter who came to Conway during the war lived in the Beaty home to protect Mrs. Beaty and the children while Beaty was away at war. Years later, the reporter described the town as he found it in 1861 and said of his hostess, "Mrs. Beaty was a northern woman, with some peculiarities, but well informed and intelligent."

Between 1852 and 1859 Tom and Mary had four daughters and a son. In 1859, within two months of each other, three-year-old May and seven-year-old Clara died, leaving Cora, six, Frederica, four, and Henry Brookman, a babe in arms. When she was only fifteen, Cora fell in love with Charles Bolton, a lawyer and newspaperman who worked on Tom Beaty's paper, and they married in 1869. Their honeymoon trip on a river steamboat ended tragically. The boat grounded on a sandbar and mosquitoes attacked. Cora's young groom contracted hemorrhagic fever, to which he succumbed several weeks later. She returned to the family home on Kingston Lake, a young widow who had had no real chance to be a wife.

On July 2, 1870, her younger sister was bathing in the waters of Kingston Lake under the watchful eye of a servant. Some accounts say she fell off the dock, and others that she got into trouble while swimming. The servant went to her rescue but could not save her. Cora, who had heard their screams and run to the dock, jumped in to help. All three, Cora, Fredrica, and the servant, drowned. The grieving parents buried their daughters in Kingston Presbyterian Church cemetery, a short distance down the lake from their home.

On September 15, 1871, fifteen months later, Mrs. Beaty was at home alone with her son, Brookie. In the early evening, she saw him into bed and went to her sitting room to work on her mending. She later told friends she became aware of a choir of angel voices. Her attention was drawn by a discordant note. She recognized Cora's voice among the singers, and asked, "Cora, why have you come back?"

Cora's reply, "Mother, we have come for Brookie," sent Mrs. Beaty rushing to her son's bedside. She found him stricken. He died the next day, September 16, 1871. Again invitations were sent around the town by hand. They read: "FUNERAL NOTICE. The friends and acquaintances of Mr. And Mrs. T.W. Beaty are respectfully invited to attend the funeral of H. Brookman, their only son, and the last of their children, from their residence, to-morrow at 9 o'clock, A.M. All Sunday School Scholars are especially invited to attend the remains of their little class-mate to its last resting place. Saturday, Sept 16, 1870 [1871]."

In the Kingston Presbyterian Cemetery the glass-enclosed recumbent statue of two little girls entwined in each other's arms marks the graves of May and Clara, the daughters who died in infancy. A tablet marker lists without dates the names of all the family of Thomas W. And Mary Brookman Beaty, including their son-in-law, Charles Bolton.

Thomas and Mary Beaty lived on, overcoming their grief by contributing to the life of the town and county. Thomas Beaty continued his business affairs and practiced law. He served in the South Carolina Senate from 1880 to 1884.

When Thomas Beaty died on April 18, 1886, Mrs. Beaty assumed the management of the businesses she had inherited, benefiting from the advice of his friends and the help of Braxton Brown, her Negro foreman. By all accounts, she was a good businesswoman as well as an outspoken member of the community.

The year after her husband's death, the railroad finally came from North Carolina to Conway. Mrs. Beaty watched as construction workers laid the track to bring it down Main Street. She probably welcomed this opening into the greater world outside Horry County. One morning, as she watched, she saw the construction crew preparing to fell one of the large oaks at the edge of her front yard—the very tree under which Gen. Wade Hampton had addressed the crowds when he was stumping for governor in 1876. Mary Beaty did not hesitate. Grabbing her gun, she advanced on the construction men and persuaded them to spare the old oak.

Mary Brookman Beaty, a strong and resilient woman, survived her husband by fifteen years. When she died in November 1901 her obituary said, "Mrs. Beaty was a woman with more than an ordinary mind. She was always well informed on current events, and was thoroughly conversant with the leading questions pertaining to her adopted State, and also affairs of material importance." Both the Methodist and Presbyterian ministers officiated at her funeral when she was laid to rest at last with her husband and five children in Kingston Church Cemetery.

D. ALLEN SPIVEY: CONWAY'S BANKER COLONEL

The opening of a McDonald's fast food outlet in Conway was remarkable in several ways. Although committed to golden arches on the outside, the franchisee decided on a local history theme for the interior decor. He was a Northern transplant and came to the public library for help. There he looked through pictures of old Conway and selected images he thought best summarized the history of the town and the county. For several, among them the sailing ship *Henrietta* and a portrait of Gen. Peter Horry, he commissioned a Columbia artist who painted them especially for the restaurant. It was, remarkably, the first time that a portrait of the man for whom this county is named was hung in the county seat.

Then the franchisee had old photos copied and framed—an early locomotive, street scenes, old stores, and Col. D. Allen Spivey. He thought Colonel Spivey in his summer attire—white suit, white Panama hat—was the essence of the Southern gentleman, the epitome of the old South. The whole display attracted a good deal of favorable comment from locals and visitors alike.

Doctor Allen Spivey and his twin, William H., were born August 25, 1868, in the Cedar Grove community west of Conway in Horry County. "Hop" and "Dock" were sons of William Alexander and Frances C. Hughes Spivey. Unlike most Horry men of his generation, Dock Spivey had the benefit of a college education. He received a scholarship to the Citadel, the first from Horry to do so, and in 1891 he graduated with honors.

Spivey joined the local militia, the Horry Hussars, and, enabled by his military training at the Citadel, helped make them prominent among the militia units at annual statewide encampments. It is not from this service, however, that the title by which he came to be called is derived. When he became a well-known businessman and political leader, several governors honored him by appointments to their staffs. He also served on the Citadel Board of Visitors. Each of these appointments carried the honorary title of "Colonel."

Banking institutions had been slow to establish themselves in Horry County. Even though there had been a number of false starts, the need was obvious. D. A. Spivey was one of a group of up-and-coming businessmen who organized the Bank of Conway in 1893. For him it was the beginning of a career in banking which spanned more than a half century. Some called him "the young Vanderbilt" because he seemed destined for success. He participated in the founding or management of several banks, most prominently the Peoples National Bank of Conway (now NationsBank). During the banking "holiday" of the Great Depression, when many of the country's banks closed, Conway had two sound institutions. In 1895 he married Mary Essie Collins, the daughter of B. G. Collins, partner with F. G. Burroughs in the prominent firm of Burroughs and Collins.

Fairly early in his career Dock Spivey entered local politics. From 1901–

1903 he was mayor of Conway. He served in the South Carolina House of Representatives from 1908-1912 and in the South Carolina Senate from 1925-1928.

Colonel Spivey developed a personal style of dress and grooming which made him stand out in a crowd. He wore his thick curly hair long, carried a cane and wore pince-nez glasses on a black ribbon. A watch chain decorated the vest, and there was usually a flower in the buttonhole of his three-piece suit. He wore dark suits in winter and solid white in the summer.

His business career was primarily in banks, but he also founded the Horry Land and Improvement Company, still in business, and operated a hotel and warehouse, among other enterprises. He and his brother John C. Spivey were early investors in Myrtle Beach. They purchased and developed a large tract around Withers Swash as Spivey's Beach.

There is a story about him and feisty Mary Brookman Beaty. After there had been words between them, he ordered a cake of ice to be delivered to her with the message that she "should sit on it until she cooled off." After her death, he acquired her property on Kingston Lake from her heir. He had always admired the house, so he made his home there and subdivided the large front lawn into lots for business purposes. In 1935 the U.S. Post Office was built on the corner with Fifth Avenue. Family businesses and the bank with which he was associated most of his life occupy other parcels.

When his son, Collins A. Spivey, succeeded him as president of Peoples National Bank in 1936, Colonel Spivey became chairman of the board of directors and remained in that office until his death on May 24, 1945. He is buried in Lakeside Cemetery, Conway.

VIRGINIA DURANT YOUNG: EARLY FEMINIST SHOOK CONWAY

Some wonderful mysteries and spellbinding stories lie hidden in the land records of Horry County. One in particular had the potential of disaster for Conway in 1901 when the heirs of William Durant brought suits against some prominent residents and landowners. Their claims had roots in early history.

On November 19, 1817, John Durant received by grant from the state of South Carolina 1,000 acres on the north side of the Waccamaw River adjacent to the village of Conwayborough. The grant boundaries lay alongside the Deep Gully, just southeast of Ninth Avenue, Kingston Lake, and Waccamaw River. At other places it joined the lands of John Rogers, the William Waller estate, John Sing, John Beaty, and John Sarvis. John Durant's son Henry received this land from his father in 1821.

Trouble followed because Henry Durant wished to control the future of his land. Fifteen years later on November 24, 1836, when he realized that his end might be near, Henry made his will. He left the bulk of his estate to his son William with his brother, John Durant, and his friend, Eleazar Waterman, as trustees. Evidencing some mistrust of his son's business acumen, he specified that the estate should not be subject to William's debts nor to any contracts William might make. The estate was to be preserved for any son William might name Henry, or, absent a namesake, divided among William's heirs.

In January 1838, less than two years later and in spite of his father's will, William did sell his inheritance to Col. James Beaty and then moved to Marion County. Beaty, in turn, conveyed portions of it to various buyers, including the Conwayborough Academy, the firm of Perkins and Barnhill, Samuel Bell, E. T. Harrison, William A. Burroughs, William H. Jones, Elizabeth Inman, and Timothy Cooper.

William Durant died December 15, 1896, leaving eight daughters. Under the provisions of their grandfather's will, the women would have inherited a large section of the most valuable property in Conway. Believing that the will would prevail under the law, they argued that the land had been sold unlawfully by their father when they were minors, and they brought suit against the current owners to reclaim their inheritance.

Among the prominent defendants were the estate of F. G. Burroughs, the Burroughs and Collins Company, W. R. Lewis, Benjamin G. Collins, Jeremiah Smith, and D. T. McNeill. McNeill was the defendant in the first suit which came up. The judge dismissed the jury and issued a directed verdict, giving the Durant family the victory. This decision threatened great financial loss, if not ruin, to many people who had bought parcels of this property in good faith. They appealed the verdict, and the South Carolina Supreme Court reversed it on July 10, 1907, and remanded the case to the lower court for retrial.

The courts had taken six years to get this far. In the meantime, development in the heart of Conway stood still. Several defendants, anxious about potential financial loss, apparently made settlements with the plaintiffs out of court to get clear titles. After the Supreme Court opinion it became apparent that the defendants would prevail. A consent order filed in the McNeill case effectively settled more than one hundred cases.

Virginia Durant Young, the most active of the eight sisters responsible for this chaos, made several trips to Conway during the time the cases were being heard. She described the town in her newspaper, the *Enterprise*, as the "residence of millionaires. It has thirteen big mercantile companies, whose yearly business foots up from $25,000 to $200,000 a year. The sworn statements of the Bank of Conway, issued in September of this year [1905], show deposits of over a quarter million of dollars." On visits to Conway to attend to legal matters, Mrs. Young looked for landmarks associated with her grandfather, Captain Henry Durant, including his plantation, Crabtree, and the Durant Chapel.

Born March 10, 1842, she married twice. Her second marriage to Dr. William J. Young, a physician in Fairfax, was happy but childless. Virginia Young developed interests to which she devoted her considerable energies and intelligence. She wrote four novels: *Loruhamah* (1874), *Beholding as in a Glass* (1895), *A Tower in the Desert* (1896), and *One of the Blue Hen's Chickens* (1901).

In 1888, she joined the Women's Christian Temperance Union. The next year, when she went to Chicago to its national convention as South Carolina's only delegate, she heard Frances Willard speak. It had a great effect on her. In 1890 at a suffrage conference in Greenville, she pledged herself to work for the enfranchisement of women in South Carolina. The same year, she began the weekly *Fairfax Enterprise* with an all-female staff.

She and other feminists addressed the 1895 South Carolina Constitutional Convention, hoping to have a woman's suffrage amendment adopted. It failed overwhelmingly. She contributed a chapter on the history of women's rights in South Carolina to *History of Woman Suffrage* (Anthony and Harper, eds., 1902). On January 31, 1902, she became the first woman to speak to the South Carolina House of Representatives.

Ironically, Mrs. Young died November 2, 1906, before the Conway land title suits were withdrawn, but it would be many days before Conway would forget the averted disaster.

JESSE P. AND CORA WILLIAMS: THE RAILROADING MAN AND HIS LADY

The railroad president's private car rolled into Conway and onto a siding at the old depot near the present site of the chamber of commerce on a Friday in late April 1914, just as World War I was getting underway. The visit probably had more impact on the town than the war in Europe.

The president was a woman, the only female railroad president in the United States at that time. Cora V. Taylor, daughter of W. H. P. Taylor of Tampico Plantation in Dog Bluff Township, grew up in Horry County. In 1879, she married J. P. Williams, then a successful entrepreneur at Port Harrelson on Bull Creek. He had died a little more than six months before her visit to Conway, and she had inherited his position as president of the Georgia, Florida and Alabama Railroad.

Jesse Parker Williams was born in Wayne County, North Carolina, on December 27, 1842. His ancestors had fought in the Revolution and the War of 1812, and he himself served long and devotedly in the Civil War, organizing and commanding at least two companies. After the end of the war he came, penniless it was said, to Horry County. For about a year he worked as bookkeeper to James S. Burroughs, a Conway merchant. He then worked for about a year in the same capacity for Beaty and Holliday, a naval stores firm at Cool Spring. By the third year, he had begun a timber business of his own there.

About 1872 he moved to Port Harrelson and entered the mercantile business. Sailing ships came into its harbor on Bull Creek to load naval stores and lumber. Port Harrelson was a bustling port, the first village actually incorporated in Horry County. There were homes, accommodations for visitors, a Methodist church, a Masonic hall, several stores, and other amenities which attracted the people from a large area around.

In 1873 Williams married Rowena Olivia Outland; she died April 4, 1875, probably in childbirth. She was only nineteen at her death; her grave is in an old cemetery near Port Harrelson. In 1879 he married Cora V. Taylor, who was born in Dog Bluff Township in Horry County.

About 1880, convinced of the need for a knowledgeable middleman to facilitate negotiations between the distillers of naval stores and Northern commission buyers, he sold his successful business and moved to Savannah, where he became a commission merchant or factor for naval stores and cotton. According to one Georgia source, it was the "oldest naval stores house in the South." The firm's name was Williams and Watson, later incorporated as J. P. Williams and Company with a capital stock of $3.5 million. He diversified his business interests, branching out first into a wholesale grocery business. Later, he began to purchase pinelands worn out for turpentine use, but valuable for their timber.

His foresight again paid off and led him into the railroad business. He was among the promoters of the Middle Georgia and Atlantic Railroad, which became Central of Georgia. Then on his own he began the construction of a line which became the Georgia, Florida and Alabama (originally called Georgia Pine). Seeing that he would need produce to haul on his railroad, he combined the extension of rails into fresh territory with a liberal policy toward settlers. He actively encouraged immigrants from other states to take advantage of land which he offered at a good price along his right of way.

Meantime, back in Savannah, he turned his attention to nearby beaches and helped to organize the Tybee Hotel Company and the Tybee Island Beach Company. He also got into banking with the organization of the National Bank of Savannah and the Oglethorpe Savings and Trust. He and Mrs. Williams had a home in Savannah and one "for occasional use" in Statesboro, where her parents lived.

Nor did he neglect his civic and religious duties. He was active in Methodist church projects and served for some years as a trustee and chairman of trustees at then Emory College.

He died on August 5, 1913, "after suffering for several years from a form of insanity which had rendered him incapable during his last years of attending to business affairs." His widow inherited his fortune, including his personal railroad car.

Mrs. Williams had celebrity status when she returned to Horry County. Old friends in the area were invited to visit her aboard the car during her stay. They described for their friends who were not so lucky the splendors of the traveling apartment. Sometimes she ventured abroad to visit the scenes of her childhood. Years after she had returned to Georgia, Conway people talked of her visit.

CAPTAIN CAUSEY AND MISS JULIA

From a conversation with Evelyn Mayo Snider, granddaugher of John Mayo, I learned that the cottage at 605 Laurel Street, Conway, was built by John A. Mayo, the merchant whose store stood just across Main Street from city hall on the corner of the present parking lot. Mayo was a brother-in-law of Franklin Gorham Burroughs and followed him from North Carolina to Conwayborough. *Horry County Survey of Historic Places* (*IRQ*, April 1973) does not give the date the cottage was constructed, but since Mayo died in 1896, the structure is about a century old. For many years it was home to Coleman S. Causey, a riverboat captain, and his wife, Julia E. Skipper Causey, a milliner.

They married on May 9, 1894, when each was about forty-two years old. The beautiful little cottage may have been ready for them to occupy at that time. The house is typical of modest nineteenth-century homes in the old town. Few of them remain, so Conway is fortunate that this one has been preserved almost intact. A bay window has been added to the north side, but otherwise its exterior has not been changed. The place has architectural charm, distinguished by the decorative "banjo" boarding on its porch.

It catches the eyes of passersby in any season of the year, but never more than in the fall when a beautifully shaped sugar maple beside the street in front became a golden flame—one of the most beautiful trees in Conway, now gone.

Captain Causey was born about April 11, 1852, the son of W. G. And Margaret W. Causey. He was captain of steamboats on the Congaree, Wateree, and Waccamaw Rivers, including the Waccamaw Line of Steamers' *Ruth*, a side-wheeler. After his marriage to Julia Skipper, he left the river and operated a mercantile business. He was also the innkeeper of the Kingston Hotel. The town admired him for his decided opinions, his honesty, and his reliability. According to his obituary, he was "never known to be concerned in the intermeddling that sometimes takes place in a community. His death ended a long and useful life" (*HH*, 18 September 1924).

Miss Julia was also born about 1852, the daughter of Sheriff Abijah H. Skipper and his wife, Sarah Caroline. She was a talented milliner, and her shop was well patronized. Her handiwork graced the heads of Conway ladies in an era when new bonnets were made individually to suit the wearer. A new hat was the mark of a new season and received careful consideration of materials and style by the milliner and her customer. Captain Causey helped his wife with the business end of her millinery. Since they married late, the couple had no children.

Mrs. Virginia Burroughs Marshall has told the story of how F. G. Burroughs, her grandfather, asked Miss Julia to make a cushion for his coffin. He had commissioned the coffin, thinking to save his wife that responsibility at the time of his death. When it was delivered, he found it lacking in comfort, so he selected the material (some say red velvet) and called the milliner in to make a comfortable support for his remains. He found her cushion much to his liking and sent the finished coffin home to be stored. His wife, not willing to live with it in the house, sent it back to him at the Gully Store, where it remained until his death in 1897.

Near the main entrance to Lakeside Cemetery is a mausoleum with no names, dates, or other identification on it. It is the resting place of Captain and Mrs. Causey. Captain Causey did not wish to be buried underground, so although he died on August 22, 1924, his body was not interred until the mausoleum could be finished. His funeral therefore did not take place until August 28. His widow lived on with her dogs in the little cottage for nearly a decade before she died on November 22, 1933. The undertaker followed instructions to lock the door and throw the key inside after Miss Julia was laid beside the captain.

H. KEMPER COOKE: BACKWOODS STATESMAN

Senator Henry Kemper Cooke flaunted his kind of Horry independence on the local scene and in Columbia. At the time of his election to the Senate in 1932, the *Charleston News and Courier* described him as "medium sized, wiry, fast walking, fast talking" and added, "The voters of Horry County, whether friend or foe, knew when the deciding returns flashed they would have the most colorful representative in the State Senate that had been there for many years; that he would speak his mind and that he has enough mind to keep him speaking."

Cooke was born December 30, 1866, in Marion District, the son of Henry B. Cooke and Catherine Carolina Ayers. He grew up in the Galivants Ferry area and attended high school in Conway and in Fair Bluff. From 1890 to 1892 he attended Furman University, but a severe case of influenza cut short his studies.

After his father's death in 1898, he operated Lake Swamp Farms. Cooke relished the life of hunter and fisherman and always kept a pack of good fox hounds. In the agricultural depression of the 1920s, he lost much of what he had accumulated.

Late in his life, Cooke turned to politics, making his first successful race for the House of Representatives in 1930 when he was sixty-four. Cooke called himself the "Backwoods Statesman." He was a "tell-it-like-it-is" anti-establishment politician whose bluntness won him no friends among the professional politicians and their backers.

He won the senate race in 1932 against Marsden G. Andersen. Andersen challenged the election, claiming that Cooke was not a registered voter when he ran and therefore not a qualified elector. The local board of canvassers refused jurisdiction in the dispute, and Andersen took his case to the state supreme court.

The court also found reason not to judge the dispute, so the decision fell to the South Carolina Senate. Andersen, represented by Cordie Page, asked the Senate to vacate the seat and hold another election. When the vote did not carry, Edgar Brown of Barnwell made the motion to seat Cooke. The senate leadership assigned him to the agriculture, claims and grievances, education, engrossed bills, federal relations, and fish, game, and forestry committees.

Ten days later, the Senate had cause to wonder about the wisdom of its decision. Cooke spoke in opposition to a resolution and held the floor until 10:05 the next morning. According to one of his colleagues, he conducted all-night filibusters nine times.

Cooke opposed anything proposed by Ben Sawyer of the highway department. A month after his first filibuster, while speaking against reducing the cost of auto driver licenses, Cooke charged certain senators had received favors from the highway czar. Seventeen colleagues demanded that he provide proof. Never one to back down, Cooke read his reply, giving specifics.

On March 22, 1934, he leveled charges that senators were accepting bribes from lobbyists. York senator W. M. Dunlap introduced a resolution to require the senator from Horry to furnish proof. In his lengthy reply Cooke named the senators who had relatives on state payrolls, the relatives, the departments, and the salaries received. No one need be surprised that the senators voted he had not made his case against them. Senator Dunlap then moved to expel the senator from Horry. The result was 23-17 in favor of expulsion, not quite enough votes for the two-thirds majority needed to carry.

That year Cooke ran fifth in a field of eight in the Democratic primary for governor on a platform advocating popular election of judges, local option on liquor, a practical school curriculum, and the elimination of "ring" rule—the last an obvious jab at the "Barnwell ring" then prominent in state politics.

He returned to the Senate, but on March 27, 1935, asked for a leave of absence because of illness. On Sunday, July 14, 1935, Kemp Cooke and K. L. Mishoe stopped at J. H. Johnson's filling station about six miles from Conway on the road to Myrtle Beach to get out of a rainstorm. Another motorist who had trouble starting his car after the rain asked Mishoe to help him push it. Cooke was walking along the pavement toward them when he was struck by a car driven by Wallace Floyd. He died two days later.

Five hundred people attended his funeral at Galivants Ferry Baptist Church near his home, but the requisite eulogy in the Senate for a deceased member was pointedly brief. Paul Quattlebaum, who succeeded the backwoods statesman as senator from Horry, read into the record a piece that had appeared in the Charleston paper, and Cooke's old college roommate, that day the presiding officer of the Senate, made "remarks." The people of Horry County have shared with each other the stories that keep the memory of H. Kemper Cooke alive.

WORLD WAR II TRAGEDY: THE NORTON TWINS

The Norton twins were Conway's golden boys, handsome, rugged, athletic. They were the last children born to Dr. And Mrs. James A. Norton, a couple greatly loved in the town. Dr. Jamie was a dedicated physician, untiring in his attention to his patients. Miss Ed was a pillar of Kingston Presbyterian Church.

Dr. James Arthur Norton (1876-1950) graduated from the Medical College at Charleston in 1902 and came back to Conway to join his father's practice. Perhaps to differentiate him from his father, Dr. Evan Norton, he became known as Dr. Jamie. He married Edward Robertson, "Miss Ed," daughter of a Presbyterian minister.

They had seven children, but two little girls died in infancy. When twin sons were delivered August 18, 1920, one was named for the father, one for the mother. James Arthur Jr. And Edward Robertson Norton, known by their nicknames "Wack" and "Hogie," were never separated, not even for a night.

As little boys, the twins were fascinated by flying. They built and flew model airplanes. Gas models were too tame for them when they reached high school. When their mother refused to let them buy a secondhand motorcycle, they persuaded her to let them buy a secondhand airplane. Dr. Norton purchased land for an airfield and helped them build a runway. By the time they graduated, they had some fifty hours flying time apiece as student pilots. They traded their old plane for a new one.

Together they graduated from Conway High School and together they went to Clemson, where they excelled in football and track, particularly the high jump. After two years they decided to enter the Army Air Corps. Accepted for pilot training on November 19, 1941, they trained at Arcadia, Florida, and Greenville, Mississippi. Not until they got to the Columbus (Miss.) Army Flying School did they have roommates other than each other.

The United States declared war after the Japanese bombed Pearl Harbor on December 7, 1941. The twins received their wings and commissions as second lieutenants nine months later, September 6, 1942. The local newspaper, which had followed their progress closely, declared, "Double trouble is in store for the Japs and Nazis when [the twins] begin doing their stuff from Uncle Sam's bombers."

They were assigned to the 322d Bombardment Group activated at MacDill Field, Tampa, Florida. When the group went to England toward the end of that year, Lts. James and Edward Norton went with it to Rougham near Bury St. Edmunds in Suffolk. When the base reached full American strength, the British turned the field over to the Americans on April 23, 1943. The group was ready to fight.

On May 14, 1943, the 322d Bombardment Group undertook its first low level bombing mission, the destruction of a power plant in Holland.

The Norton brothers were not assigned to this mission, but flew on the second, three days later. On May 17, 1943, eleven B-26s took to the air in two flights. Lieutenant E. R. Norton was pilot of one of the six bombers in the first flight. His brother flew as his copilot. As they approached the target at Ijmuiden, the Netherlands, they met heavy flak which seriously damaged the aircraft. Nevertheless, the B-26 completed its mission. It turned toward home, but went down in the North Sea. Reports listed the crew as missing in action. Sixty men from the aircraft on the mission failed to return. One survivor eventually turned up as a prisoner of war.

In Conway, on May 19, Dr. And Mrs. Norton received first one dreaded message and then a second. "Missing in action." A pall fell over the whole town. For months there was no further word. Eventually Dr. Norton discovered that the bomber had gone down over the North Sea. In September 1945 he learned from the mayor of Haarlem, the Netherlands, that the body of James washed ashore July 26, 1943. He is buried in the military cemetery at Margraten, Holland. His brother's body was never found.

Conway mourned with the parents. People told and retold stories of the twins—how they loved flying, how promising they were, how they were never separated. In the Norton family plot at Lakeside, cenotaphs, one on each side of their parents, remind the town of the loss of these devoted brothers. Their names also appear on the memorial tablet in the Horry County Memorial Library in the company of other Horry County men lost in World War II.

FLORENCE THEODORA EPPS: "I LIVE IN A WORLD OF MY OWN"

She was born in the house in Conway where she lived and died. Callers reached the house by descending from the sidewalk to a vine-shaded path through a lovingly organized chaos of natural shrubbery, trees, and flowering plants. The house was built in 1903, shortly after her parents came to Conway. James H. Burroughs's mural depicting their arrival aboard the *F. G. Burroughs* in 1902 is displayed high on the wall of the dining room.

A finicky housekeeper who might describe her home as cluttered would totally miss the point. The house held curios and mementos of the places she had been and the people she had known, as well as priceless memories of Conway's past and its people. Years ago, when she went to New York to seek her fortune, one of her first jobs was modeling. "I had a good jaw," she was fond of saying. Good bones are not surprising when one was, as she claimed, a descendent of Thomas Jefferson.

Shakespeare said of Cleopatra, "Age cannot wither her, nor custom stale her infinite variety." When Florence Theodora Epps died in 1988, Conway lost something of its distinctive flavor. Everybody who knew Florence had a favorite story. Groups of her friends vied with each other to tell the best—some true, some maybe! Many outrageous.

One favorite story dates from the 1960s when the Theatre of the Republic was young. After the new group had put in almost a year of organizational work, Florence had the responsibility for putting together the first program meeting. Late one night, her favorite time to work, a neighbor answered her phone and heard Florence's distinctive voice, high pitched, slightly querulous. She explained she was getting together casts for reading famous scenes from great dramatic works. These would make up the first public program given by the Theatre. She had the neighbor in mind to read the part of Elizabeth I in the scene in which the queen confronts Essex in the Tower of London on the night before his execution.

Now, the woman she called had never had any interest in performing upon the stage and said she could not possibly do what Miss Epps wanted. Florence insisted. Anyone who knew her knows how difficult it was to fend off her arm twisting. The woman declined; Miss Epps persuaded. Finally, with more than a little exasperation, her victim asked, "Florence, why me?" "Well," she said in that distinctive voice, "in this scene Elizabeth is no longer young." The unwilling neighbor finally agreed to do the part. When the scene was done, Florence Epps came to the front of the stage and critiqued her performance as lacking in royal "presence"—she had not "dominated" the stage in portraying the great queen!

Florence Epps worked to give the children of Conway an opportunity to see and participate in theater, and many with graying hair in Conway remember participating in plays in the little cottage behind her home and in the auditorium of the public library when it opened in 1949.

She was one of the people who dreamed and worked to bring a local little theater group into being. Among her most devoted fans were those who worked with her to "birth" it, and they honored her by calling her its "fairy godmother."

Florence had a knack for dominating every stage she trod upon. During her life she never confined her interests to her career. She was known for her devotion to the theater, her love of literature, her aptitude for quoting from her wide reading, her interest in history, particularly the past of Conway and Horry County, her love of nature and her passion for growing things, her fondness for travel, and the friends around the world with whom she visited and who visited her. She was a legendary hostess, witty, engaging, acerbic, wonderfully entertaining. Her menus were often unusual, their presentation imaginative. She owned and used grape scissors with aplomb.

One Sunday afternoon in January 1968, she had a tea for three ladies from out of town who were descendants of General Robert Conway, for whom the town was named. They brought his silver watch with them to show. Florence went into action when she saw it and can be credited with persuading them to give it to the city of Conway, a decision they finally made some years later.

Florence Epps was the first editor of the *Independent Republic Quarterly* when the Horry County Historical Society founded its journal in the fall of 1966. She drew on her wide acquaintance of people and history, and within three years the American Association for State and Local History recognized the *Quarterly* with a certificate of commendation. It bore the stamp of her opinions and personality for five years and became a valuable repository of stories, pictures, documents, and lore.

Toward the end of her long teaching career she was not in the traditional schoolroom, but traveled about the county providing corrective training to students with speech problems. One of them, a farmer, many years later expressed his appreciation for what she had taught him. He told her how, when he was angry or hurt, he would go into the fields and shout aloud "them purty words."

No matter on what ground you encountered Florence Epps, you were not likely to forget her. Consider the television talk show host who thought he had invited her to discuss conservation on behalf of the garden clubs. Will he ever forget that, instead, she read poetry which she attributed to her poodle, Pago, beloved companion of her last years?

After all, when Miss Epps wore strawberries in her hair, friends would only remark, "Isn't that Florence all over?"

ANDREW WASHINGTON STACKHOUSE: USEFUL MAN

On Friday, April 5, 1963, the police were directing traffic at Highway 501 and Racepath in Conway. On an ordinary day there would have been no reason for them to be there. Even at the height of the tourist season in those days traffic along this artery would have moved steadily and at a good pace through town.

This was not an ordinary day. A funeral for one of the most visible men of the black community, the Rev. Andrew Washington Stackhouse, was about to be held at Cherry Hill Baptist Church. He worked for the Latimer Funeral

Home, was a frequent guest in pulpits around the county, and was a man who made himself useful.

Mr. Stackhouse was especially well known for the help he gave less well educated, and sometimes intimidated, blacks with the "system." He made himself familiar with the workings of the Social Security Administration, for example, and with the welfare department, the health department, the probate court, the police, and, of course, local politics. If a man or woman was confused by the actions of one of these agencies, or thought some injustice had been done, the Reverend Stackhouse would accompany him to the office to determine the facts. Sometimes the client had misunderstood; sometimes the agency had misunderstood or ignored information provided by the client; sometimes there had been an injustice done. Sometimes Stackhouse was able to help the client understand that the ruling had been made according to regulations and would have to stand.

He became known as someone a black citizen could turn to for help. Conditions in the early 1960s in Horry were such that many people sought his advice and services. Needless to say, over time this useful man became well known and well respected among the black population. He also became well known in the white community as an advocate for blacks.

The Reverend Stackhouse was a member of a prominent black family in Floyds Township. He attended Morris College and was an ordained minister, active particularly in the associational affairs of Baptist churches. For more than twenty-five years he was general superintendent of the Kingston Lake Baptist Association and held that position at the time of his death. Mr. Stackhouse had been pastor of a number of churches, but because he had narcolepsy was not in the active pastorate at the time of his death. Instead, it might be said that he was pastor-at-large to the black community of Horry County, not just Conway.

It was not just the service he had done the community, however, or even the love and respect in which he was held, that caused the unusual interest which surrounded his death and funeral.

Early in the morning of March 29, the Reverend Stackhouse, age fifty-eight, had accompanied the funeral home hearse into the country to pick up a body. On the way back into town the driver noticed that the flow of conversation was all in one direction. Checking out his companion in the passenger seat, he found him dead.

The day before Stackhouse had gone to the courthouse and filled out his own death certificate, saying that he would not live through the night. Two months earlier he had ordered a casket made to his own design and had set the arrangements for his funeral. The wake took several days. Between eight and nine thousand people, black and white, visited the funeral home to view his remains.

The casket was made to sit upright and was four and a half feet tall. It was lined with champagne-colored velvet. The front opening was half glass behind which the deceased sat on a chair. He wore clerical robes of his own design and his customary small, brimless hat.

After several days the funeral ceremonies began. Several churches organized services at which the body in its unusual coffin sat in state. The funeral at Cherry Hill was the most elaborate. Among those who offered remarks were Dr. E. A. Finney of Whittemore High School and Dean H. E. Hardin of Morris College. (Dr. Finney's son and namesake is Chief Justice Ernest A. Finney Jr. of the South Carolina Supreme Court.) Reverend Stackhouse was taken back to his home in Floyds for a final service and burial at Hill Chapel.

Not surprisingly, the news went far beyond Horry. *Jet Magazine* carried the details, but neither the *Sun News*, the *Conway Field* nor the *Horry Herald* carried one word or picture. Those were the days of black invisibility.

4

Self-Help as a Way of Life

EDUCATION IN HORRY COUNTY BEFORE WORLD WAR II

From the opening of this corner of South Carolina to European settlers in 1735 until 1808, no records regarding education, either private or public, are available. Given the times, it may well be that there was little or no formal education available to anyone in the area. State (earlier province) supported education did not exist. An early school at Socastee, established by the Winyah Indigo Society, is mentioned in records in the 1830s and 1850s. Although one writer claimed that it was established before 1800, this is not confirmed in the spotty records available (Cooper, 127-32).

There may have been a few private tutors, but teaching the young was truly the province of the parents who passed on to their children such literacy as they possessed. But primarily, and more important at the time, they taught the skills and crafts necessary for frontier survival.

Not many years after Horry became a separate judicial district (1801) with its own courthouse and gaol, the building commissioners, who constituted such local government as there was, concerned themselves with the education of indigent children. The children of the affluent and the nature of the education available to them were not mentioned. On June 4, 1808, the commissioners announced that they were prepared to pay for the schooling of twelve poor children. They asked the public to let them know where schools might be found and to help identify children in need. In the usual frustrating way, the record is silent about the outcome of this resolve.

> Resolved, that publick notice be given by the advertisement that the Commissioners are ready to school twelve children and desire that the Inhabitants of the said District may be given information where schools are established and give recommendations to such poor children as are adjacent to such schools to the Commissioners at their

next meeting that they may know how to regulate the same and fix the children to the most advantage.

Resolved, that notice be given to the Teachers of the respective schools to attend at our next meeting to make contracts.—Minutes of the Horry District Commissioners of Public Buildings, June 4, 1808.

In December 1811, the South Carolina General Assembly passed free school legislation that entitled Horry District to two free schools. The next year, 1812, the Free School Commissioners of Kingston Parish, appointed as a result of the legislation, reported not two but six schools, each having upward of twenty children. Schools were established in each militia beat—that area from which a company of militia was drawn and for which it provided protection. Each beat had fifty dollars to fund the instruction of about one hundred students. Kingston Parish teachers that first year: Robert Sessions, John Harris, Josiah Gay, John Clark, John Graham, Thomas Jenkens, Jacob Parker, and John Redmon. Other early teachers were John B. Conway, Levi Gerrald, Dan E. Crawford, G. B. Granger, James Perry, John Forgaty, John McQueen, John R. Whitman, William Todd, and Josias T. Sessions.

All Saints Parish (from the Waccamaw River to the ocean) reported four schools and ninety scholars. All Saints and Kingston Parishes (sometimes known by other names) constituted Horry District. Their statistics were separately reported until the beginning of the Civil War.

There were schools at Socastee, Little River, and Sterrits Swamp in All Saints and at Brown Swamp, Camp Swamp, Lake Swamp, Gapway, Gallivants Ferry, Dog Bluff, Pawley Swamp, and Halfway Branch in Kingston in 1816 and 1817. In 1817 Kingston educated 189 children among its eight schools at a total cost of $756. Terms were six months long.

In 1822 the terms were only three months long, except in Josias T. Sessions's case; he taught a four and a half month term. School enrollment ranged from five to twenty scholars, the average being just under twelve. In the comments column of the commissioners' official return, John Sarvis, chairman, and Josias T. Sessions, secretary, commented, "We believe that this institution [i.e., public education] is good and we think in a few years that it will be plainly seen by every eye that this institution is good."

Robert Mills's invaluable *Statistics of South Carolina*, published with his *Atlas* in 1826, noted for Horry District that "from 10 to 15 private schools are established in various places; price of tuition from 10 to 20 dollars a year. There are 6 public or free schools, supported at the expense of the state, where the children of the poor are taught gratis. The report of the commissioners states, that the last two years, the benefits of education have been afforded to 438 pupils, and the expense eight hundred and twenty-two dollars and twenty five cents."

There were more private than public schools, even though they required tuition. While fathers of typically large families might have favored sons over daughters in providing schooling, they would have wanted to treat their sons equally. The tuition for even one child would have been prohibitive for most parents in an economy that was largely based on barter.

School commissioners met when necessary at the courthouse to examine the qualifications of teachers and to distribute the funds according to the number of pupils reported. While overseeing all public education, the commissioners favored subsidizing only the education of the children of the poor, with the result that gradually public schools became stigmatized as institutions for the poor only. In his history of Conwayboro Academy, Dr. Evan Norton says that in the period preceding the Civil War the subsidy amounted to five cents a day or a dollar a month (Evan Norton. *History* repr. *IRQ* 7:4/7:6).

Since the general level of education was low, the level of preparation demanded of teachers was also low. Many were itinerants who moved from community to community, holding classes in some convenient place in each for as long as the money of local parents held out and then moving on to the next.

For a long time there was no school located in the district seat. The Harlee map of Horry District in 1820 shows a school a little north of the village. In her *Memoirs* Ellen Cooper Johnson of Conwayborough mentions several schools she attended (*IRQ* 15:2: 4-17). One was two miles from town at the old Campground on the Georgetown road—a long walk, she remembered, for a little girl. Silas Sessions taught another, which seems the first to have been in the village, in a small house probably located on Elm Street between Fifth and Sixth, near the large oak which juts out into the street.

The first little schoolhouse in Conwayborough probably was not built until the late 1840s or early 1850s. Considering that there is no evidence of a church building in the village from the time a storm destroyed one about 1798 until the first Methodist structure in 1844, the lack of a school building is not astonishing. It does not mean that there were no worship services or that no schoolmasters or schoolmistresses had pupils in the village during this period. It argues, rather, that the people felt no need to create institutional buildings but probably chose to use their homes for these special purposes.

The first schoolhouse was probably not elaborate, nor sturdy, and was certainly not kept in repair. Its dilapidated condition caused men of the village to meet on December 16, 1856, to organize an association to improve the building. Nineteen citizens, John Readmon, John R. Beaty, Thomas W. Beaty, Thomas H. Holmes, William H. Buck, Bethel D. Beaty, James S. Burroughs, Thomas F. Gillespie, Samuel Pope, Henry Hardee, Henry Buck, B. F. Smith, W. H. B. Taylor, C. F. Malloy, J. A. Stone, J. J. Richwood, J. T. Walsh, J. F. Harrell, and Jehu Causey, who subscribed from ten to one hundred dollars each to underwrite repairs, chose Thomas W. Beaty, William H. Buck, John R. Beaty, Samuel Pope, and Charles F. Malloy for the first trustees. They employed the Rev. James Mahoney, pastor of the Methodist church, as teacher for 1857 at a salary of eight hundred dollars for a term of ten months, to be paid in quarterly installments due in April, July, and October 1857 and January 1858.

Although the trustees hired Joseph J. Marlowe to work on the old building, it soon became apparent that repairs would not serve. The association met again and determined to build a new schoolhouse. Otis Eaton, who would become the chief builder of Kingston Presbyterian Church the following year, was the contractor. The new Conwayborough Academy building cost $364.50. Subscribers to the building fund were Charles F. Malloy, W. H. Buck, J. T. Walsh, Charles Alston Jr., James S. Burroughs, B. H. Gurganus, Thomas H. Holmes, J. W. Holliday, W. R. Freeman, W. J. Taylor, W. L. Graham, Robert Munro Jr., W. H. Johnston, P. C. J. Weston, Samuel Anderson, Jane Norman, and Henry Hardee (*IRQ* 7:2/3: 7-8).

The three R's constituted the basic curriculum in Horry District schools, but Conwayborough Academy offered, in addition, some history, geography, and English grammar. Trustees pleaded with the parents of the community to "take advantage of the means of education now at its disposal and give that gift to their children, which neither misfortune, distress, nor all the world can take away." The school year had two terms, the first to begin in January and end in August, the second to run from late September until just before Christmas. This arrangement allowed "a vacation of 40 days during the sickly season of the year." When it did not work out, the terms were changed and shortened, probably in response to strain on the pocketbooks of the parents.

In the beginning the trustees limited the student body to forty children, but in fact forty-six were enrolled in 1857. A year later only twenty-five enrolled. Tuition was low: $1.60 a month for first graders and $2.40 for second graders. The trustees were always struggling to meet quarterly salary payments for the instructor. The Academy Association frequently supplemented the income from tuition. The trustees recruited students from outside Conwayborough, noting that "Good board can be obtained in town and neighborhood from six to ten dollars per month." Their members were C. F. Malloy, Jehu Causey, H. Buck, Thomas W. Beaty, W. H. B. Taylor, James Beaty, Alexander Elliott, H. Hardee, W. H. Buck, J. E. Dusenbury, Joseph T. Walsh, P. C. J. Weston, U. A. DeLettre, John LaBruce, Charles Alston Jr., James S. Burroughs, B. H. Gurganus, S. N. Anderson, Jane Norman, Thomas Randall, W. H. Johnston, Thomas H. Holmes, J. W. Holliday, W. R. Freeman, W. J. Taylor, W. I. Graham, S. M. Stevenson, R. Munro Jr., and Joseph F. Harrell.

In his history, Dr. Norton commended the practice of having local doctors instruct children in basic physiology and hygiene, stressing that this knowledge would save them from "the awful and calamitous consequences attendant upon and resulting from careless and youthful indiscretions." The first physician to offer his services was Dr. J. H. Norman, of whom Norton said, "[He] possessed a bright mind and had only a short time graduated in medicine. . . . [He] started with splendid opportunities and brilliant prospects, but his devotion to piscatorial pastime in connection with other unprofitable habits allowed his light to be obscured and his talents buried." Dr. Norman would not be the last Horry man to prefer fishing to working.

The most significant observation to be made about the education of Conwayborough children in this period is its discontinuity. After the first two years when Mahoney was principal, the trustees contracted to several different people the right to conduct schools in the building during the years before the Civil War. None lasted long, and none was financially successful. In all probability, formal schooling ceased entirely during the Civil War years.

So hard were the times that the war had been over two years before the Academy Association members met on June 3, 1867, to consider the restoration of the school. Only two members of the prewar board, Thomas W. Beaty and Joseph T. Walsh, survived to restart the school. The association elected James S. Burroughs, Thomas H. Holmes, Jehu Causey, S. N. Anderson, and Dr. Joseph F. Harrell to fill the vacancies.

When local Masons signaled a willingness to run the school and to appropriate money for the education of the orphans of Confederate soldiers, the trustees accepted the offer, and Jesse Thornton, a Georgia native, operated the school for three terms, 1867-1870. Dr. Norton said of him: "he was a very voluble, plausible talker without very profound knowledge of any subject. He followed the old system of governing schools by absolute authority, that if a child did not willingly receive and appropriate instruction, he would force it into the child's mind by the rod."

Joseph T. Walsh became the first commissioner of public schools under the new (1868) South Carolina Constitution. A lawyer and dedicated Presbyterian layman, Judge Walsh attempted to build during Reconstruction a whole new educational system that included for the first time the education of black children. Whittemore Academy, named for the carpetbagger B. F. Whittemore, was established for them. Whittemore was from Massachusetts. He represented Darlington County in the South Carolina Senate but fled the state after the 1876 election. (*BDSCS,* 3:1718-21). The new system went into effect before means became available to pay the teachers, who were sometimes required to wait more than a year for their money.

The school system, shaky and uncertain, did not provide a dependable education for the children of the village. Terms were generally from thirty to sixty school days, or from a month and a half to three months. Teachers received compensation according to the grade level, not their training or competence. First grade teachers were paid fifty dollars a term, third grade teachers only half that—the argument apparently being that if children were well taught in the first grade, the work of teachers in the following years would be easier and therefore worth less money.

Toward the end of the Reconstruction period, young Confederate veterans who had come home and started families now had children in need of competent schooling. Conwayborough was the county seat and an active riverport. Opportunities for business enterprise were better in the town than anywhere else in Horry but depended upon men with some education to take advantage of them. The old Academy Association had gone out of existence, and there was no one to turn to who had authority to rescue the school.

One Confederate veteran in particular had established a promising business with a succession of partners and was determined that his children should have competent schooling. Franklin G. Burroughs, who had received only minimal education himself, recognized that good schools are absolutely essential to a flourishing business community. He personally undertook to salvage the village school. Norton said that "in starting the school he assumed all responsibility" and continued to do so for two decades. He provided an adequate facility and adequate pay for the teachers, supplementing the income from the pupils' tuition from his own pocket. He hired A. P. McCormick, the first principal, who used the old academy building. Burroughs eventually selected a site and built a new school on Main Street at the corner of what is now called Kingston Lake Drive.

After McCormick retired in 1879, Burroughs asked his business partner, B. G. Collins, his brother-in-law, J. A. Mayo, and Dr. Evan Norton to join him in the management of the school and the selection of the next headmaster or principal. The board of trustees was self-perpetuating. When death or resignation took one man off, the others selected a replacement, inviting only proven members of Conway's tight leadership group to participate in the management of the school. They did not incorporate Burroughs school until December 23, 1889.

Norton, who provides a running, sometimes amusing, assessment of the teachers and principals, described A. B. Bethea, who was in his early twenties when he succeeded McCormick, as "a very good teacher, somewhat irritable and peevish." He lasted three years, 1879–1882. This was to become the pattern: schoolmasters employed by the Burroughs School did not stay in Conway long. Always from outside the county, they were usually qualified academically but varied considerably in their temperamental suitability for the administration of the school and particularly for discipline of students. Principals in turn were T. E. May, M. Herndon Moore, John M. Knight, J. H. Dysinger, A. B. Riley, A. J. Bradshaw, R. B. Clarke, Zach McGhee, Dr. W. S. Stokes, W. A. Dagnall, M. C. Woods, and S. W. Carwile, who was responsible for creating District 19 as qualifying for taxing authority.

Usually their assistants were women, some of them local and connected with the members of the school board, who instructed in music, embroidery, and the like. The ladies were variously "healthy," "quiet and unobtrusive," "attractive in person," etc., except for one lady from Charleston whom Norton described as "a most excellent little woman, but a veritable assembly of nerves."

Burroughs, who had propped up the Conwayborough school, died in 1897. The next year South Carolina passed laws permitting school taxes which would eventually make it possible for taxes to supplant the private support he had provided. S. W. Carwile, the school principal, spearheaded the move to create a school district which would have the power to levy taxes for the support of the school. The district, authorized October 29, 1898, included approximately 12 square miles of Conway township.

The law required two-thirds of the three mills tax voted by the citizens for support of the District 19 school to be shared with schools in the rest of the county. So began the distribution of tax funds collected in one jurisdiction to poorer schools in other jurisdictions in order to provide them some of the benefits the wealthier are able to afford.

Universal free public schooling really did not exist. However advanced the Conway schools may have seemed by the early twentieth century, compared with earlier times, the schools in the rest of the county continued to struggle to provide even basic reading, writing, and ciphering. Terms varied with the ability of the community to pay—two weeks, a month, three months. The time of year school was held varied with the availability of schoolmasters, usually itinerants, who moved from community to community. Students sometimes followed a teacher from one place to another, boarding with relatives or family friends, to get more training.

The *Horry Herald* editorialized on January 2, 1902, that "the census of 1900 discloses a situation that ought to interest every man in Horry County. The percentage of illiteracy is greater in this county than in any other county in the state. Out of a total white male population of voting age, of 3537 there are 751 who cannot read and write."

The 1895 constitution provided for elected county superintendents of education. The Horry superintendent in 1903, E. Van Best, had so little authority that he was in his office only on Saturday of each week and his work consisted mostly of record keeping. The county superintendent's greatest assets were his political skills and his powers of persuasion. Every community chose its own trustees from among its powerful and influential men, who hired the teachers, set the pay, raised the money, made the rules, and oversaw the operation. These men were the movers and shakers, known to candidates for elective office as the men to see to win support in the rural communities. The boards also became the breeding and training grounds of Horry politicians, rivaling the law as a desirable background for political success.

Any community with the will and wherewithal could have its own school. Trustees determined the length of the school year and the grades that would be offered. Schools moved about from place to place within the community according to the number and location of children who needed schooling. In 1910, according to the *Herald* (October 13), there were ninety-five [white] schools in operation.

In rural Horry there were reasons to have schools close by. Few families had a horse or mule and a wagon or buggy to spare from work all day for the use of their children, so there was little school transportation save shank's mare. Few roads were worthy of the name, so young scholars mostly used trails through the woods, crossing swamps and branches by footlogs.

Over time wealthier rural communities built substantial schoolhouses. The grades offered depended on the level of the students living in the community at any time, but few schools offered more than seven grades. Nearly always the completion of classes offered by the local school signaled the end of formal schooling for the sons and daughters of rural families. Few families could afford to send even promising children to high school.

Parents kept children out of school for reasons which seem unreasonable now: the inability of the family to pay, the seasonal press of work on the farms, the lack of parental enthusiasm, or the illness of a family member. William J. Rowe wrote in his memoirs, "No one knows like a schoolboy who loves to attend school how it feels to hear the school bell ring at the beginning of a school year when he knows he cannot return" (*IRQ*, April 1972, 6:2:6).

Older Horry men and women have few memories dearer than those which surround their school days. Even when they were educated in primitive and harsh conditions or under nearly illiterate teachers or those who spared nothing when it came to discipline, most of them remember those experiences warmly. Through the glow, one can nevertheless glimpse the hardships that children suffered in pursuit of basic education: daily treks through all kinds of weather, rooms filled with rough benches and desks and heated by a potbellied wood stove, outdoor privies, inadequate books. Of the available memoirs not one displays resentment of these conditions. These men and women accepted them as part of the hard times which prevailed generally, and they tended to be grateful for what schooling they got.

Socastee Academy joined Burroughs High School in 1890 and Loris High School in 1900. The Loris school disappeared after a few years, was reestablished after 1915, but was not accredited until 1920.

A hunger for education also manifested itself among rural people. A few boarded in Conway and attended Burroughs School. Two denominations attempted to supply the need. In 1916 Horry Industrial School was established in the Horry Community by Methodists and Pee Dee Academy in 1921 in the Wanamaker Community by Baptists. Both tuition-supported schools went under in 1928 when the county established high school districts, which assured that free high school education would be available over the whole county. Horry Industrial became Aynor High School and

Pee Dee Academy was supplanted by Floyds High School. In the struggle to establish and maintain these early high schools is a clear foreshadowing of the determination shown later by the people of Horry to establish a college and a technical school.

During this same period, black parents were struggling to improve the education of their children with the aid of Northern philanthropists. The Julius Rosenwald Fund, the Slater Fund, and the Anna T. Jeanes Fund provided financial help to build better school facilities and a county teacher who traveled to rural schools to oversee classroom teachers and help them improve their skills.

Still, on the eve of the Second World War most Horry County schools can be described as backward. When Thurman Anderson became superintendent of education in 1941, the first order of business, according to one official, was to locate the schools in operation. In 1946, a survey conducted by George Peabody College for Teachers pronounced Horry seventy-five years behind the times.

There were eighty-five school districts, seventy-seven elementary schools, and eight high schools, many of which operated both white and black schools. Anderson moved toward consolidation. He visited trustees and held public meetings in communities with small schools to persuade them that their children would be better served if they combined with other small schools or with a larger one nearby. When adequate bus transportation became available, they were more likely to agree, but it was still wrenching to a community's pride to give up that part of its identity. Under this consummate politician the consolidation movement accelerated until Horry ultimately achieved a single countywide district.

Anderson was a product of rural schools. He knew the ground over which he had to fight his campaign for better schools. He knew intimately the mind-set of school patrons who identified with their own communities, who worked hard to build institutions within them, and who resisted any effort to force them into unfamiliar territories. He cajoled, persuaded, and enticed with such carrots as he had at his disposal. It is doubtful that an administrator without such a background could have achieved the same result.

During Mr. Anderson's long tenure (1941–1973) came the passage of a state sales tax for school support, bus transportation, a better school lunch program, stricter accreditation for teachers, an elected board that appointed the county superintendent, and integration of black and white schools. His term constitutes a clear transition between the way public education was and the way it has become.

From this time and place, the hard times, the struggles, the inadequacies of public education in Horry County before World War II are remarkable. Not to be overlooked are other, equally true, conditions. Some fine and talented schoolteachers taught many apt and ambitious students who became successful men and women here in Horry County and in the outside world. It is also worth remembering that few members of the community were more honored by the affection and respect of children and parents alike than those teachers. None struggled more by example and precept to mold the character of the society by molding the character of its children.

Early schools enjoyed community involvement and pride, not to say partisanship. If they sometimes lacked another essential ingredient—competent instruction—that would be remedied with time. Community support continued to be given to the consolidated system. It assured funding for schools and curriculum designed to instill curiosity and the habit of lifelong learning and to prepare the young to compete in the world into which they are born.

YANKEE PHILANTHROPY AIDED BLACK SCHOOLS

Between 1900 and World War II, Northern philanthropists contributed greatly to improving educational opportunities for black children in the South. Their benevolence included Horry County.

On October 30, 1917, Julius Rosenwald, then president of Sears, Roebuck, and Company, committed twenty thousand shares of his stock in the company to the Julius Rosenwald Fund to further "the well-being of mankind." This fund helped poor blacks in South Carolina build five hundred school buildings, several of them in Horry County. A full list is not available, but in 1927 (perhaps the peak year) and in 1928 eleven were constructed here. The fund required local groups of black citizens to have fee simple title to at least two acres, to submit plans for a building, and to deposit with the local county treasurer sufficient money to finish, paint, and furnish the school. The fund's consultant had several floor plans to offer depending upon the size needed. The simple, functional, and attractive buildings are easy to spot among pictures of schools of that era.

The Negro Rural School Fund, Anna T. Jeanes Foundation, was established in 1908 to provide teachers to needy schools. Jeanes, a Quaker spinster of Philadelphia, was the last survivor of her immediate family and thus a considerable heiress. She committed $1 million to a foundation to aid the education of poor blacks in the South. Jeanes teachers were usually women. The report of the South Carolina state superintendent of education for 1920 commented, "The Jeanes supervisors visit the schools of the county giving instruction in home industries and sanitation, encouraging the people of the neighborhood to improve their school conditions and conducting gardening clubs and other clubs for the improvement and betterment of the schools and neighborhoods."

In 1926 the thirty-nine black schools in Horry had average terms of five months. The Jeanes teacher reported to the county superintendent of education but was not given a desk in his office; she traveled from school to school, teaching special subjects and helping other teachers develop lesson plans and improve their teaching skills. She received six hundred dollars a year from the fund for her work.

Mrs. Nellie Adelaide Burke Levister, Horry County's first Jeanes teacher, held the post from the early 1920s until she retired in 1958. Born in Elizabeth City, North Carolina she attended Hampton Institute. She came to Conway when her husband was appointed pastor of Bethel African Methodist Episcopal Church. The great respect Horry County's black citizens had for her caused the new "separate, but equal" school for black students built in Aynor in the 1950s to be called Levister Elementary (renamed Aynor Elementary in the unified county system).

The Slater Fund, created by John F. Slater in 1882, placed emphasis on teaching manual and domestic skills through which blacks could lift themselves out of poverty. Its training schools did not prepare students to continue their education beyond the high school level. Indeed, the Slater Fund withdrew assistance from one school which offered a liberal arts curriculum that would have prepared blacks for college.

The Slater Fund imposed stringent requirements. The recipient must be a public school to which the local school district contributed at least one thousand dollars annually for salaries, have an eight-month term, and teach some form of industrial work. Local blacks gave sacrificially to match grants. Charley Watson of Loris is known to have mortgaged his home to provide matching funds. Sympathetic white friends gave land or money to demonstrate the support of both communities. In Loris, the J. C. Bryant family gave land for the Loris Training School.

By 1931 the General Education Board of New York was funding staff positions for black educators under the South Carolina state superintendent of education. This allayed whatever suspicion white officials might have had and provided for coordination between the work of the General Education Board and the South Carolina Department of Education. Their particular responsibility was the oversight of all foundations operating in the state.

Horry County received $450 from the Jeanes Fund, $250 from the Slater Fund, and $400 from the Rosenwald Fund in 1931. Not much in today's terms, this money helped educate 2,871 black children that year, 81 of them in high school. The state superintendent also reported in 1931 that "during the last ten or twelve years" black citizens had contributed a half million of the total value of nearly $3 million in buildings, whites had contributed $200,000, and public school funds another $1.5 to $2 million. The black citizens of South Carolina had made a remarkable effort on their own behalf.

PEE DEE BAPTIST ACADEMY

In Floyds Township, in northwestern Horry County, is Wanamaker Community, named for the man who was U.S. postmaster general when its post office was established in 1889. Near the junction of State Road 400 and State Road 44 stand Wanamaker Baptist Church and, close by, the old Pee Dee Baptist Academy, an early effort of the people of that area to provide secondary education.

In the years following World War I, there were high schools at Loris and at Conway. Nearby Marion and Mullins across the Little Pee Dee River in Marion County had high schools. Most Horry County schools, including those in Floyds Township, offered only seven grades. Young people whose parents could afford the expense left their communities and boarded near the high school they chose to attend.

In about 1915 Horry Community, west of Conway, established the Horry Industrial School, later taken over by the Methodist Conference. In 1919, perhaps encouraged by that example, the Baptists of the Waccamaw Association led by the Rev. W. J. Wilder, pastor of Wanamaker Baptist Church, sought help from the South Carolina Baptist Association to establish a high school for the benefit of students from all over the Pee Dee region. After World War I, South Carolina Baptists established seven such schools around the state.

The Reverend Wilder became chairman of the board of trustees, which included as members E. M. Meares and W. C. Hooks. Wilder reported to Waccamaw Association in the fall of 1921 that J. D. And W. J. Anderson had donated 57-plus acres of land. The community had pledged $17,000, with $5,310.16 already in hand. A home (still standing) had been constructed on the grounds for Dr. John Hampton Mitchell, the principal. His alma mater had already honored Dr. Mitchell, a graduate of Furman University as well as of the Southern Baptist Seminary, with a doctor of divinity degree.

The school opened October 3, 1921, with instruction in grades eight through ten. Classes met on the second floor of the two-story Wanamaker School building. Forty-one students enrolled on the first day. By the time of the Reverend Wilder's report there were forty-four. In the fall of 1922 classes moved to Wanamaker Church, and William Franklin Hagan became principal. For reasons unknown, all students repeated their grades that year.

Construction plans called for an academic building, one dormitory for men and another for women, and athletic fields. The eight-classroom building never was completed, but for the next six years Pee Dee Baptist Academy provided high school and college preparatory training. The first graduating class, in May 1924, numbered eleven. A short unsigned history of the school says "more than 100 pupils . . . Attended during the six years of operation." Graduates went on to the University of South Carolina, Furman and Clemson Universities, Winthrop and Limestone Colleges, all in South Carolina, and to Mars Hill and Women's College, Greensboro (now the University of North Carolina at Greensboro).

The academy on its isolated site lost out to hard times and the encroachment of the public schools. Enrollment never reached the expectations of the founders—highest enrollment in any session was about fifty students. Consolidation of rural public schools lured paying scholars from the private school. The South Carolina Baptist Association decided to close it in 1926 and ordered the land and buildings sold to satisfy indebtedness, primarily salaries owed the teachers. Classes did meet in 1927, but after that students had to continue their studies elsewhere. Horry County established seven public high school districts in that year. Floyds High School (now Green Sea-Floyds) opened in 1928.

The building has been idle since then except for storage and, briefly, as a residence. It still stands, a handsome derelict, a reminder of the hunger of Horry people for education and their determination to go it alone if necessary—the same spirit that gave birth to Coastal Carolina Junior College (now Coastal Carolina University) in 1954 and to the technical education school, now Horry-Georgetown Technical College, in 1965.

LIBRARIES FOR "THE ENTIRE PEOPLE"

Although there were some excellent private libraries, and some small school and church libraries in Horry County prior to 1934, there had been no public library. It was then that a movement spearheaded by Mrs. H. L. Buck, a former president of the South Carolina Library Association (1929), gained support. As a result of her efforts and those of a small group of leading citizens, a public library was opened in Conway on March 4, 1938. Supported by private funds and a town appropriation of twenty-five dollars per month, the library was housed on the second floor of the town hall. The nucleus of the book collection came from the private library of Dr. J. A. Norton and his brother, J. O. Norton.

Before the public library in Conway was opened, a Works Progress Administration countywide library project was initiated with the cooperation of the Horry County Board of Education. Mrs. Sophie Blanton of Green Sea was director of this effort. For the first time, a bookmobile brought library service to the rural areas of the county. When WPA funds were withdrawn in 1942, the board of education assumed full responsibility for the service, and the books which had been purchased by the WPA were reassigned to a serviceman's library at the Myrtle Beach Air Base. The Horry County Board of Education purchased a collection of books in order to continue rural service and operated it until the establishment of the Horry County Memorial Library.

Convinced of the value of countywide public library service, the County Library Committee continued to work vigorously for a county library and, in so doing, enlisted powerful political support. In 1944 the county Legislative Delegation appropriated the first fifteen thousand dollars towards the construction of a library building. In 1946 the delegation introduced the legislation which established the Horry County Memorial Library Commission, appropriated fifty thousand dollars for a building, and levied a one mill tax for support of the library.

Senator Frank A. Thompson is generally credited with being the chief sponsor. (He said that his defeat in the next election was in large part due to his support, which was seen as "more for Conway, less for the rest of the county.") Later Senator Thompson would add 20 percent of the county rebate of beer, wine, and liquor taxes and one-half of the marriage license fees to the funds generated by the millage for county library service. Surely no public library ever had a more imaginative funding structure! All sources were bound to grow with the population and the economy of the area.

At the time the library was established, Mary Parham, a qualified professional librarian, was appointed, and during the period of building construction, she ordered the books, organized the book collection, and established a public relations program essential for understanding the services the library would provide.

The Horry County Memorial Library was the first public library building to be constructed in South Carolina after World War II. Beautifully designed, handsomely (though sparsely) furnished, and containing a small book collection, it was dedicated on July 1, 1949.

The beautiful small auditorium that was a feature of the new building quickly became a popular place for dramatic and musical programs. For many years before it was sacrificed to the growth of the book collection, this facility housed many important community meetings, including the one at which Coastal Carolina Junior College was conceived.

Chapin Memorial Library, the only public library in South Carolina still funded by a municipality, opened on June 1, 1949, exactly a month before the county system commenced public service on July 1. The opening day collection incorporated the library which had been used by servicemen stationed at Myrtle Beach Army Air Base during World War II. Shirley Walker Boone became the first librarian at Chapin and continued in that role until her retirement in 1990.

There had been some conversation between the county system and the Chapin Library Board of Directors about its becoming a part of the new county system. The Chapin board members may have feared that the countywide system, struggling to plant service all over this large county, would not be able to give the Myrtle Beach library the support which they were prepared to muster. The Chapin Foundation promised to provide support beyond the budget granted by the city. While they decided to go it alone and it has continued as an independent library, Chapin Memorial cooperates with the county system in many ways.

The county library immediately assumed full responsibility for rural library service, using as its first bookmobile the one transferred from the Horry County Department of Education. Bookmobile service not only served adult readers but provided collections of books and direct service to the schools of the county. Soon there were two bookmobiles and parallel services were provided for white and black patrons. In the 1960s federal grants made it possible to establish outreach service to institutions and service points where help was provided for the poor.

Shortly after the first county librarian came on duty, the new county library commission authorized the inauguration of a branch for the black citizens of Conway, which was housed in Whittemore High School. It was later moved to a house on Racepath in Conway and was finally closed in 1965. Integration of the schools and other public agencies made it possible to discontinue the Conway Branch Library and the second bookmobile.

Until the 1960s there was dual service for whites and blacks. The legislation which established the Horry County Memorial Library stated the purpose of the county system in simple eloquence. It was to provide free public library services to "the entire people" of Horry County. Early in the period of racial integration, when some public libraries closed their doors rather than serve a mixed population, the wisdom of this wording was especially apparent. Horry County was spared by the wording of the enabling act. The library commission, relying on it, acted to welcome all citizens to its libraries.

Local groups in towns throughout the county sponsored and supported branch libraries. The Loris branch opened in 1949, Aynor in 1950, the Grand Strand branch (in Crescent Beach, later North Myrtle Beach) opened in 1958, and Surfside in 1978. Between 1976 and 1980 Horry County constructed almost a building a year to replace old branch facilities and initiate new ones.

When the Elementary and Secondary Education Act came into effect in the early 1960s, schools around the county established libraries (later called media centers to reflect the heavy utilization of audiovisual materials). The public library staff took on an advisory role during this period, but eventually the new school libraries relieved the public library system of responsibility for direct service to schools and freed resources for other purposes. The establishment of libraries to serve Coastal Carolina Junior College in 1958 and Horry-Georgetown Technical College in 1968 further increased the information resources available to people in Horry County.

Horry County Memorial Library was dedicated to the memory of all servicemen from Horry who have served their country. It seemed natural that the headquarters library became a focal point for an active community interest in local history. Carrying out a responsibility specifically mentioned in the library's enabling legislation, the staff assembled a large and varied local history collection through gifts from the public and by purchasing books and periodicals which bear on local history.

The strength of the county library system in its first four decades lay in the development of a strong central collection and a professional staff at the headquarters library in Conway. The branches were connected by telephone and later by computers so that instant access to the headquarters' resources was available in every branch library. The bookmobile and outreach services provided access for people isolated either by their place of residence or the condition of their lives.

THE BIRTH OF A UNIVERSITY: THE FOUNDING OF COASTAL CAROLINA

In 1954 there was no institution of higher education closer to Horry County than Coker College. Few high school graduates were able to go away to college. Numbers of public school teachers did not have four-year degrees. The longtime Horry County superintendent of education, Thurman W. Anderson, and J. Kenyon East, who was on his staff, were concerned with the general level of education, with training a workforce, and with the continuing education and training of the teachers in the school system. Credit for the idea of Coastal Carolina is due primarily to them. They convened a group of community leaders at the Horry County Memorial Library auditorium on July 23, 1954, to discuss the need for making available to students of the county the first two years of education beyond high school.

The men present at that historic meeting, in addition to Anderson and his staff, were James P. Blanton, the Rev. Cecil Dubose Brearley Sr., George W. Bryan, Edward E. Burroughs, William F. Davis, Ralph H. Ellis, the Rev. Morgan B. Gilreath, Dove Walter Green Jr., James C. Hipp, Joseph W. Holliday, Jesse M. Lee, Harold S. "Jack" Reese, Harold S. Rogers, Dr. R. Cathcart Smith, Ernest F. Southern, and E. Craig Wall Sr. On that very evening they determined to proceed with plans for a junior college, laid the groundwork for the Coastal Education Foundation, Inc., to govern and finance the institution, and pledged their own financial resources to the task.

The founders offered the University of South Carolina the honor of being the junior college's nurturing mother. The university declined. The founders employed Drs. Edward and Margaret Woodhouse from Chapel Hill, North Carolina, to teach and assist in administration, and classes began September 20, 1954. Classes met after regular school hours at Conway High School. Coastal Carolina Junior College had opened with little more than faith and determination to sustain it.

The students were in the main those who could not afford to go away to college or who for other reasons could not leave Horry County to further their education. Older men and women, established in full-time employment, enrolled to qualify for further advancement in their careers or for personal enrichment. Apart from financial considerations, students sometimes could not qualify academically for regular college admission without special assistance. Open admission, giving the marginal student a proving ground to establish that he or she could keep up with the demands of college-level work, became the policy of the new college.

The founders approached George Grice, president of the College of Charleston. He was sympathetic to their appeal and agreed to oversee the fledgling school—but only for three years. Grice sent Dr. George C. Rogers Sr. To direct the operation. During that time Coastal utilized its sponsor's accreditation to facilitate the transfer of its students to senior colleges. The faculty and administration began the exacting process of qualifying for Southern Association of Colleges and Universities accreditation, which required a minimum of three years.

When the College of Charleston ended its supervision the process was well along, but in this interim period Coastal required the approval of its faculty and courses by the University of South Carolina, the accrediting agent of the state of South Carolina. If the university did not give its seal of approval, students lost valuable credits when they sought to transfer to senior colleges. The university's oversight committee regularly visited in Conway and negotiated with the CCJC faculty and administration about which course work could be accredited.

The little college enjoyed great popular enthusiasm. Its faculty and administrators were in demand to speak about the college and its future. In 1958 the people of Horry County voted by a margin of four to one to impose on themselves a three mill tax to support the college and established the Horry County Higher Education Commission to administer the funds generated by the levy.

In the second year of independence large questions confronted the founders. Should they continue to struggle alone or should they align themselves with a stronger institution? In the fall of 1958, they decided to invite experienced educators to come to a conference on the future of the junior college. The program was designed to provide information to the founders, the administration, and the general public. It was held February 6 and 7, 1959, in the auditorium of the Horry County Memorial Library in Conway. Presentations covered the history of the junior college movement; curricula, administration, and finance; public or private support; and the relative benefits of independence or affiliation. After each presentation a lively question-and-answer session allowed everyone to participate.

On Saturday morning, as the conference was winding down, a brief and memorable moment occurred when Dr. Nicholas Mitchell rose and asked to be recognized. He was director of the University of South Carolina Extension Division, the man in charge of an ambitious program of establishing branches of the University across South Carolina. Its rationale was that the first two years of college work could be offered more economically to greater numbers of underclassmen at local institutions, relieving pressure to accommodate ever greater numbers of freshmen and sophomores on the Columbia campus. Graduates of these branches would be "fed" into the senior college and graduate schools of the university. Clemson College was engaged in a similar extension program.

Dr. Mitchell was not on the program, but, in the light of subsequent events, his short speech may have been the most critical given in two days. A man of rotund figure and blunt speech, Mitchell outlined the university's aggressive plan and declared, without softening the statement into an invitation, that CCJC was a takeover target. He made it perfectly clear he meant to absorb the independent college into the university system. USC's power to grant or withhold accreditation until the college qualified for the approval of the Southern Association put teeth in the "invitation."

The Horry County Higher Education Commission signed a contract with the University of South Carolina in 1960 which made the junior college a two-year branch campus. The people of the county continued to support the school loyally. In 1962 ground was broken for the first building on a new campus east of Conway. There was a great fundraising drive to which the people of the county responded generously—Burroughs Timber Company and International Paper Company donated land; some contributed large amounts of money, and some with fewer resources pledged amounts as little as $5.00 a month to raise $317,000.

The student body and the faculty grew steadily. Two years were increased to four years by 1974, and later some graduate studies became available. Buildings on the campus multiplied.

With a certain eye to historic irony the Coastal Educational Foundation, Inc., and the Horry County Higher Education Commission met together on July 23, 1991, thirty-seven years to the day after the founders had held their first meeting, and voted to seek legislative approval to separate Coastal from the University of South Carolina. From those who had been there from the beginning there was an almost audible sigh of approval. With persistence and superb help from legislators, the college was declared Coastal Carolina University on July 1, 1993. Ronald R. Ingle was inaugurated the first president on October 22, 1994.

THE SWAMP THAT TEACHES:
PLAYCARD ENVIRONMENTAL EDUCATION CENTER

Playcard Environmental Education Center is committed to fostering knowledge of the relatedness of plants, animals, soil, water, and human beings through teaching the natural sciences in the special world of a black water swamp. Its mission statement begins:

> The land is fragile, all its parts interrelated. It is not possible to create more of it. There is no substitute for it. Our continued life on earth

depends upon it. How we use—or abuse—the land affects our present and our future.

In Horry County our land and water have too often been used for present profit and pleasure without regard to the future and the welfare of those who will live here after us. Short and long term strategies to save our natural resources—strategies which will require major sacrificial efforts by individuals, businesses and governments—will not happen unless we educate ourselves and our children to respect and protect the land and to make the hard decisions now that will enable future generations to live here in an environment that is healthful and productive.

Swamps are part of Horry County history and heritage and are an essential part of the way nature works in this place. They control flood waters, replenish the underground water system, filter pollution out of our waters, and provide habitat for plants and animals, some of them endangered. Like the seashores and marshes, swamps are important to people who live here now and those who will come after us.

Planning for the center began in 1981 with the establishment of the Horry County Conservation Foundation. The moving force behind it was James P. Blanton, farmer, businessman, banker—a man with an abiding faith in education. The founding directors were men engaged in farming, government, and business, all with agricultural connections, all convinced that Horry's natural resources must be wisely used to protect future generations. In addition to Blanton, they were James E. Griffith, Shelton T. Hayes, S. F. Horton, Ernest W. Johnston Jr., Sam B. McQueen, Robert L. Squires, Arden L. Stephens, and W. D. Witherspoon.

The Horry County Conservation Foundation issued a straightforward statement of purpose: "To provide sufficient data, analysis, and publicity so the people of Horry County understand the condition of the county's natural resources and realize the need for effective conservation." The foundation supported projects aimed at teaching adults and children to understand, appreciate, and protect the natural world in which we live. A connection with the educational system existed from the beginning.

Playcard Center was established in 1987, an outgrowth of the foundation's mission. After James P. Blanton gave the foundation 80 acres of land along Playcard Swamp that he had acquired by purchase and long-term leases on 120 acres more, the foundation invited a group of educators, professionals from agricultural agencies, and interested citizens to become members of a board of directors to govern the operation of the center. Laura Blind became temporary chairwoman while the members organized to develop plans. The first permanent chairman was Mack Sarvis. A plain, practical, and efficient building, constructed on high land at the edge of the swamp on Highway 19 just off Highway 410, was introduced to the public at Swampfest '87, the first annual open house.

The Horry County School District agreed to provide a teacher to conduct classes on site. From 1987 to 1996, Laura Blind, the first on-site teacher, instructed thousands of public and private school students who have visited Playcard. Many of their teachers have attended special workshops at the center. While Playcard Center is focused on the people of Horry County, adults and students alike, its success has made it a model for groups interested in environmental education in other places across South Carolina and beyond. Visitors to the center have marveled at the richness and beauty of the swamp ecosystem. Professional biologists and other specialists have been invited to study it and make recommendations for learning programs based on it.

This central asset has been enhanced by James Blanton's personal development of land his family holds across Highway 19 from the center itself. A tobacco barn on the property evokes the way of life farm people have known during the twentieth century. It shelters farm equipment, including a wagon which provides rides for children on special days. Blanton has provided and helped to stock a barn which houses farm animals and a pond which provides a habitat for waterfowl. This project has unleashed a wave of nostalgia among Playcard Center's rural neighbors, who have contributed artifacts from their farming past. Millstones, straw brooms, and a dugout boat are among the exhibits which allow students to imagine a way of life that has changed greatly in two generations.

Playcard Center separated from the Horry County Conservation Foundation in 1989 when it was chartered by South Carolina as a not-for-profit corporation. In January 1990, the foundation and the center entered into a lease which allows the center to manage its property and conduct educational activities. Memberships dues, sponsorships, and income from fundraising programs and user fees provide the operating funds. In 1993 the patrons and friends of the center gave funds to purchase another critical 51 acres.

The center runs on volunteer energy provided by its board of directors and volunteers who are interested in the work it does. The board runs

Playcard in a hands-on manner, because there is, as yet, no permanent staff. The board, therefore, not only establishes policy and makes all major decisions about the program and budget, but individual board members put many hours of actual labor into the development and upkeep of Playcard Center. To run the special programs put on several times a year hundreds of volunteers are needed, and they have always been there.

MEDICAL CARE BEFORE MODERN HOSPITALS

Horry County was on the frontier of South Carolina until the twentieth century. Early settlers drifted into the area in family groups or as single individuals. They brought with them the folk medicine of their homelands, to which in time were added Indian and African knowledge. Not until seventy years after settlers came to the area does the first mention of a doctor occur.

A "Dr. Blith" (perhaps Dr. Joseph Blythe of Waccamaw Neck) evidently purchased land when lots were first sold in Conwayborough in 1802. He conveyed them to Anthony Pawley without proper titles. In 1808 the district board of commissioners ordered one of their number to "wait upon" him and demand payment. Dr. Blith may have been a speculator in real estate who had hoped to turn a profit, not a resident.

Dr. Randolph Seawell, on the other hand, was a landowner in the Red Bluff area along the Waccamaw River. He came from Whiteville, North Carolina, about 1827 and is known to have had a practice. His recorded receipt to John Durant on June 19, 1845, for forty dollars ("it being in full of all medical account up to the present date") furnishes documentary proof. A writer in the local newspaper recalled him as practicing in the 1840s and described him as a man "who used many little bad words, but was counted a good physician."

The same writer recalled Dr. John Grant, his contemporary, who had a "large practice and was very successful, was liked by all who knew him." The area north of Conway where he lived became known as Grantsville. The 1850 census lists only Grant, M. G. Hart, and W. K. Cuckon as doctors, one doctor per 2,550 persons in Horry District's 1,200 square miles. Dr. Hart apparently practiced in the Maple area. Dr. Cuckon's practice was in Little River. His account book for 1856-1869 has survived.

A decade later Dr. D. B. Campbell, Dr. Joseph H. Harrell, and Dr. J. H. Norman had joined Dr. Grant and Dr. Cuckon. Dr. Hart is not listed in 1860. That census lists Anzy Vaught as a midwife, though there must surely have been many more midwives or granny women who aided the "birthing" of Horry's growing population.

Dr. James H. Norman, allied by blood to the powerful Beaty family and by the marriage of his sister to the wealthy Henry Buck of Bucksville, was practicing in Conway shortly before 1860. He became captain of the Brooks Rifle Guards, a militia group which merged into the Tenth South Carolina Volunteers after the Civil War began. After the Battle of Shiloh, he resigned his commission and returned to Conwayborough. At the end of the war his brother-in-law, Henry Buck, asked him to go to Charleston to request from the military commandant a unit of soldiers to restore order in the Independent Republic.

Shortly before the war, Joseph Harrell came from the Whiteville, North Carolina, and set up practice in the Grantsville area, perhaps even succeeding to the Grant practice. After some years, Dr. Harrell returned to Whiteville, where he died in 1903.

In 1871 Dr. Evan Norton (1841-1914) began practice in Conwayborough. He became a leader in education and religion as well as in medicine. Most physicians of the period concocted their own medications, but Dr. Norton established a pharmacy. His Norton's Biscuits became a popular over-the-counter remedy for malaria. Dr. Archibald Hector James Galbraith (1840-1905) and Dr. J. S. Dusenbury (1866-1933) joined Dr. Norton in Conway. County records also list Dr. J. W. Johnson as "qualified" at that time.

Trained doctors were available around the county by the late nineteenth and early twentieth century. R. G. Sloan and J. A. Stone located in Little River and S. P. Watson in the Round Swamp area, where he treated patients from Loris to Little River and Conway. A. D. Lewis, who qualified in 1897 according to county records, settled in the Green Sea area. John Kelly Stalvey (1873-1950) practiced in the Bucksport-Eddy Lake area. P. K. Bethea and Sam Mace practiced for a time in Loris before moving on. Homer Hope Burroughs, a Conway native, practiced there after qualifying in 1900 and was a warden (councilman) in the first city government of the town when it was incorporated in 1902. Others in Loris were a Dr. Robinson, D. O. Dubose, P. P. Chambers, Charles Rhett Taber, and H. T. Kirby. Dr. Huger Richardson located in Loris in 1912 and Dr. John Dorsey Thomas in 1915. Dr. William Eugene King (1887-1951) practiced in Aynor from August 1914 until his death.

Conway had four doctors and two dentists by 1905. There were now enough physicians to form the Horry County Medical Society. Dr. J. S. Dusenbury became the first president, Dr. J. W. Floyd the vice president, and Dr. J. A. Norton (Dr. Jamie, son of Dr. Evan Norton), secretary-treasurer. In the same year (1905), a public interest in health matters resulted in the formation of the Conway Board of Health. Young Dr. Norton was the medical adviser to the board, which consisted of Jeremiah Smith, J. C. Spivey, S. T. Sessions, and H. H. Woodward. Dr. Jamie Norton also gave lectures on personal health and hygiene at the high school.

Dr. Henry L. Scarborough (1886-1945) graduated from the Medical College of the University of South Carolina in 1911. He moved to Conway the same year, opened his practice, and built at Sixth and Elm an office for himself that also housed his family and provided rooms for operating and for short-term patients. This was the first time such an arrangement was offered to the sick in this area. Doctors had always tended patients in their own homes, sometimes remaining in residence for days while ministering to them.

Dr. Burroughs (1874-1926) moved his practice from Loris to Conway. In 1913, he applied for a charter to operate a hospital. His nurse, Miss Esther Faircloth, R.N., and his sister, Nina Burroughs, R.N., signed the application. Burroughs converted the old Gully Store at Ninth and Elm Streets, which Burroughs and Collins had vacated, to patient rooms, treatment and operating rooms, and offices. The need for skilled assistants was soon apparent. It was not long before Miss Faircloth began to train students.

Dr. Burroughs began his hospital in a period of growing prosperity for Horry County. The traditional reliance on turpentine and timber had given way to tobacco as the main source of money. The towns were growing as the number of professional, government, and business people grew. Contacts with the world outside the county were increasing.

The people of Horry County, however, even this late—on the eve of World War I—depended in illness and injury upon folk remedies, the devoted care of relatives, and stoicism. In 1914 the Civic League of Conway offered sunflower seeds free to all citizens provided they would grow the plants to ward off malaria and other fevers in the town.

When medical help was available in the community, doctors customarily came to their patients' homes. Many people were reluctant to enter a hospital, regarding it as a place to go to die. Among the people, the only familiarity with hospitals belonged to war veterans who had experienced the summary care of military or field hospitals. Furthermore, many people could ill afford even modest costs, and doctor bills were often paid in produce or services.

Dr. Burroughs became disabled in 1922, and his hospital was forced to close. In 1924 Dr. Scarborough closed his office and patient care at Sixth and Elm. Conway was once again without a facility for care of the sick.

That year James Archibald Sasser graduated from the Medical College of South Carolina and returned to Conway. He, Dr. Scarborough, Dr. Dusenbury, and Dr. Stalvey began to offer patient care at Dr. Scarborough's Sixth and Elm building. These men were all from Horry families, deeply rooted in the community. The doctors cooperated in administration, operations, and patient care, often foregoing individual fees. They continued in this location until 1926, when they secured the old Burroughs Hospital site at Ninth and Elm.

At the time, of course, the races were segregated. On May 29, 1926, the Horry County Colored Hospital and Training School received a charter to operate a hospital and a training school for nurses. This effort grew out of work Dr. Archie Sasser did among blacks. A. L. Rainbow was president, Horace Johnson, vice president, B. F. Levister, secretary, and C. A. Jones, treasurer. Paul Smith, J. A. Bines, and M. C. Conner were directors. Sarah Buck Lloyd operated the small clinic on Racepath, which apparently ceased operation when the new hospital opened in 1930.

Dr. Hal B. Holmes graduated from the Medical College of South Carolina in 1926 and joined the Conway group in the operation of the hospital. These practitioners had served internships in good hospitals and knew that patients needed a better facility than the local physicians alone could afford.

The Duke Endowment had begun to take an interest in health and put Dr. Watson Smith Rankin in charge of assisting the construction of modern hospitals throughout the Carolinas. Early in January 1928, Dr. Archie Sasser put before the Conway Chamber of Commerce the possibility that Conway might qualify for financial assistance. After all, Dr. Rankin had a local connection, a brother, Harry W. Rankin, who lived in Allsbrook, close to Dr. Sasser's boyhood home.

The chamber immediately appointed D. M. Burroughs, L. D. Magrath, and M. A. Wright as a committee to pursue this opportunity. Almost at once the Kiwanis Club of Conway named W. A. Stilley Sr., J. E. Watson, and Hoyt McMillan to assist.

No time was wasted. On January 13, Stilley, Magrath, Burroughs, Wright, and Dr. Sasser met with Dr. Rankin in his Charlotte office and received information about what should be done to qualify for Duke Endowment help. Soon thereafter, the Horry County Legislative Delegation promised ten thousand dollars in county funds provided the people of Conway Township would bond themselves by referendum for the remainder of the funds.

A local newspaper editorially opposed the bond, saying it was unfair that Conway Township should bear the burden alone when all the county would benefit from the hospital. The sponsoring committee tried in vain to counteract the opposition, but the election held April 6, 1928, failed by a vote of 69 to 134.

Still, Duke Endowment's offer was good until November 1 that year. Hospital advocates regrouped. They began a successful campaign to raise $25,000 to match Duke's $25,000. By October 18, almost at the deadline, $3,600 was still lacking. The campaign went over the top when the doctors at the Conway Hospital offered to donate equipment valued at $6,000 to make up the deficit. A pledge form run in the newspaper brought additional gifts after the deadline. Despite its former opposition to the bond proposal, the newspaper joined in the general jubilation, publishing a headline on November 8 that read, "Hospital Is Now Assured."

Once the sponsors secured money, they moved quickly to complete the formal organization. Although the existing institution was called Conway Hospital, there was no charter. The application filed with the South Carolina secretary of state on November 7, 1928, listed H. L. Buck as president, W. A. Stilley Sr. As vice president, and M. A. Wright as secretary-treasurer. H. W. Ambrose and A. C. Thompson completed the board of directors. The stated purpose of the corporation was to "construct, establish, own, manage and operate a hospital at or near the Town of Conway, S. C." (An amendment of the charter on November 3, 1938, changed the formal name to Conway Hospital, Inc.)

In March, 1929, Dr. Rankin came to Conway to confer on suitable sites. A few weeks later, on June 26, 1929, Buck signed a deed conveying a lot on Ninth Avenue to the hospital. It measured 250 by 736 feet and contained 4.22 acres. Constructing and furnishing the building consumed the next year. The Duke Endowment laid down specifications to assure that it would be both functional and economical to operate. The town government cooperated by providing water, sewer, and street improvements.

The paper made much of the fact that the hospital would be managed by the board of directors and that patients would have absolute freedom of choice in the selection of their physicians. The medical staff (Dr. J. A. Sasser, chief of staff; Dr. H. L. Scarborough, assistant chief of staff; and Dr. H. B. Holmes, secretary) invited specialists from the region to become the consulting staff. All local doctors of high professional and ethical standing were eligible for membership on the active staff. Katherine O. Altman became the first administrator in 1929.

Not to be outdone by the men of the town, the ladies of Conway formed a Hospital Auxiliary. On May 30, 1930, they held an open house to introduce the hospital to the community before it was formally occupied.

The new hospital had accommodations for thirty-one patients in single rooms and wards. The first floor contained the public reception areas, housekeeping areas, nurses' dining room, the storage rooms, the emergency operating room, and rooms for colored patients. The latter had their own entrance in the right wing. The second floor had only private rooms and wards with their accompanying nurses' stations and other functional areas. At each end was a solarium for the enjoyment of the patients. The surgical rooms were on the third floor with more patient rooms and wards and the nursery, which held six bassinets. Dumbwaiters connected the second and third floors to the main kitchen; chutes connected the upper floors to the laundry and incinerator on the first floor. It was a facility in which all concerned took great pride. The nursing school graduated its first class from the new building.

The American College of Surgeons granted the hospital provisional approval in 1935 and full approval in 1936. Clearly, Horry County had entered a new era in medical care with the opening of Conway Hospital.

In Loris Dr. Wilbert K. Rogers started a clinic in the old Bullock home in 1943. Planning was going forward for the establishment of a hospital in Loris. The Civitan Club, which included most of the town leadership, undertook sponsorship of the movement and canvassed the townships that would comprise the primary service area. Civitans secured enough signatures to persuade the Legislative Delegation to establish a special tax district, and the Loris Community Hospital became a reality. The members of the first hospital commission were S. F. Horton, C. A. Lupo, E. W. Prince Sr., Lundy Vaught, and Eldred E. Prince, chairman. Prince served in that capacity for thirty-six years. Dr. Rogers' limited care facility closed when the Loris Community Hospital opened on May 15, 1950.

Myrtle Beach's Ocean View Memorial Hospital, though chartered in 1949, did not open until July 2, 1958. Its first site on Ocean Boulevard was abandoned when an outside corporation bought the hospital and built a new facility, Grand Strand Memorial, on Highway 17. In 1994, it underwent an extensive renovation and expansion and changed its name to Grand Strand Regional Hospital.

LET THERE BE LIGHT

Katherine Hammack Heniford, brought up close to the bright lights and display windows of Broad Street in Richmond, arrived in Loris in the 1920s. She was dismayed by the dark streets of Loris. Even fifty years ago, the candlepower now expended along the Grand Strand each night could not even have been imagined by its inhabitants.

There is some doubt about where electric lights were first used in Horry County. Eddy Lake on Bull Creek, now vanished with hardly a trace, is sometimes said to be the first community to provide electric lights. Others claim that honor for Allentown, now another ghost village north of Conway on the railroad. Outsiders engaged in harvesting Horry County's vast timber resources founded both communities and brought the technology with them, probably a Delco or some other similar kind of generator.

Country people had no electric lights (except the few who had Delco generators) and necessarily quit most work at sundown. The cooling capacity of springs or wells provided the only refrigeration. The farmwife's world had none of the myriad electrical appliances which now make her chores easier. Farmers labored without the help of electric equipment.

Some used candles or perhaps light from the fireplace in winter, but most people relied on kerosene lanterns or lamps, which had to be trimmed, cleaned, and filled regularly. Outside lanterns were of sturdy metal with glass surrounding the flame. Lamps used inside varied from plain glass holders with clear chimneys to the most elaborate glass or porcelain, their chimneys etched with designs. The Sears, Roebuck catalog of the time shows a wide range of choices.

Paul Quattlebaum, son of Conway's first mayor and later to become a state senator, graduated from Clemson in 1906 and brought electric lights to Conway in 1908. To be sure, the Conway Light Company provided a fitful light, and the newspaper often complained of its unreliability.

President Franklin Roosevelt authorized the Rural Electrification Administration to bring electricity to rural America, one of the most transforming events in the history of the United States. Prior to this time, power companies felt it was not cost effective to extend lines into sparsely populated areas. Instead of allowing existing companies to borrow money to serve rural areas, the REA encouraged groups of rural people to form self-governing cooperatives to borrow at low interest the money necessary to bring the electric lines to their homes.

South Carolina decided to work through vocational agriculture teachers in each school district. The national authority preferred to work through county extension agents. Competition between the two action plans caused some friction, and the national authority sent an agent in to do the organizing. At a meeting at the Burroughs School auditorium, the little group of founders picked Mansie Gause, a respected farmer, to solicit members. Working with county extension agent V. M. Johnston, Gause succeeded in recruiting enough men from all sections of the county to form the Horry Electric Cooperative, Inc. On April 24, 1940, they elected a president, Pearly S. Page, and district directors: W. Hal King, D. M. Grainger, P. L. Elvington, U. A. Johnson, H. L. Lupo, W. J. Jordan, H. E. Stevens, and T. C. Hardee. The nine district directors each put up five dollars to give the fledgling cooperative forty-five dollars of operating capital. These were the men who made the hard sell in bad economic times to recruit enough members to start the lines. Few farmers felt they could afford to pay the $1.50 a month. Eventually, however, 627 signed up, enough to begin.

According to Hal King, there was at first one transformer, located in Aynor, and two cutoff switches in the whole system. "One was on a pole in the Bucksport area. When that switch was knocked out, the best way to cut it back on was to hit the pole with an ax. This would jar it back on. Before the pole was replaced, it was most beat in two."

The cooperative bought electricity at first from Carolina Power and Light, but switched to Santee Cooper when the state-owned system was completed. The first staff had quarters in the Wright building at the corner of Fourth Avenue and Laurel Street in Conway. The present building is at 1708 Oak Street in north Conway. Lloyd Williams, a native of Bucksport, who had worked four years with the Florida Power and Light Company, was the first manager. H. Otis "Tab" Stogner, also a native of Horry, succeeded him January 1, 1957, and was succeeded in turn by Charlie Webster in June 1977 and James Patrick Howle in 1994.

It would be impossible to reckon the difference electricity (and, of course, the men who struggled to bring it to Horry) has made in the lives of rural people.

5

The Civil War and Its Aftermath

CIVIL WAR REFUGEES IN CONWAYBOROUGH

Plowden Charles Jennet Weston, a prominent rice planter in Waccamaw Neck, recruited the Georgetown Rifle Guards, Company A of the Tenth Regiment, South Carolina Volunteers. At his own expense he outfitted the entire company with all gear, including English rifles and uniforms for summer and winter. He also put slaves ("Pioneers") in uniform to precede the company clearing away the underbrush. Three drummers and one fifer, also slaves, supplied military music.

Weston's great wealth has become legend in Waccamaw Neck. One story relates how Captain Weston led his company to the coast to intercept an enemy landing. It was a false alarm. On the way back to camp, he sent word ahead to the servants at Hagley Plantation. They prepared and served his company of 150 men with a seated full-course meal, served on fine china with crystal and silver. Wine was supplied from rare vintages in his cellar. The beautiful stained glass window behind the altar in Prince George Winyah Episcopal Church, Georgetown, originally graced a chapel he built for his slaves on the plantation.

While he was away at war, Mrs. Weston supervised the plantation with the help of trusted slaves. Emily Frances Esdaile Weston was an Englishwoman from Cothelestone House, Somerset. Plowden Weston had been at Harrow with her brother. They married August 31, 1847. Miss Elizabeth Collins, a young Englishwoman, came to Hagley to be her companion just before Christmas 1859. Collins later published a book in England, *Memories of the Southern States* (Barnicott, 1865), about her experiences with the Weston family.

In pursuit of his military duties in Confederate service, Weston was away from home for long periods. Mrs. Weston feared that Federal forces would come up the Waccamaw from Winyah Bay and pillage Hagley. Having heard in January 1862 about the possibility of a cottage available for her use in Conwayborough, she had Prince, her coachman, drive her the forty-mile distance. Arriving toward evening in the 'Borough, she discovered that Judge Joseph P. Walsh was in charge of most things while the men were away in service of the Confederacy. He showed her the cottage on Snow Hill, and they agreed to a rental fee of $120 a year. Its outhouses and stables were very much in need of repair, but it had 8 acres of cultivated land and an orchard of peach trees among the 100 or so acres of pine.

Mrs. Weston and her husband agreed to leave some slaves at Hagley with an overseer and to find a farm upstate to which they could be sent should the need arise. They buried some valuables at Hagley; others went by flat upriver to Conwayborough, accompanied by a crew of slave carpenters to build housing for the slaves as well as to repair the buildings already at Snow Hill. On January 22, 1862, Mrs. Weston took up residence in her refuge, a spartan place compared to Hagley. Prince was heard to say, "Conwayboro' [shortened form of the name] must have been the last place God made."

In April Captain Weston and his men were dispatched to Corinth, Mississippi. There many men of the Tenth died in epidemics of measles and mumps. In May Federal troops did raid Waccamaw plantations, and the Hagley slaves, under the supervision of a slave overseer, were sent to land purchased near Winnsboro for their refuge.

In June Mrs. Weston welcomed the Rev. William Malet, who had come from England through the Northern lines to visit his kinswoman and bring her news of her family. This clergyman also published a journal of his visit in *An Errand to the South in the Summer of 1862* (Richard Bentley, 1863). At Knoxville Captain Weston left the Tenth to return home. His health, impaired by the hardships of the march and camp, forced him to take time after his arrival in October to recuperate. Although Weston bought the house at Snow Hill, he soon returned to Hagley, and Mrs. Weston quickly joined him there.

That winter Weston was elected to the state legislature. When the lieutenant governor died in office, he ascended to that position without a dissenting vote. Still his health did not improve. He died on January 25, 1863, and was buried at All Saints Cemetery. His tombstone is one of the first to be seen on the left as a visitor enters the old graveyard. In September Mrs. Weston returned to England to live the rest of her life.

After the Civil War F. G. Burroughs bought the home in which the Weston family had lived for their short time in Conway. It has been moved twice and is now on Applewhite Lane.

COMPANY B, SIEGE TRAIN, CSA

Warren T. Alford, Civil War veteran, was buried in the old Heniford burying ground in the Live Oak Community not far from Loris. His stone bears no dates and no epitaph, only his name and one line, "Co B Siege Train CSA." Thomas Heniford, buried in the same cemetery, was also a veteran of this outfit, but his grave does not have the Confederate service marker.

By definition, a siege train is a collection of pieces of artillery combined into a special force for a specific purpose, in this case to break the hold of Northern forces on Charleston. Its purpose fell somewhere between that of the field artillery and the seacoast artillery. The commanding officer of the South Carolina Siege Train was Maj. Edward Manigault (pronounced *Man-i-go*). He and his brother, Arthur Middleton Manigault, were the youngest sons of Joseph and Charlotte Drayton Manigault. He grew up in the handsome house, which is now the Joseph Manigault house museum near the Charleston Museum. Arthur became a major general in the Confederate forces, and Edward became a major.

Major Edward Manigault was born March 8, 1817. He attended South Carolina College, forerunner of the University of South Carolina, graduating in 1835. As captain of the Twelfth Infantry Regiment, he served in the war with Mexico, was promoted to major on July 16, 1847, and moved to the Thirteenth Regiment.

He served as South Carolina chief of ordnance with the rank of colonel and petitioned to lead a battalion in defense of Charleston and South Santee. Appointed major on October 31, 1861, Edward Manigault received command of the Sixth Infantry Battalion, South Carolina Volunteers, which became known as Manigault's Battalion. On May 18, 1863, impatient with his relatively inactive role in the fighting, Major Manigault requested command of a unit of artillery to be formed and called the South Carolina Siege Train. He assumed his new command June 22, 1863. When Federal troops attacked Morris Island, the siege train moved from Charleston to James Island.

Severely wounded and left for dead at the Battle of Grimball's Causeway on February 20, 1865, Major Manigault surprised the attendants in the makeshift operating room where they removed his leg. Official records actually reported his demise. He received his parole on May 10, 1865.

After the war Manigault, who never married and of whom no portrait has been found, settled in Georgetown County as a planter. He died October 2, 1874, when the buggy he was driving overturned. His remains lie among his ancestors' at the Huguenot Church in Charleston.

A short article in the old *Horry Herald* for February 19, 1914, lists Horry members of the South Carolina Siege Train who were still living at that time: Tom Barnhill, Jim Bryant, C. A. Causey, Mitch Edge, J. H. Grant, H. L. W. Johnson, Waterman Johnson, Bryant Moore, Henry Moore, G. W. Sessions, J. M. Sessions, W. J. Sessions, and E. B. Tompkins. The memory roll of Confederate veterans at the South Carolina Department of Archives and History lists 173 men from Horry County in Company B, Eighteenth Heavy Artillery Battalion, the South Carolina Siege Train.

THE TWO GREAT BATTLES OF CONWAYBOROUGH

Horry County's geographical isolation worked to its advantage during the Civil War. It was not ground fought over and destroyed by battle. Its men went to fight—almost all of them. It was said that eight hundred Horry men were eligible for service and twelve hundred volunteered. Conditions on the home front deteriorated while they were away. Judge Joseph Travis Walsh recalls that he had "only a peck of rough rice and a few potatoes on which to live that week" before Lee surrendered.

As the Civil War was winding down to its inevitable conclusion, Confederate forces disintegrated on faraway battlefields. Survivors, seeing no point in trying to find other units to join, returned to Horry and hid out in swamps near their families. Because they had not been properly discharged, they were technically deserters. They seized provisions from nearby farmsteads, sometimes with the collusion of owners, sometimes by force or stealth. Law and order had broken down. The sheriff could neither enforce the law nor punish offenders. Some communities were terrorized.

In February 1865, Federal troops took over Georgetown. Rumors flew about the Yankees coming to Conway. The town had only a few defenders, most of its men being still away at the war. Those who were available were under the command of Capt. Samuel Bell and Lt. John Robinson Beaty. It seemed to them that the enemy must come by river and that the logical place to station their men was on a big bend in the Waccamaw River at the foot of Elm Street at the spot now occupied by the Conway Marina.

The defenders arrayed themselves in ambush beside the river. Walsh, who because of a physical handicap had not served in the military, was among them. After night fell, a sudden alarm caused the local men to begin shooting. In the confusion and shooting that followed, three men were seriously wounded, Lieutenant Beaty being one of them. Beaty, who was thirty-eight years old, had served in the army and had finally come home to the pursuits of civilian life. He was wounded by one of his own men, his dear friend, Samuel Bell. Beaty was carried to his home at the corner of Sixth and Main Street and given tender care, but he died within a day or two. He left a widow and children. The first "battle" of Conwayborough ended tragically for the townspeople and for Beaty's family.

Normal life could not be resumed in the chaotic state which prevailed in the district. Henry Buck, eager to restart his profitable lumber business down at Bucksville, sent his brother-in-law, Dr. James H. Norman, to Charleston to talk to the military commandant about protection for people here. He promised help.

One damp day some while later, two young boys, one of them Edgar Beaty, Lt. John Beaty's son, went rabbit hunting on the Musterfield. The place where the local militia drilled was on the edge of the settlement beyond Elm Street and the Racepath. A high board fence separated the field from the road to Georgetown. Having had no luck hunting, the boys began shooting at knotholes in the fence. Even when they heard movements beyond the fence, they kept up their target practice.

This time the Yankees had come! Their boat had grounded on a sandbar in the Waccamaw, so they had marched through mist and rain along the Georgetown road and were now approaching their objective. Hearing shots, the commanding officer believed his men were being fired upon and gave the order to return fire. The result could have been disastrous to the young hunters, but for the bad weather. Their ammunition was damp from the rain, and the Yankees were unable to obey.

About this time it dawned on the boys that something was wrong—badly wrong. They peeked through a knothole and saw enemy troops. Edgar Beaty, recalling the incident later in his life, said that jackrabbits could not have made better or more secret time than the boys did in making their escape. The second great "battle" of Conwayborough had ended ludicrously!

The boys stayed out of the reach of adults until it was time to go home to supper. As young Beaty approached the house on Main Street, he saw Yankee soldiers on the front steps and porch. Sure that they had come to arrest him, Edgar had visions of being put against a wall and shot. The soldiers, however, were only being quartered in the house, one of the finest and largest in town. They posed no danger to the boys.

The occupying troops from a Maine regiment were welcomed by the townspeople, even though they were Yankees and therefore enemies. Walsh said they behaved themselves with great kindness toward the suffering poor. Their presence restored order. Soon some of them became emboldened to court local girls. One even paid romantic attention to Miss Izzie, daughter of Lt. John R. Beaty, who had died defending the town. Local legend says that, outraged at the thought of a Yankee with his daughter, Beaty came back from his grave to break up the pair. His ghost is said to be heard even now, stomping up the steps of the house.

HORRY BLACKS HELPED WRITE 1868 CONSTITUTION

At the end of the Civil War the political leaders of South Carolina put in place a constitution designed to retain control of the state in white hands. With carpetbaggers and black freedmen or newly freed slaves in control of the legislature, its repudiation was inevitable. Indeed, in order for South Carolina to recover its full statehood in the union, it would have to adopt a constitution which enfranchised blacks.

Across the state the Republican Party sponsored Union Leagues for blacks. Their purpose was to register voters and, of course, to control the way in which those voters cast their ballots. In preparation for the convention, every effort was made to register black voters. The registration books show for the first time the surnames which former slaves had taken for their own.

Georgetown voters elected Franklin F. Miller, Henry W. Webb, and Joseph H. Rainey to represent them. Rainey would later become the first black man elected to the national House of Representatives. The voters of Horry elected the Rev. Henry Wallace Jones and Augustus Reeves Thompson, both black. Biographical information about these former slaves appeared in the *Marion Star* on February 26, 1868, supplied by an occasional correspondent who signed himself "Waccamaw." Its contemptuous tone reflects white bitterness at that time. On January 14, 1868, elected representatives met in Charleston to draft the second constitution for South Carolina since the end of the Civil War.

According to this account, Jones was born about 1829 (1880 census) in North Carolina on a "turpentine farm" and came to Horry in 1852 "in the service of Ruben Wallace." He ran a still in which the pine gum was broken down into spirits of turpentine and rosin. According to "Waccamaw," he dealt in other kinds of spirits as well. He also had quite a reputation as a fiddler until he converted and joined the Conway Methodist Church. His religious fervor caused him to become an exhorter. This led him into conflict with the Reverend Mr. Mahoney, a white Irish minister in Conway, who tried to have him put out of the church. His owner sold him to a "Mr. Beaty," perhaps Thomas W. Beaty of Conway. His skills in distilling turpentine would have made him valuable to Beaty, who owned a still located on Kingston Lake near Fourth Avenue.

In spite of opposition from Mahony, he became a preacher, building a strong following among blacks. By virtue of his leadership ability he became after the war the founder of Bethel, the first African Methodist Episcopal church in Horry. He also became one of the organizers of the Union League. He operated a small grocery store.

Augustus Reeves Thompson was "born the property of Amon Thompson, a man of considerable station" about 1815 (1880 census). When Thompson died, William S. Reeves bought Augustus in an estate sale to satisfy the debts of the deceased. According to the *Star* correspondent, he was six feet tall, thin, and spare. He could neither read nor write. Amon Thompson evidently thought highly of his slave's ability. He made Augustus captain of his flat boat running between Red Bluff and Bucksville, transporting naval stores on the first leg of their journey to market. He also was responsible for rafting logs to the mill.

The delegates to the Constitutional Convention were a mixed group. Seventy-six of the 124 were black, 57 of them former slaves; 67 were former freedmen either from the state or from the North. Other delegates were mostly whites from the North who had settled in the state either before or after the war. Many delegates were illiterate, but a few able men took control.

Before the convention adjourned on March 17, 1868, the members had drafted a constitution which was enlightened in many ways. It gave the vote to all men, black and white, and removed the property-owning qualifications for holding public office. It outlawed dueling and legalized divorce. And, while not giving women the vote, it did grant them limited control over their own property.

Among its last acts, the convention set in motion an election based on the new rule. In Horry County the Republicans nominated Henry W. Jones for the Senate and Gus Thompson and Steven H. Thompson to the House. The Democratic ticket named Capt. Henry Buck for the Senate, and the Rev. Zadoc Bullock and W. W. Waller for the House. Horry County was the only eastern county in South Carolina to go Democratic.

THE 1876 CAMPAIGN SOLUTION

The gubernatorial campaign of 1876 in South Carolina brought Confederate general Wade Hampton out of retirement to save his state from the cumulative problems of Reconstruction and continued occupation by Federal troops. The General Assembly was corrupt; the state was bankrupt. Since the end of the Civil War, South Carolina had endured a decade of occupation and a Radical Republican government determined to ruin the old order.

Hampton campaigned in every district [county] of the state. Local Horry dignitaries attired in red shirts, the insignia of his campaign, met him on horseback at Galivants Ferry and escorted him into Conwayborough. On October 1, 1876, he stood beneath an oak tree near Main Street to speak to the crowd gathered at a public picnic on the grounds of the Thomas W. Beaty home. That evening at their request he appeared before black citizens at Bethel A. M. E. Church and asked for their support.

The Republicans (the party of carpetbaggers, scalawags, and newly freed slaves) conducted a strong campaign to register black voters. Local Democratic politicians, equally determined, wanted Horry to do its part to see Hampton elected. They campaigned throughout the district and endeavored to have their own people assigned at the local precincts to assure that the other side did not steal the election from the Democrats.

The Democratic leaders were a tight group of men, prominent in the civic, professional, and religious life of the community. Among them were Judge Joseph T. Walsh, Col. I. T. Gillespie, Capt. Thomas W. Daggett, Dr. Evan Norton, and C. P. Quattlebaum. None were native-born Horryites, but all were strongly entrenched in local leadership positions.

Judge Walsh had come to Conwayborough in 1854. His mentor, the judge under whom he had read law, had advised him to come to Horry to establish his practice here. "The people," the judge told him, "though poor and primitive, are true as steel." He practiced law, became a judge, and helped establish Kingston Presbyterian Church. As the first superintendent of education under the 1868 constitution, he had for the first time helped to establish schools for black children. He was clearly a religious and civic leader.

Col. I. T. Gillespie and C. P. Quattlebaum were also lawyers, both greatly respected in their profession. Quattlebaum, who had come to Horry only two years earlier (1874), later became the first intendant (mayor) of Conway. Dr. Evan Norton had come to Conway about 1870. He established a successful medical practice and pharmacy, edited a local newspaper and was an active Methodist layman. Later he would be deeply involved in education as a trustee of the Burroughs School.

Although a native of Massachusetts, Captain Daggett had a distinguished Confederate war record. He had been in charge of Confederate coastal defenses from Winyah Bay to Little River during the conflict. He had been the engineer whose crude floating mine sank the *Harvest Moon,* flagship of the Yankee Admiral John A. Dahlgren. Now he lived in Conwayborough and commanded the federal dredge boat charged with keeping the Waccamaw and Little Pee Dee Rivers navigable for paddlewheel steamers and other river traffic.

As the election approached, these men watched developments closely. Not long before the election, they discovered that Republicans were urging their adherents to "vote the eagle ballot." The Republicans, who were afraid that illiterate voters might mark the Hampton ballot by mistake, secretly printed a ballot which identified their nominees by a spread eagle at the top of the candidate list.

The Conway group notified the state party of this subterfuge. They met in the newspaper office to consider a counterstrategy. It turned out not to be too difficult. On a wood block Daggett and Quattlebaum together fashioned a passable copy of the Republican eagle. They used it to print Democratic ballots which looked like those the opposition was distributing. At the last moment, only the day before the election, the Democrats learned they had not discovered one key element of opposition strategy. Republicans ballots were printed on colored paper, not the traditional white. There was no time to coordinate a statewide counterstrategem.

Still, something might be achieved locally. Again the friends met around the stove at the newspaper office. Gloom hung heavy in the room. No paper available to them was anywhere near the color sported by the Republican ballot. Doctor Norton's supply of pharmaceuticals had no chemical which would dye the paper they had. What to do?

Captain Daggett went outside in response to nature's call. When he returned he took one of the white Democratic ballots and dipped it slowly into the fluid in the can he carried. It came out the exact color needed. Captain Daggett had had a physical examination that day which included a litmus test. He applied that knowledge to the ballot problem. Now the Democrats had a solution, but no supplies. Two thousand colored ballots were required. Word went out of the urgent need. For the rest of the evening good men, fortified by lemonade and coffee and assisted by nature, contributed to the supply of dye. Ballots were dried by the stove. Before dawn supplies of the new ballots were dispatched to the precincts.

Hampton carried the state by 1,134 votes. He carried Horry by 1,352— more than the victory margin. The results were, of course, hotly contested by the incumbent, Governor Daniel H. Chamberlain, and the final results were not secure until the spring of the next year. Horry and Marion were the only low-country districts Hampton carried.

How it was done in Horry was told and retold. Two of three versions in print (by Laura Quattlebaum Jordan and Marion Wright) are attributed to C. P. Quattlebaum, who was rewarded by two appointments to Governor Hampton's staff. W. W. Sellers (*A History of Marion County*, R. L. Bryan, 1902) said of Daggett's role in the winning strategy, "To him should be erected a monument in the hearts of the people of the State more enduring than brass and marble."

6

Memorable Murderers

A MAN AND HIS WORD

In the old days farmers fenced their crops in and let their livestock roam free. Only when they were being fattened for slaughter were hogs, for instance, penned. Many a dispute arose about ownership of hogs and other livestock when it came time to slaughter them.

Such a quarrel erupted at a place in the woods near Cool Spring in the fall of 1849. Two brothers and their families each claimed the hogs. On September 4, Abram Rabon Sr. And his sons, Duke and Little Abe, confronted Willis Rabon, Abram's nephew, at the pigpen. Neighbors who heard but did not see the altercation told the coroner that the old man urged his sons to kill their cousin. Someone did indeed stab Willis Rabon to death. Abram Rabon and his sons were charged with murder and taken to jail in Conwayborough. They were still there awaiting trial when the census taker came around in 1850.

When they came up for trial, all three men were convicted of murder and sentenced to be hanged. In the appeals process the state dismissed the cases against the father and the older son. No actual proof had been presented to link Duke Rabon to the crime scene. The record is not exactly clear how the father's case was decided, but one researcher thinks he was pardoned by the governor. From the testimony, it appeared that it was Little Abe who had murdered his cousin. The higher court upheld his conviction and gave the order for his execution in the fall of 1851, probably in November.

Abram Sr. went to the judge privately and appealed to the judge to let him take the boy from jail. He pleaded that he had a crop in the ground and needed the boy to help him work it, saying that it would be a great hardship on the rest of the family if he lost the crop. The judge agreed. He named a date and allowed the condemned man out of jail to go home with his father. Naturally, word of the bargain struck between the judge and the

180

father had gotten around the county. Wherever people met, they talked about the unusual circumstances. When the time set for the execution of the young man came, a great crowd gathered in Conwayborough for the event. Curiosity drew men, women, and children to the place where the hanging was to occur. The judge, the sheriff, and the hangman assembled on the local militia's muster field somewhere near the corner of Sixth Avenue and Elm Street in Conway.

The time set for the execution was noon. As the time drew near, the crowd grew more tense and expectant. Someone spied a wagon coming along the road from Cool Spring, and the word spread quickly from person to person. As the vehicle came still nearer, some recognized the man on the driver's seat as Abram Sr. Then those nearest as it passed saw that there was a coffin in the body of the wagon. Atop it sat the condemned man and his sisters!

When the wagon came to a stop near the cluster of officials, the father turned his son over to Sheriff W. H. "Hickory Bill" Johnston. The execution proceeded on schedule. The father took the body of his son when it was done and placed it in the homemade coffin. In the rain he drove slowly away along the Cool Spring road toward home and the burial of his son.

Aside from the official records, there is a written eyewitness account of this execution. Little Ellen Cooper, taken by her father to witness the hanging, recalled the event and wrote in her memoirs in 1924, "This was many years ago, and was the first hanging I ever heard of in Conwayboro, and the only one that I ever saw. My father took me and my little brother with him to see the man hung. The gallows stood where the Baptist Church now stands. It made such an impression that I have never forgotten it. I am now an old lady, but I remember well how it all looked, and I have never wanted to see such a sight again."

Ellen Cooper Johnson's account suggests that Abram Rabon came to the hanging expecting his own execution as well as that of his son. Later in her memoirs she referred to him as the man who came to his own hanging, which suggests that the governor's pardon came at the last moment.

Nearly a decade and a half later, toward the end of the Civil War, she was staying with her sister, Mrs. Louisa Cooper Barnhill, and Mrs. Barnhill's children at the sister's farm near Cool Spring. They were the victims of raids by Confederate deserters who hid in the swamps nearby. Their store of food was reduced almost to nothing. Then the raiders tried to burn them out by setting fire to the outhouses of the farm. The women had only two freed slaves to assist them.

One day, when the women were desperate for help, a wagon drove up to the gate of the farm. The driver offered to take what was left of their food stores and keep it for them until the raids stopped. He reassured the women that the raiders knew him and knew that he would not hesitate to shoot anyone who tried to take anything from his farm. Ellen recognized him as "the man who came to his own hanging." As good as his word still, Abram Rabon guarded their food and returned it in due time, as promised.

Alas, the old man did not die peacefully in his own bed, but met death at the hands of a son-in-law in a family dispute.

MUDDY FOOTPRINTS

It was the morning of June 23, 1905. In a community near present-day Allsbrook and Bayboro, the Rev. Harmon D. Grainger finished his breakfast and early chores around house and barn. He harnessed his mule to the plow and made his way to the cotton field.

About nine o'clock his wife heard two shots. Other firing had been heard in the neighborhood, but these shots came from the direction of the field where Grainger was plowing. As Mrs. Grainger and her son and daughter approached, they saw Grainger slumped between the handles of the plow in an attitude of prayer. The mule stood as though awaiting further instructions.

For years there had been an unofficial but often violently enforced line that ran from west of Loris to south of Galivants ferry, marking an area where black people were not allowed. Recently someone in the community had shot at Negro field hands, workers employed by the Reverend Mr. Grainger, for violating the "deadline." With reason to fear they might be in harm's way, his family halted at the edge of the field and remained in cover some while before sending for help.

Sheriff B. J. Sessions and Dr. H. H. Burroughs, the coroner, arrived late that day by train. Burroughs impaneled a coroner's jury from among the curious who had gathered at the scene. A trained bloodhound summoned by Sheriff Sessions picked up a scent which led to the home of Charlotte Simmons, across the branch from the Grainger place.

On her porch was a pair of muddy shoes. Gossip had it that Commander Johnson, who had made threats against Grainger, had moved in with her. The Reverend Grainger had threatened to lodge an accusation of adultery against them. When Johnson had testified before the coroner, he seemed so agitated that the sheriff had quietly sequestered him among the chief witnesses.

Officials took the shoes to the field where, according to witnesses, they matched perfectly with the track of the presumed murderer. Johnson's "pigeon toed" track found at the scene, the worn shoes, and probable motive were sufficient evidence for the sheriff to take Commander Johnson and Charlotte Simmons to Conway and lodge them in jail.

Trial began September 14, 1905, with B. Wofford Wait for the defense, Solicitor Monroe Johnson, and Judge Ernest Gary. The judge named W. M. Booth foreman of a jury consisting of L. M. Ludlam, J. M. Nixon, W. H. King, M. A. Royals, Charles Dusenbury, W. E. Williamson, S. M. Lane, William Booth, B. K. Doyle, F. W. Jernigan, and R. M. Prince.

The solicitor carefully marshaled the evidence against Johnson with a parade of more than thirty witnesses led by Widow Sarah Grainger. She testified to bad blood between her husband and the accused. She believed that Commander Johnson was the one who had shot at the Grainger hands. Mrs. C. L. Johnson testified that Commander Johnson had said that if Grainger got in his way, he would "bloody his shirt." Others told of the quarrel Grainger and Johnson had over cross-tie timbers. Dr. Burroughs testified that he had found twenty-nine shotgun pellet holes in Grainger's back. Clerks from the J. R. Allsbrook store testified that Johnson had been interested in shotgun ammunition of the kind that killed the preacher. Paper wadding used in the shotgun shells taken from the crime scene included a piece that bore the Allsbrook name.

Several offered testimony suggesting that at least one other person had recently quarreled with Grainger. Testimony that Charlotte Simmons's father, Daniel Prince, walked with one foot turned in mitigated somewhat the damning evidence of the pigeon toes.

The trial ran into the second day. When the prosecution rested, Attorney Wait called no witnesses for the defense. The jury did not take long to reach a verdict that Johnson was guilty of murder. The jurors also found Charlotte Simmons guilty but recommended mercy.

Judge Gary denied a motion for a new trial, but in an unusual move told Wait to produce his witnesses right then. D. L. Hewett testified that certain people had conversed with the jury overnight. The suggestion of jury tampering did not impress Gary, who sentenced Johnson to die. He, however, did grant Charlotte Simmons a new trial.

The South Carolina Supreme Court upheld the verdict; and the United States Supreme Court declined to hear an appeal. Judge J. C. Klugh sentenced Commander Johnson to die between the hours of noon and two o'clock on Friday, October 19, 1906. Defense lawyer Wait made a final appeal to Governor C. D. Heyward, who refused to intervene.

On Wednesday before the date set for execution, Sheriff Sessions and Deputy Leon H. Burroughs went by train to Marion, where Johnson had been taken for safekeeping, and brought the condemned man back to Conway. The newspaper reported that he seemed in good spirits and joked with the crowd that watched his transfer from train to jail.

The sheriff made sure that everything there was in order with the gallows. Family members and local clergy visited the prisoner, who still protested his innocence. Crowds filled Conway's streets at one o'clock on Friday, when the sentence was carried out in the presence of a few witnesses. The newspaper said Sheriff Sessions, who felt sorry for the family, provided the casket. Later another man confessed to the murder for which Commander Johnson had suffered the ultimate penalty. Johnson was the one who planned the murder, he claimed, but had not actually committed the deed.

Charlotte Simmons was eventually freed for lack of evidence of her complicity in the death of Preacher Grainger. The judge's order banned her from Horry County, but she eventually came back to Conway.

THE TRIALS OF EDMUND BIGHAM

Three times South Carolina prosecuted Edmund Bigham for the murder of his mother, his brother, his sister, and his sister's two children. The present (1908) courthouse in Conway was the setting of the last two trials. No others ever held there have generated more interest over a longer period.

Events leading up to and resulting from the 1921 murders span generations. The Bigham family was prominent in old Marion County, the part that is now in Florence County. Florence elected one of them, Smiley Jr., the first state senator from the new county. Concentrating only on events that occurred in the senator's immediate family, the story begins with his death. The community suspected that his wife, Dora, "had done him in" with poison. Neighbors whispered horrendous stories about how members of the family mistreated servants, including the murder of one young boy by driving a nail into his ear.

Dr. G. Cleveland Bigham and William Avant stood trial for the murder of the senator's daughter-in-law, Ruth, Cleveland Bigham's wife, at Murrells Inlet in 1909. The jury found the husband and his accomplice guilty of manslaughter. The judge sentenced Cleveland Bigham to three years and released him on bond, pending appeal. When the higher court upheld the verdict, he left the state without serving his sentence.

Memorable Murderers

On January 15, 1921, the Bighams' neighborhood near Pamplico became aware that something was wrong at the Widow Dora Bigham's house. All about the place lay the bodies of shooting victims. Of the whole household, only Edmund Bigham, his wife, and daughters remained alive. He claimed that, before she succumbed to a wound in the head, his mother had told him his brother, Smiley Jr., had done the murders. Edmund claimed that Smiley had then killed himself.

Edmund Bigham's first trial in Florence County began on March 21, 1921. It resulted in a death penalty. A higher court set aside the verdict and ordered a new trial, not to be held in Florence County. The court judged Bigham could not get a fair jury there. In October 1924, Bigham went on trial in Horry County. Conway took on a carnival atmosphere. Because of his notoriety, seats in the courtroom were in great demand.

The trial lacked nothing one might ask in suspense and drama. Bigham cursed court officials and all who testified against him. "They've lied on me, and every one of them will die before I do." Following this, one witness had a heart attack and died in the box. In all, four would die before the end of the trials. One prosecuting attorney thrust the skull of Dora Bigham toward her son's face and begged him to acknowledge his guilt. Two opposing lawyers engaged in fisticuffs in the courtroom. Bigham called down the wrath of God against his enemies and the rains came—and came. The "Bigham flood" or freshet that nearly drowned Conway during the trial has become a legend.

Once again the jury rendered a guilty verdict, and the judge sentenced Bigham to the electric chair. Again the sentence was set aside and a new trial ordered. At the beginning of the third trial, the court announced a delay. Rumor said Bigham's wife was pregnant. A special term of court met in April 1927 for the continuation. Again, a short delay occurred. The spectators were tense with anticipation of some new dramatic twist. Finally the judge announced that Bigham had pleaded guilty in exchange for a sentence of life imprisonment. Suddenly, the courtroom drama was over, but the Bigham story was not.

Edmund Bigham did outlive the prosecuting attorneys, who died in a car wreck, and most of the jury. He did not die in prison. In spite of the plea bargain, Senator Ralph Gasque of Marion succeeded in having Bigham paroled to his custody in 1960. The old convict lived the last two years of his life in Marion.

Dora Bigham's skull remained in an evidence box (actually an old-fashioned round, deep hatbox) in the Horry County courthouse for many years.

A later senator from Florence, Tom Smith, got a court injunction to claim it for reburial. Somehow, though, the skull passed into private hands. Some years later members of Pamplico community finally buried it there on April 14, 1990, more than sixty-nine years after Mrs. Bigham's murder.

Two books—*The Last of the Bighams*, by J. A. Zeigler, and *A Piece of the Fox's Hide*, by Katherine Boling—recount this bizarre story. It has also been the subject of many newspaper and magazine articles and several television programs. Neither of the books is satisfactory, and for the most part both lack the local lore which has kept the memory of this remarkable trial alive in Horry County.

7

You Would Not Expect It in Horry!

THE *HENRIETTA*

Once upon a time sailing ships visited Horry County. Coming up the Waccamaw River from Winyah Bay, they called at riverports to load lumber and turpentine, furs, and cotton. Mrs. Flossie Sarvis Morris, when she was interviewed in her nineties, remembered seeing them load lumber at Port Harrelson on Bull Creek as late as about 1905. Sailing ships could come up the Waccamaw as far as Pot Bluff a few miles below Conway. The river was kept free of obstacles to accommodate them. And once upon a time ships for the world trade were built at Bucksville. Skilled mechanics and ships' carpenters from Maine, experienced in their crafts, came south to do this work.

The largest of the sailing ships built at Bucksville was the *Henrietta*, which was launched with great fanfare in May 1875. She was named for the wife of Capt. Jonathan C. Nichols of Searsport, Maine, who was the master mariner in charge. She measured 210 feet long, 29 feet wide, 24 feet deep, and registered 1,203 tons. The man in charge of the crew that built her was Elisha Dunbar.

Henrietta was a marvel, even during construction. Drawings of her have been found in the Penobscot Marine Museum in New England. In them the buildings of the village of Bucksville can be seen clearly behind the ship on the ways. The launching was a gala event. According to eyewitness Charles Dusenbury, "there were 5 steamboats there, all come loaded with people and people came in every conceivable vehicle for, I would say, 50 miles around. That night we took two head-lights out of the mill and put one in each end of the ship, between decks, which brightly lighted it. We had a string band from Georgetown, and the young folks at Bucksville, with those who remained over for the night danced about all night."

Unlike some launchings, everything happened as it should have. As the crowd watched from boat and bank, Master Dunbar knocked out the wedge which held the *Henrietta* in place on the ways. "This wedge loosened everything, and the ship left the land, and with all ease and grace she stepped into her new home—the water."

The *Henrietta* sailed the seven seas for nearly two decades under command of famous Searsport captains Charles Melvin Nichols, Edward D. Blanchard, James Clifford Gilmore, and Andrew McGilvery Ross. In 1894, she was in Japan. At Yokohama she loaded 800 tons of crockery and manganese ore and went on to Kobe to complete her load before heading back to New York. A typhoon overtook her there, and she went ashore. Although all hands were saved, the great ship was lost, utterly shattered by the storm. The book *Searsport Sea Captains* says, "All hands landed safely and later the *Henrietta* was floated and towed to Kobe where everything was sold for the benefit of all concerned. Eventually the hull was broken up, the frame being cut into kindling wood and sold in small bunches." What an ignominious end for a proud ship!

The villages of Bucksville and Port Harrelson have disappeared. The cottages and public buildings, the active waterfronts, which once made them important places in Horry County, are gone. As the lumber and turpentine trade declined, so did the villages they helped to build.

COLONISTS CAME OUT OF THE WEST

"Why do people seek the south?" asked a Chicago magazine in 1896. According to the *Farm, Field and Fireside* editorial, southern migration was "in obedience to natural laws." Farmers of the Midwest, in particular, should move into "sunnier latitudes" because of the variety of crops which could be grown, comparatively light costs, essential services from business to government to schools already in place, and so on.

Farm, Field and Fireside, which claimed a circulation of 150,000, was already engaged in turning its editorial position into reality. As early as 1885 it had organized and sponsored a colony called Roseland in Tangipahoa Parish, Louisiana. Others followed in California, Florida, and North Carolina. The success of its Sunny South colony at Chadbourn, North Carolina, led it to investigate nearby sites for still another. The scouting party selected land north of Conway owned by Addie Burroughs, widow of Franklin G. Burroughs, and in 1898 secured a three-year option to sell land for the Homewood Colony. The site was in the area called Grantsville.

Farm, Field and Fireside announced the new colony and invited settlers to apply. Adventurous land seekers took an excursion in April 1898 which left by train from Chicago and came to Horry County via Indianapolis, Cincinnati, and Richmond. Round trip from Chicago cost twenty-five dollars, sleeping cars five dollars extra. After a day's rest stop in Wilmington, the first party reached Conway on the fourth evening. One traveler wrote, "To one coming from a region where there is no climate, but only 'weather,' it was a joy just to breathe the delicious air of the pines and the ocean mingled."

The April 30 issue of *Farm, Field and Fireside* claimed that 3,087 acres had been spoken for and 1,500–2,000 more acres were expected to go. The first settler was John Dolphin of Sheridan County, Nebraska, who bought 39.6 acres for $237.67 on April 25, 1898. He set to work to build a house the same day. Others came from Ohio, Iowa, Idaho, Wisconsin, Michigan, Illinois, Pennsylvania, Colorado, Massachusetts, South Dakota, Kansas, and Oregon. One wrote back that "many people seemed to think we were a lot of volunteers on our way south to fight the Spaniards in Cuba. Some of our party have seen the smoke of battle and one at least saw the inside of several Confederate prisons, including Andersonville."

In August 1898, *Farm, Field and Fireside* quoted a local paper enthusiastic about the colonists: "Our western and northwestern visitors ... have been favorably impressed with Horry's soil, climate and people, and with some few exceptions, all have bought land and will come among us to live. ...We have no doubt but that the new ideas they bring and the energy they possess will be very helpful and profitable to our people."

Excursions ran in May, June, July, August, and September. A year later settlers were still arriving. Some bought land individually, but most joined the Homewood Farm Association, a cooperative venture managed by L. L. Seiler. Under the plan a farmer bought as much land as he chose and received stock in the association based on the amount of land owned. Members could also cultivate land for nonresidents on a profit-sharing plan. The farmers joined forces to clear land and plant crops on a large scale, using modern farming and marketing methods. The cooperative aspect of the Homewood Colony did not last long. The association dissolved itself in 1900. Some colonists left, but many became a permanent part of the Horry County population.

As the nineteenth century ended, a number of profound changes were taking place in Horry County. The longleaf pine forests had been so depleted they could no longer support the naval stores industry, which moved on to Georgia and other states along the Gulf of Mexico. Many families followed it. Although the timber industry continued to employ many men, prime stands of pine and cypress were gone.

Agricultural change, influenced in part by the farming know-how of the colonists and in part by the introduction of commercial cultivation of tobacco, altered the way farmers thought about themselves. Where previously they lived on their farms, grew some livestock, a little cotton, some corn, and their vegetable plots, and worked in the timber or naval stores woods, they now saw their small holdings as the means to acquiring money. As one commentator writing in the *Southern Workman* (October 1905) said, "For the first time they are learning how to farm . . . crops which sell for a big profit." One new crop was tobacco.

LONELY WOMAN: CHARLOTTE BRONTË

Young people in the Epworth League at Conway Methodist Church decided to organize some sort of library for themselves and others. They had no funds, but their minister, the Rev. Albert Betts, was hopeful that northern charities might come to the rescue. He knew about Pratt Institute in New York, which had one of the earliest library schools in the United States. Pratt and other Yankee benevolent groups would send discarded books to organizations in the South that acted as libraries or book distribution centers.

A shipment of books arrived in three barrels sometime in 1911. Some were in poor condition; some were considered not to be of interest to local readers. Young people gathered once a week to cull the useful from the useless and arrange the books for readers. The life and works of Robert Burns was put aside as of no interest. Another, literally falling to pieces and considered inappropriate for Conway youth, was *Confessions of an English Opium Eater*, the lurid best seller by Thomas de Quincey.

Lucille Burroughs (later Mrs. S. G. Godfrey), one of the group, took both of these discarded books home since neither was deemed useful for circulation. Later she discovered hidden in the volume of Burns's poetry a letter written by Charlotte Brontë, author of *Jane Eyre*, sixty years before. Aware of the treasure she had in her hands, she secured it between sheets of glass to preserve the fragile paper.

Dated August 25, 1851, at Haworth, the letter is addressed to Ellen Nussey, a friend of Charlotte's school days. Only Charlotte and her father, the Rev. Patrick Brontë, were left of their family. Mrs. Brontë died in 1821. Maria and Elizabeth died of tuberculosis in 1825. Branwell, the much loved and indulged brother, who was a painter, succumbed to opium and drink in 1848. Emily, author of *Wuthering Heights,* caught cold at his funeral and died of tuberculosis in December 1848. Anne, author of *Agnes Grey,* died of tuberculosis in 1849. As Charlotte wrote to Ellen Nussey, Patrick Brontë was recovering from an illness and Charlotte herself was recovering from a severe cold. Ellen had evidently expressed concern about not hearing from her friend. The explanation is poignant.

"I am silent," the thirty-five year old Charlotte wrote, "because I have literally nothing to say. I might indeed repeat over and over again that my life is a pale blank and often a weary burden—and that the future sometimes appalls me—but what end would be answered by such repetition except to weary you and enervate myself? The evils that now and then wring a groan from my heart lie in [illegible word] not that I am a single woman and likely to remain a single woman—but because I am a lonely woman and likely to be lonely. But it cannot be helped and therefore imperatively must be borne—and borne with as few words about it as may be."

Charlotte's spinsterhood was not for lack of suitors. She is known to have had at least four suitors, one of them Ellen Nussey's brother Henry, a clergyman. She had placed devotion to her family before her own happiness. In June 1854, nearly three years later, she did marry her father's former curate, Arthur Bell Nichols. By all accounts this was a happy marriage. She looked forward to children despite her age, but in 1854 Charlotte Brontë fell ill with the disease which had plagued the family, tuberculosis. This, coupled with the stress of pregnancy, caused her death March 31, 1855.

Of all this talented family Charlotte received the most recognition in her own lifetime. Both movies and television have adapted *Jane Eyre*, her most famous novel, and new generations of readers discover with pleasure its poignant story. The discovery of her letter was the most exciting fruit of an early attempt to provide a library in Conway. Although several groups attempted to establish reading collections, the first that was really successful was a private circulating library run by the ladies of the town. It opened in 1938 upstairs in the city hall. A decade later, this collection became the foundation of the Horry County Memorial Library, a county funded public library, which opened its main library on July 1, 1949.

AND YOU THOUGHT IT WAS A NATURAL PART OF THE LANDSCAPE!

It's hard to remember that the Intracoastal Waterway, so much a part of our lives and local geography, appeared on maps little more than sixty years ago. The section through Horry County was the last in its entire length to be constructed. The gala national opening was held at Socastee on April 11, 1936.

George Washington dreamed of an intracoastal waterway. The great canal building era in this country resulted in the Erie and other westward-looking canals that connected major waterways and provided safe passage for barges that transported goods and people. The maturing of the railroad system eroded their importance, so that the Intracoastal Waterway was almost an anachronism as a commercial enterprise when it was completed. During World War II it had strategic importance for defense by providing passage safely away from enemy ships and submarines. Pulpwood barges, local shrimp and fishing boats, and pleasure boats of various sizes and elegance now make up the chief traffic on Horry County's stretch. The luxurious "snow birds" going south in the fall and north in the spring provide a show.

In the nineteenth century local citizens gave thought to a short canal from the Waccamaw to Little River, a distance of some five to seven miles. It seemed logical to construct a water passage for barges, rafts, and small sailing craft that transported timber and turpentine. The topography unfortunately made this unfeasible, but most people didn't realize that. They thought this route would be selected when plans for the waterway began to take shape in earnest about 1930. It would restore Conway to its former status as a riverport in the days of the steamboats and provide new revenue to the county seat. Imagine their chagrin when the U.S. Corps of Engineers decided to make a straight cut through some of the highest land in the county from Little River to Socastee Creek, the longest man-made ditch in the entire length of the Intracoastal Waterway.

Our section begins at the north in Little River, along which it runs for 5 nautical miles. It then follows the Pine Island Cut for about 24 miles before it intersects Socastee Creek. The cut altered the natural drainage patterns along its route, leaving some land dry which had been swamp and bay. The cut, 90 feet wide and 8 feet deep, lays bare our geological history, creating a fossil hunter's paradise. Here can be found the fossil remains of ancient land and sea animals that have in different ages inhabited this area.

Leaving Pine Island Cut, the waterway follows Socastee Creek until it joins the Waccamaw River near Enterprise Landing. The Waccamaw swamps provide the black water characteristic of this section of the waterway. Tannin in tree roots and in other vegetation colors it. Hydrologists say that water from the Waccamaw flows back along the waterway to Little River, taking six days to reach Little River Inlet!

From Enterprise to Winyah Bay is 22 nautical miles. A book about the waterway, written by Allan Fisher for the National Geographic Society in 1973, says, "Since the time of the Indians, boatmen have been groping for superlatives to describe the Waccamaw. Many believe it to be the loveliest part of the southern Waterway." Before the waterway was dug, trails wandered from the interior toward the ocean in many places. There are now only three places where automobile traffic can cross the waterway. At Highways 9, 501, and 544, high-rise bridges allow boat traffic without interrupting the flow of automobile traffic.

Along the route the Corps of Engineers has reserved spoilage sites where it dumps mud, sand, and other debris that it continues to dredge from the canal to keep it open for navigation. No permanent structures can be built on these easements as long as the corps controls them. Recently the corps has begun to negotiate with Horry County to release some sites for development.

Several guides are available for private boaters who wish to cruise the ICW. Local tour cruises leave marinas in North Myrtle Beach, Socastee, and Georgetown, but at the present time no local tours cover the entire length in Horry County. Cruise ships that travel the waterway take on passengers at strategic points such as Norfolk, Savannah, and Miami.

WHAT A SWELL BIRTHDAY PARTY!

It was South Carolina's three hundredth birthday party. You had to be here in 1970 to feel the excitement, the exuberance. A Tricentennial Commission had been formed to plan a statewide celebration. Laura Quattlebaum, Conway High School history teacher and daughter of former state senator Paul Quattlebaum, was named the commissioner from this area to plan for the state and to help organize the celebration in Horry County. Each county had its special time during the yearlong observance, and for Horry it was the week of August 9, 1970.

A professional firm, the Rogers Company of Fostoria, Ohio, was hired early in the year to organize and promote an extravaganza for Horry County. On the advice of the Rogers representative, a local committee incorporated as a not-for-profit group to handle the business details of the celebration.

The company sent a fill-in-the-blanks script, which was given to Catherine Lewis and Florence Epps. They submitted episodes and characters in the history of Horry which had dramatic possibilities and sent the company's writers the information necessary to create the framework for a musical. A dynamic man, James La Rue, dispatched to be their man on the ground, hit the county like a whirlwind. One participant said, "His meteoric appearance in Conway created a theatrical commotion...." Men signed up to grow beards and were known as Brothers of the Brush. Ladies became Celebration Belles, Kingston Belles, Gay Gibson Belles, etc.

Although LaRue's primary responsibility was the production of a theatrical pageant, he spread excitement in all directions in advance of the main event. Every Friday afternoon for several weeks before the focus week, there was a promenade of people in costumes in the towns of the county. Participants could buy a costume, pull an heirloom out of an old trunk, or make one for the occasion. They could hark back to any historic era, so there were flappers, Gibson girls, and pioneer women, as well as the hoopskirted belles.

A Kangaroo Kourt tried those who failed to appear in proper costume or who were hauled before it for pie throwing, bottom branding, and barrel dunking, all prearranged. Souvenirs were created and sold to help with the expenses incurred. There was a bronze medal, a special commemorative plate, and *The Independent Republic of Horry*, selections from the *Independent Republic Quarterly*, published by the Horry County Historical Society and distributed as a program at the outdoor drama.

The week opened with an exhibit of Jimmy Burroughs's paintings sponsored by the Fine Arts Club on Sunday afternoon, August 9, in Conway and an address by C. B. Berry at Little River. That night the religious leaders of the county, black and white, led rain-soaked worshippers in an outdoor service at the Coastal Carolina stadium. Chairmen of this event were the Rev. S. George Lovell and the Rev. Rufus J. Daniels.

August 10, Pioneer Day, had special events for senior citizens. Leo Knauff of the Horry Electric Cooperative coordinated the events with the help of Mrs. Hester Medlen and Mrs. Hal Holmes. They were assisted by the Kingston Belles, the Light Belles, and the School Belles. The flirtiest girl, the greatest sport, and other superlatives, including oldest citizen, were chosen. In Myrtle Beach there was an Old South Rice Planters' Ball for which the Tommy Dorsey Orchestra played on the night of August 11. In Conway that day there was a kiddie parade on Lakeside Drive. Children dressed in costumes of the past or suggested by their favorite books.

The centerpiece of the whole celebration was the outdoor drama, *Horry County—Our Independent Republic*. It was rained out on opening night, August 12, but played to packed houses at Coastal Carolina stadium the rest of the week. Many attended more than one performance. The drama was played on six stages, including two towers, all of which had to be fashioned during the five weeks of rehearsal. It had been a casting and property nightmare, requiring 350 people, oxen and horses to pull wagons, and a goat to be milked, as well as all the necessary props, including a train!

Thursday afternoon, August 13, there was a garden party at Snow Hill on Kingston Lake which featured a fashion show of old clothes owned by local people: uniforms, an 1870s dress, wedding dresses from various eras, school dresses, a graduation dress, and bathing attire and clothes from the 1920s.

A grand parade on Saturday afternoon, August 15, preceded the final performance of the drama that night. After the lights were dimmed the last time, a little girl wrote, "I wish it had never ended." LaRue and the people of Horry had pulled it off, in spite of the odds and the rain, in the heat of summer and at the height of the tourist season.

DEATH OF THE JERRY

In 1992, Conway witnessed the last days of an institution and a tradition. The Jerry Cox Company on Main Street closed. The old Burroughs and Collins flagship store offered everything—even its fixtures—at discount prices. For nearly a century "The Jerry" had offered its customers a wide range of quality merchandise and unmatched service. We won't see its like again.

Burroughs and Collins owned the store for most of its existence. The firm maintained its corporate headquarters next door, but there really was a Jerry Cox. He hailed from the Red Bluff area and with Alfred Burroughs Lundy owned the Cox-Lundy firm, which originally occupied the premises at 316 Main Street. Jerry Cox remained in charge until his death in 1931. The name of the store was changed to the Jerry Cox Company about 1924.

Until the construction of the Founders Center behind Myrtle Square in Myrtle Beach, a small suite of offices adjacent to the Jerry Cox Company was the nerve center of a diverse economic giant. Clerks, managers, and owners were equally accessible to the public at the counter of the front office. The walls were lined with pictures of the old firm's owners, stores, and staff.

Walter Cox, a nephew of Jerry Cox, recalled that at age 15 (1919) he went to work in the store and never left it. His early duties were mostly janitorial, but he was allowed to do delivery work and then to become a clerk, and finally to rise to vice president. Walter Cox recalled that in his early days the store opened at 6:30 A.M. And stayed open until 8:00 P.M. weekdays and 11:30 P.M. on Saturday. These were typical hours for stores in the town and country alike.

A good many years ago "The Jerry" had wrapping paper imprinted with verse which described its wares. The list of merchandise could apply to country stores all over Horry County. The "pome" is anonymous.

> Clothing for the naked,
> Glasses for the blind;
> Shoes for the barefooted,

Horry County, South Carolina, 1730 – 1993

Gloves that are lined.
Curtains for the windows,
Shoestrings and Laces;
Lamps, Wicks and Oil
To light the dark places.
Dried Fruits, Canned Goods,
Everything to eat;
Caps for the head
And Socks for the feet.
Calico of the finest,
That never fades;
Woolen Goods for Dresses,
Ribbons for old maids.
Tobacco for menfolk;
Hats for the ladies;
Toys for the children;
Bottles for the babies.
Queensware, Glassware,
Pitchers and Bowls;
Leather for harness
And Leather for soles.
Straps and Strings,
Buckles and Screens;
The finest of silks,
And the coarsest of Jeans.
Potatoes and Apples,
Lard and Meat;
Butter from the country,
Fresh and sweet.
Tea and Coffee,
Sugar and Rice,
Beans and Crackers,
Cheese and Spice.
Oysters and Salmon,
Flour and Meal;
Mouse Traps—and Cats
To make the mice squeal.
Powder for faces,
Powder for hunters;

You Would Not Expect It in Horry!

Axes for Choppers,
And Remedies for grunters,
Chewing Gum, Candy,
Corset and Bustle;
The people come trading,
And how we do hustle.
Medicine to make you sick,
Medicine to make you well;
In fact, we have everything
That the best stores sell.

Acknowledgments

"Whatever Happened to Hugerborough?" appeared in *IRQ* 19:4 (Fall 1965): 27-35, where it included the names of the signers of the petitions, a valuable list of the heads of households in 1801.

"Horry County Courthouses" combines *Sun News* columns which appeared May 12, 1990; October 6, 1990; January 5, 1991; and January 4, 1992.

"That Damned Independent Republic: A Nickname is Conferred." Some of this material appeared in the *Sun News*, April 13, 1991.

"Natural History." I wish to thank Laura Blind for checking the accuracy of this. We have traditionally been rural and agricultural people. Observation and appreciation of the natural world is ingrained in us.

"Horry County Historical Society." A shorter version appeared in the *Sun News,* November 21, 1992.

"Little River: First Village" was prepared for the First Atlantic Bank shortly after it was founded. The full version appeared in *IRQ* 24:4 (Fall 1990): 6-17. C. B. Berry has contributed many articles on this area to *IRQ*. I am indebted to him for much of this information.

"Conway: Riverport and Seat of Government" originally appeared in "Discover Conway," published by the chamber of commerce in 1987.

"Conway: Around City Hall." This information was compiled originally at the request of then city administrator William Graham. It appeared in the *Sun News* January 5, 1991.

"Loris: The Gateway City." When Loris celebrated the centennial of its establishment beside the railroad in 1887, I served on the celebration committee and wrote a short history of the town for a centennial publication. This is abridged from the book. The Horry County Historical Society distributed the book as the Winter 1988 issue of *IRQ* (22:1), and it is bound with sets of *IRQ* in the public libraries of the county. It provided background for a *Sun News* column, March 23, 1991.

"Loris: It Takes a Whole Village to Raise a Child" originated as a series of personal memories which I read for a radio audience during the observance of the town's centennial.

"Aynor: The Little Golden Town." This short essay appeared in the *Sun News*, September 15, 1990. Carlisle Dawsey and others have written about the history of Aynor. See particularly Dawsey's "The Aynor Mystery," *IRQ* 23:2 (Spring 1989): 5-6; *IRQ* 13:3 (Summer 1979), special issue on Aynor; and other articles and interviews.

"Myrtle Beach: New Town." There are so many articles about Myrtle Beach to be found in the files of *IRQ* that it is necessary only to consult the indexes which have been compiled for it. In addition the memoirs of Lucile Burroughs Godfrey, which were printed in the Winter 1980 issue (15:1), are rich with material about the early years of the town and the contributions of the Burroughs family, the Myrtle Beach Farms, and the firm of Burroughs and Collins, predecessor of Burroughs and Chapin.

"Briarcliffe Acres: A Private Town." See Dorothy Fillius Green, *Prolongation of a Vision: A History of Briarcliffe Acres, South Carolina* (privately printed, 1988), a thoroughly researched history from its inception to 1988.

"Surfside Beach: Out of the Ark." *IRQ* 24:2 (Spring 1982) contains several articles which grew out of the Historical Society's spring tour that year: "Memories of the Beach—Before Development," by Mary Emily Platt Jackson; "The Ark Plantation," by Greg Martin; and "How I Remember It," by Louise Chestnut Squires. In addition, I had the benefit of participating with Mrs. Jackson and Lacy Hucks in an interview with James Calhoun at his home shortly before his death. Mrs. Jackson transcribed the interview and owns the audiotape. I also interviewed Archie Benton, longtime member of the city council of Surfside Beach, in May 1993. The videotape and a transcript of the interview are available at Coastal Carolina University.

"Atlantic Beach: Black Pearl." Information came from the land records of the Horry County Register of Mesne Conveyance and contemporary newspaper accounts of events in the town. See also "The Black Pearl," by Eleanora E. Tate, *Myrtle Beach Magazine* 2:4 (Winter 1986): 22-27.

Acknowledgments

"North Myrtle Beach: One out of Four." Much of this information comes from research for a paper on Little River and the northern beaches prepared for Anchor Bank. Consult *IRQ* indexes for the many articles on these beaches. Those by C. B. Berry, surveyor, former mayor of Crescent Beach and renowned local historian, are particularly helpful. Contemporary newspaper files are also necessary.

"Peter Horry: 'No Man More Eagerly Sought the Foe'" appeared in *the Sun News*, December 11, 1993. Horry is included in *Biographical Directory of the South Carolina Senate*. See also his own journal, edited by A. S. Salley (*South Carolina Historical and Genealogical Magazine* 38:2 (April 1937): 49-53.

"Robert Conway." This paper, first presented February 2, 1989, was commissioned by Conway Hospital as one of three public lectures presented in celebration of its sixtieth anniversary. There is a biographical sketch of Conway in *Biographical Directory of the South Carolina House of Representatives*, vol. 4, 1791-1815 (Columbia: University of South Carolina Press, 1984). See also *The Beatys of Kingston* by Edward Stanley Barnhill (n.p., 1958) and "Robert Conway and Some of His Descendants" by C. B. Berry in *IRQ* 1:4 (October, 1967): 12-16.

"George Washington Slept Here" was originally a paper for a luncheon meeting of the DAR and SAR at Dunes Club, Myrtle Beach, on Washington's birthday, February 22, 1992. The primary source is *Washington's Southern Tour, 1791*, ed. Archibald Henderson (Boston: Houghton Mifflin, 1923).

"Where All the Women Are Strong." Most of this information is taken from the files of *IRQ* and from a paper prepared by Ernest Harper Jr. And others for an Horry County Museum exhibit of dolls representing important women of Conway's past (*IRQ* 20:4 [Fall, 1986]: 4-19).

"Henry Buck from Bucksport, Maine." This essay was a column in the *Sun News,* March 24, 1992. Many people have written about the contribution of Henry Buck to Horry. I acknowledge with particular appreciation the work of Eugenia Buck Cutts and Dr. Charles W. Joyner.

"Lorenzo Dow: Eccentric Missionary" appeared in the *Sun News*, December 19, 1992. Dr. J. A. Norton found the encounter of Horry County people with this controversial cleric fascinating and recorded it in his manuscript history of the county. The facts of Dow's life appear in standard works, including the *Dictionary of American Biography*.

"Thomas Daggett Sank the Yankee Admiral" originally appeared in the *Sun News*, June 26, 1993. Much of this information is based on an obituary found in the papers of Dr. J. A. Norton. It gave no source, but is probably from a Georgetown newspaper. The essential data is found in the *Biographical Directory of the South Carolina Senate*.

"The Irish Derhams of Green Sea." Some of this information appeared in the *Sun News*, October 3, 1992, and in *IRQ* 26:4 (Fall, 1992): 5-7. The latter article contains a photograph of John P. Derham and of his home. Other material was furnished by Col. John S. Mace, of Salem, Oregon. He corrected some information in the former articles and provided copies of his accounts of his grandfather and great-grandfather. See also *Biographical Directory of the South Carolina Senate*.

"Robert Bethea Scarborough, Lawyer-Statesman." The biographical information comes from the *Biographical Directory of the South Carolina Senate* and from obituaries which appeared in local papers at his death. His own speeches at the death of his first law partner, Judge Joseph T. Walsh, are also helpful. They are found in *IRQ* 12:4 (February, 1978): 8-12.

"Mary Beaty: A Northern Lady with Some Peculiarities." Many stories about Mrs. Beaty have been handed down in Conway's oral tradition, but much about her has also appeared in the *IRQ*. Consult the indexes. Laura Quattlebaum Jordan of Conway owns a scrapbook in which Mary and Thomas Beaty gathered the obituaries that appeared in the South Carolina press on the deaths of their last three children in 1870-1871.

"D. Allen Spivey: Conway's Banker Colonel." Biographical information appears in the *Biographical Directory of the South Carolina Senate*. The manuscript autobiography of his brother, John C. Spivey, is in the collection of the Horry County Memorial Library. See also contemporary newspapers.

Acknowledgments

"Virginia Durant Young: Early Feminist Shook Conway" appeared in the *Sun News* on June 22, 1991. For a biographical sketch of Mrs. Young by Foy Stevenson, see *Sandlapper* (February 1974): 36–42. See H. E. McCaskill, "The Durant Land Case," *IRQ* 4:1 (January 1970): 11–14, for an account of this complicated case. Consult *Horry District Commissioner of Location Plat Book B,* p. 124, and other land records in the offices of the Horry County Register of Mesne Conveyance.

"Jesse P. Williams and Cora Williams: The Railroading Man and His Lady" appeared in the *Sun News,* November 2, 1991. See also *Horry Herald*, April 30, 1914, and August 14, 1913 (obituary); *Memoirs of Georgia*, vol. 2 (Atlanta, Ga.: Southern Historical Association, 1895), p. 417; and *Cyclopedia of Georgia*, vol. 3, by Allen and Clement A. Evans (Atlanta, State Historical Association, 1906), pp. 593–98. Mrs. Williams was the daughter of Capt. W. H. P. Taylor. The *Horry Herald* (April 30, 1914) says he lived in Cades, Williamsburg County, and that she was born there, but in J. P. Williams's obituary (*Horry Herald*, August 14, 1913) it was stated that she was born and raised on Tampico Plantation in Dog Bluff about ten miles from Conway.

"Captain Causey and Miss Julia" appeared in the *Sun News* January 15, 1994. I heard the story the first time when Dickie Reesor and Ernestine Little (both, alas, now buried at Lakeside), and I cataloged that cemetery for the *Independent Republic Quarterly* about 1975.

"H. Kemper Cooke: Backwoods Statesman" appeared in the *Sun News,* April 25, 1992. Information came from interviews with his acquaintances, the *Biographical Directory of the South Carolina Senate*, contemporary newspapers, and the *Journal of the South Carolina Senate* for the period of his tenure.

"World War II Tragedy: The Norton Twins" appeared in the *Sun News,* January 26, 1991. Aside from contemporary newspaper accounts, I had access to a compilation of information about these young men owned by Capt. Henry Lee Buck of Upper Mill.

"Florence Theodora Epps: 'I Live in a World of My Own.'" My earlier pieces about Miss Epps appeared in *Sandlapper* (November 1969): 63–67 and *Alternatives* 4:2 (February 10–24, 1989): 3. She herself made the information for the *Sandlapper* article available. Personal acquaintance and her friends provided the main substance of this profile.

Acknowledgments

"Andrew Washington Stackhouse: Useful Man" appeared in the *Sun News,* May 4, 1996. There is a picture of the Reverend Stackhouse in his coffin printed in the *Independent Republic Quarterly* (9:4 [October 1975]: 19). Mr. Henry Sumpter, an artist and a grandnephew of Mr. Stackhouse, says that he helped design the coffin. He also says that Mr. Stackhouse was a victim of narcolepsy, which probably explains why he did not hold a pastorate.

"Education in Horry County before World War II" is abridged from a lecture given for Conway High School Foundation, January 18, 1994. It was published serially in the *Sun News,* March 5, March 16, April 23, May 21, and June 4, 1994.

Dr. Evan Norton's important pamphlet, *History of Conway's Schools from Conwayboro Academy to Burroughs Graded School from 1856 to 1910* (Field Job Print., n.d.) is reprinted in *IRQ* 7:2/3 (April/July, 1973) : 5-23. See also *Horry County Schools, a Survey Report*, prepared by George Peabody College for Teachers, Division of Surveys and Field Services (Nashville, 1946). *IRQ* 7:2/3 (April/July 1973) is a special issue devoted to the subject of education.

"Yankee Philanthropy Aided Black Schools in Horry" appeared in the *Sun News,* August 22, 1992. See standard American biographical reference works, the *Encyclopedia of the Social Sciences,* and publications of the organizations themselves for the information about the charities. See also the annual reports of the South Carolina superintendent of education.

"Pee Dee Baptist Academy" appeared in the *Sun News,* June 23, 1990. I interviewed Douglas B. Bailey and Gary Mincey, who attended the academy. See also W. C. Allen, "Pee Dee Academy" in *Encyclopedia of Southern Baptists*, vol. 2 (Nashville: Broadman Press, 1958), p. 1,082, and the minutes of Waccamaw Baptist Association, 1921, as well as contemporary newspapers. A one-page mimeographed history, probably written by P. L. Elvington, is accompanied by a list of people who attended the academy. It was distributed at a reunion, probably in 1952. See *Horry Herald* (June 26, 1952) for an account of this meeting. E. M. Meares purchased the academy property, which is still in the hands of his nephew, J. Monroe Meares.

"Libraries for the Entire People. " My short history of Horry County Memorial Library was included without attribution in a statewide history of public library service compiled by the late state librarian, Miss Estellene

Acknowledgments

P. Walker, *"So Good and Necessary a Work": The Public Library in South Carolina, 1698-1980* (Columbia: South Carolina State Library, 1981), p. 32. My short column on the parallel development of the Horry County Memorial Library and the Chapin Memorial Library appeared in the *Sun News*, February 8, 1992.

"The Birth of a University: The Founding of Coastal Carolina" appeared in the *Sun News,* November 10, 1990.

"The Swamp that Teaches: Playcard Environmental Education Center" draws from the mission statement and history of the center which I wrote during my tenure as chairman of the Playcard board.

"Medical Care before Modern Hospitals." This paper was commissioned by the Conway Hospital Foundation and published under the title of *From Potions to Prescriptions: The History of Medical Care in Horry County, 1802-1936* for the foundation members. Portions were published in columns in the *Sun News*, October 2, 1993, and November 6, 1993. Major resource material was found in the newspapers and in the files of *IRQ*.

"Let There Be Light" appeared in the *Sun News,* January 1, 1994. Hal King's brief account of the founding of the cooperative is in *IRQ* 14:4 (Fall 1980): 44-46.

"Civil War Refugees in Conwayborough" appeared in the *Sun News,* December 14, 1991. A long article about the Weston family, written by Susan Lowndes Allston, appeared in the *Charleston News and Courier*, November 6, 1938. In addition the pertinent sections of books by the Reverend Malet and Miss Collins appeared in the *Independent Republic Quarterly*.

"Company B, Siege Train, CSA." has appeared in versions of different length in the *Sun News* (May 16, 1992), and the *IRQ*, 26:2 (Spring 1992): 13-15. The version in the *IRQ* contains a list of the men who served in this outfit. Major Manigault's journal, edited and annotated by Warren Ripley, was published by the University of South Carolina Press, 1986. It supplied biographical information about this officer and mentions some of the members of this outfit who were from Horry County. General Manigault's journals were published as *A Carolinian Goes to War* (Columbia: University of South Carolina Press, 1983).

Acknowledgments

The land on which Heniford cemetery was located passed out of the family and the burying ground was destroyed about a year after several cousins and I made a catalog of the tombstones that remained in 1975, knowing that there had been other burials whose markers were long gone. A few salvaged stones were placed in the cemetery at Live Oak Baptist Church; Alford's stone is at Princeville Cemetery west of Loris. Others are represented by cenotaphs at Princeville.

"The Two Great Battles of Conwayborough" appeared in the *Sun News,* July 31, 1993. Dr. Norton ("Independent Republic of Horry County," manuscript owned by Horry County Memorial Library) gives accounts of both events. Judge Joseph T. Walsh recalled in his "Autobiography" (*IRQ* 12:4 [Fall, 1978] : 4-8) that Confederate deserters attacked the town. Dr. Jamie Norton wrote that rumors had been heard that Yankee forces were coming to occupy Conwayborough. See also *Memoirs* of Ellen Cooper Johnson, *IRQ* 15:2 (Spring, 1981): 12+ for an account of raids by deserters at Cool Springs.

"Horry Blacks Help Write 1868 Constitution" appeared in the *Sun News,* July 27, 1991. I was lucky to find the letter from the Conwayborough correspondent to the *Marion Star.* It is rare to have information about black citizens of this period. His account jibes with what we know from other, mostly oral, sources.

"The 1876 Campaign Solution" appeared in the *Sun News,* August 27, 1994. The Hampton oak stands at the entrance of the Horry County Museum, Main Street and Fifth Avenue. Two versions of this story, by Laura J. Quattlebaum and M. A. Wright, are printed in *IRQ* 3:4 (October, 1969): 8-11. They vary in some details. It is also mentioned in W. W. Sellers, *A History of Marion County from Its Earliest Times to the Present* (Columbia: R. L. Bryan, 1902), p. 102. This third version varies somewhat from both Quattlebaum and Wright.

"A Man and His Word." An eyewitness account of the hanging of Young Abe Rabon may be found in the *Memoirs* of Ellen Cooper Johnson (*IRQ* 15:2 [Spring, 1981] : 12+). Other information comes from court records, coroner's reports, and the 1850 census. See also "Capital Punishment," by Walt Espy (*IRQ* 18:2 [Spring, 1984]: 8.

Acknowledgments

"Muddy Footprints" appeared in the *Sun News,* May 22, 1993. It is based on contemporary newspaper accounts and on court records.

"The Trials of Edmund Bigham." The trials were covered extensively in the newspapers of the time and have been the subject of numerous articles and even a TV program or two. It appeared in the *Sun News,* December 1, 1990.

"The *Henrietta*" appeared in the *Sun News,* August 11, 1990. Master ships mechanics and shipwrights from Maine built "tall ships" on the ways alongside a deep pool of the Waccamaw River. Sailing ships appeared in Horry ports until the beginning of the twentieth century. A number of articles about the Buck family and its enterprises have appeared in *IRQ.* Consult *IRQ* indexes particularly for those by Eugenia Buck Cutts.

"Colonists Came out of the West." This fascinating episode was the subject of a long article I wrote for *IRQ* 14:4 (1980) : 17 ff. It is based on files of the *Farm, Field and Fireside* and of the *Horry Herald* of the period and on land records. It appeared as a column in the *Sun News,* July 6, 1991.

"Lonely Woman: Charlotte Bronte." See Lucille B. Godfrey and Catherine H. Lewis, "Letter from Charlotte," *IRQ* 3:3 (July 1969): 4-5. The Reverend Betts served Conway Methodist Church from 1910-1914.

"And You Thought It Was a Natural Part of the Landscape!" originally appeared in the *Sun News,* March 17, 1990. For further information, see Allen Fisher, *The Inland Waterway* (Washington, D.C.: National Geographic Society, 1973), and Claiborne S. Young, *Cruising Guide to Coastal South Carolina* (Winston-Salem, N.C.: J. F. Blair, 1985).

"What a Swell Birthday Party!" appeared as a *Sun News* column, July 2, 1994.

"Death of the Jerry" appeared in the *Sun News,* February 27, 1993. For additional background, see *IRQ* 2:2 (April, 1968): 20-24, and for a reproduction of the poem as it originally appeared, see *IRQ* 3:1 (January, 1969): 14.

Index

Abrahams, Bill, 108
Afro-Fest (Coastal Carolina University), 18
Agnes Grey (Anne Brontë), 190
agriculture, 56, 189-90
airplanes and airports, 78, 134-35
Alabama, 42, 114
Alcohol and Tobacco Tax Unit, 69
Alford, Warren T., 172
Allen (Allentown), 168
All Saints Parish, 7, 37, 46, 95, 141; church cemetery, 171
Allsbrook, 165, 182
Allsbrook, J. R., Store, 183
Allston, Josias, 37
Allston, William (husband of Rebecca), 102
Allston, William, 37, 38, 74, 86
Allston family, 86
Alston, Charles, Jr., 143, 144
Alston, John, 86
Alston, Joseph, 38
Alston, William, 103, 106
Altman, Eugene, 13
Altman, Katherine O., 166
Ambrose, H. W., 166
American Association for State and Local History, 137
American College of Surgeons, 167
American Military Biography, 92
American Revolution, 4, 5, 6, 7, 8, 10, 21, 30, 38, 86, 92, 102, 104, 128
Among the Pines, (Kirke), 111-12
Andersen, Marsden G., 132
Anderson, Gene, 30
Anderson, J. D., 152
Anderson, Samuel, 143

Anderson, S. N., 144
Anderson, Thurman, 149, 157
Anderson, W. J., 152
Anderson family, 74
Andersonville Prison, 189
An Errand to the South in the Summer of 1862 (Malet), 171
Ansel, M. F., 26
Applewhite Lane, Conway, 171
Arcadia, Fla., 134
Ark (Arke) Plantation and house, 81, 82
Asbury, Bishop Francis, 7, 20, 46, 94, 114
Ash (community), N. C., 37
Ashe's (at Little River), 3, 4, 37, 85
Ashley River, 18
Atlanta, Ga., 52
Atlantic (steamboat), 43
Atlantic Beach ("Black Pearl"), 84-85, 88
Atlantic Beach Company, 84
Atlantic Coast Line Railroad, 51
Augusta, Ga., 103
Avant, William, 184
Avery, Judge, 70
Ayllon, Lucas Vasquez de, 1
Aynor, Mrs., 73
Aynor, S. C., 11, 12, 72-74, 163
Aynor Branch Library, 156
Aynor Elementary School, 151
Aynor High School, 148
Aynor Hoe-down, 18
Aynor tract of land, 73

Bailey family (descendants of Robert Conway), 99
Baldwin, J. O., 88

Index

Bank of Conway, 125, 128
Bank of Little River, S. C., 43
Bank of Loris, 53
banking, 43, 125, 123
Barnett, John, 38
Barnhill, Tom, 173
Barnwell County, 132; "Barnwell ring", 133
barrier islands, 29
barter, 13, 28, 47
Battery Point. *See* Tilghman Point
Battery White, 116
Baxter, John, 94, 96
Baxter, Mary, 94
Bayboro community, 52, 182
Bayboro Township, 50
Bear Bluff, 3, 5
Beaty, Bethel D., 143
Beaty, Clara, 123-24
Beaty, Edgar, 173
Beaty, Elizabeth Mary Prince (Mrs. John III), 99, 105
Beaty, Frederica, 123
Beaty, Henry Brookman, 123-24
Beaty, Isabel ("Miss Izzie"), 175
Beaty, James, 127
Beaty, James ("King of Horry"), 28, 144
Beaty, John, 99, 105, 126
Beaty, John, III, 105
Beaty, John Robinson, 143, 173-75
Beaty, Mary Elizabeth Brookman (Mrs. Thomas W.), 122-24, 126
Beaty, May, 123-24
Beaty, Thomas W., 117, 122-24, 143, 144, 175, 177
Beaty and Holliday (naval stores firm), 129
Beaty family, 98, 105, 121-24, 163
Beaufort, S. C., 2
Beholding as in a Glass (Young), 128
Belin, Peter, 74
Bell, Lloyd Berkley, 13, 54, 57

Bell, Mrs. P. D., 72
Bell, Samuel, 127, 173
Bellamy, Addleton, 38
Bellamy, Eva Mae (Mrs. J. Sidney), 61
Bellamy, John, 38
Bellamy, J. Sidney ("Cap'n Sid"), 61
Bellamy, Leland: store, 87
Bellamy, Merlin, 89
Bellamy family, 38
Bellamy's Landing, 87
Belle Isle Plantation, 91, 115
Bell Tract, 88
Belvedere Plantation, 39, 100
Bennett, Hardy S., 88
Berry, C. B., 34, 40-41, 88, 194
Bertie Precinct, N. C., 86
Bessent, Abraham, 87
Bessent, Carl, 43
Bessent, Tom, 43
Bessent, William, 87
Best, E. Van, 147
Bethea, A. B., 146
Bethea, P. K., 163
Bethel African Methodist Episcopal Church, 151, 176, 177
Betts, Albert, 190
Bigham, Dora, 184-86
Bigham, Edmund, 184-86
Bigham, G. Cleveland, 184
Bigham, L. Smiley, Jr., 184
Bigham, Smiley, Jr., 185
Bines, J. A., 165
Bingham Military School, 118-19
Black Mingo Creek, 6
Black Pearl. *See* Atlantic Beach
blacks, 137-39
Blanchard, Edward D., 188
Blanton, Mrs. James, 34
Blanton, James Paul, 54, 57, 157, 160-61
Blanton, Mrs. Sophie, 154
Blind, Laura, 161

208

Index

Blythe, Joseph, 162
Boling, Katherine, *A Piece of the Fox's Hide*, 186
Bolton, Charles, 123-24
Bolton, Cora Beaty (Mrs. Charles), 123-24
Bonney, Anne, 36
Booth, Tom, 49
Booth, William, 183
Booth, W. M., 183
Boundary House, 5, 39
Boyd, D. O., 51
Boyd, John L., 54
Boyd, Thurman, 64
Bradshaw, A. J., 146
Brantly, Anthony, 40
Brearley, Cecil Dubose, Sr., 157
Briarcliffe Acres, 79-81
Briarcliffe Acres Association, 79, 80
Briarcliffe Mall, 81
Briarcliffe Realty Company, 79
Briarcliffe West, 79
British Isles, 4, 7, 38, 45
Brontë family, 190
Brooker, N. W., 119
Brookgreen Gardens, 40, 101, 102
Brooks Rifle Guards, 163
Brooksville, 61
Brown, Braxton, 124
Brown, Edgar, 132
Brown, Mrs. Russell, 34
Brown, William J., 73
Brown Swamp, 29
Brown Swamp School, 141
Brunswick County, N. C., 102
Bryan, George W. ("Buster"), 82, 157
Bryan, Lucian, 43
Bryan, Nelle, 34
Bryan, W. A. D., 38
Bryan, W. L., 26
Bryant, J. C., 51, 52, 53, 119, 151
Bryant, J. C., Company, 53

Bryant, J. D., 53
Bryant, Jim, 173
Buck, Frances Norton Norman (Mrs. Henry), 107, 110, 111, 122
Buck, Henry (of Maine), 107, 122, 143, 144, 163, 163, 173, 176
Buck, Capt. Henry Lee, 112
Buck, Sen. Henry Lee, 112, 166
Buck, Mrs. H. L., 153
Buck, W. H., 144
Buck, William H., 143
Buck, William L., 112, 116
Buck Cemetery, 112
Buck Creek, 50, 57
Bucksport, Maine, 111, 112, 122
Bucksport, S. C., 111, 163, 169
Bucksville, S. C., 111, 112, 176, 187
Bull, William, II, 2
Bullard, Raymond, 51
Bull Creek, 30, 128, 168, 187
Bullock, Agnes Richardson (Mrs. Montgomery J.), 55
Bullock, Montgomery J., 54, 55, 59
Bullock, Zadoc, 176
Bullock home (in Loris), 167
Burns, Robert, 190
Burroughs, Adeline Cooper (Mrs. Franklin Gorham), 75, 108-10, 131, 188
Burroughs, Ben, 34
Burroughs, Donald M., 76, 165
Burroughs, Edward E., 157
Burroughs, F. G. (steamboat), 135
Burroughs, Frank, 76, 109
Burroughs, Franklin Burroughs (first in Horry), 75, 108-9, 110, 127, 130, 131, 144, 171, 188
Burroughs, Homer Hope, 12, 51, 163, 164, 182, 183
Burroughs, James H. ("Jimmy"), 135, 194
Burroughs, James S., 129, 143, 144

209

Index

Burroughs, Leon, 184
Burroughs, Nina, 164
Burroughs, Ruth, 75
Burroughs, William A., 127
Burroughs and Chapin, 110; Founders Center, 195
Burroughs and Collins Company, 12, 72, 73, 75, 76, 77, 127, 164, 195
Burroughs family, 82, 108-11
Burroughs High School, 148
Burroughs Hospital, 164
Burroughs School, 17, 177; auditorium 169
Bury St. Edmunds, Suffolk, England, 134
Busbee, Carl L., 49
Butler, D. J., 51
Butler, Pierce, 103
Byers, Charles W., 88

Cadiz, 112
Calabash, 45
Caldwell Company, 82
Calhoun, James A., Jr., 82, 120
California, 112, 188
Camden, S. C., 40, 104
Campbell, D. B., 162
Camp Swamp School, 141
canals, 190-92; from Little River to Waccamaw, 42, 44
Cannon, A. F., 53
Cape Fear River, 37, 39, 85; region 1, 2, 50, 51
Carolina bays, 17, 30
Carolina Power and Light, 169
Carter, John Robert, Jr., 13, 54, 57
Carter, John Robert, Sr., 54, 57
Cartrette, John P., 34
Cartrette, Richard K., 88
Cartwheel Swamp, 29
Carwile, S. W., 146
Catawbas, 2, 104
Causey, C. A., 173

Causey, Coleman S., 130-31
Causey, Jehu, 143, 144
Causey, Julia E. Skipper (Mrs. Coleman S.), 130-31
Causey, Margaret W. (Mrs. W. G.), 131
Causey, Needham, 56
Causey, W. G., 131
Cawsway, Jane, 96
Cedar Creek, 38
Cedar Creek Cemetery, 40
Cedar Lane Farm, 113
Central of Georgia Railroad, 129
Chadbourn, James H., 72
Chadbourn, N. C., 188
Chadbourn family, 47, 51
Chadbourn Lumber Company, 50
Chamberlain, Daniel H., 118, 178
Chambers, P. P., 163
Chapel Hill, N. C., 157
Chapin, Simeon B., 76, 110
Chapin Company, 76
Chapin Foundation, 155
Chapin Memorial Library, 155
Charleston, College of, 13, 157
Charleston (Charles Town), S. C., 2, 5, 6, 7, 8, 18, 20, 24, 42, 45, 49, 56, 85, 86, 93, 97, 101, 102, 103, 114, 115, 172
Charleston City Gazette, 93, 98
Charleston Museum, 103
Charleston News and Courier, 131
Charlotte, N. C., 104
Cherry Grove Beach, 38, 44, 86, 87, 87, 89
Cherry Grove Inlet, 86
Cherry Hill Baptist Church, Conway, 137, 138
Chesterfield County, 120
Chestnut, James, 82
Chestnut High School, 44
Chicora, Francisco, 1
Cincinnati, Order of the, 101
Citadel, 125

210

Index

Civic League of Conway, 164
civil rights, 13, 15
Civitan Club of Loris, 167
Civil War, 10, 13, 28, 40, 46, 47, 62, 73, 81, 86, 107, 108, 111, 112, 115, 117, 122, 163, 173, 177-78; deserters, 10, 30, 173, 181-82; federal occupation of South Carolina, 176-77; refugees, 109, 116, 170-71
Clark, John, 141
Clarke, R. B., 146
Clemson College (University), 1, 12, 134, 153, 158, 168
Clifton Plantation, 103
clothing, 108, 125, 126
Coastal Carolina Junior College, 13, 14, 153, 156
Coastal Carolina University, 153, 153, 156-59
Coastal Education Foundation, 157
Cochran, James, 8, 39, 101, 102
Cochran, James G., 23
Coker College, 156
Collins, Benjamin Grier, 75, 110, 127, 146
Collins, Elizabeth, *Memories of the Southern States,* 170
Collins, Laura Jane Cooper (Mrs. Benjamin Grier), 110
Columbia, S. C., 52, 72, 82, 103, 104
commerce, 11
commissary stores: Myrtle Beach, 76; Surfside Beach, 82
Confessions of an English Opium Eater (De Quincey), 190
Congaree River, 131
Conner, M. C., 165
Connor, Edward, 23
Continental Line, 5, 91
Conway, Ann Causey (Mrs. John Baxter), 99
Conway, Ann Daniell Goodbee (Mrs. Daniel), 93

Conway, Coast & Western Railroad, 42, 72
Conway, Elizabeth, 99
Conway, John, 93
Conway, John Baxter, 94, 96, 99, 141
Conway, John Bennet, 93
Conway, Juliana (daughter of John Baxter Conway), 99
Conway, Juliana Easton (Mrs. Robert), 93, 94, 97, 98
Conway, Margaret, 99
Conway, Mary Baxter, 94, 96
Conway, Rebecca Beaty (Mrs. John Baxter), 99
Conway, Robert, 7, 21, 22, 23, 46, 93-99, 137
Conway, S. C., 11, 45-50
Conway, Susannah Beaty Crowson (Mrs. Robert, *later* Mrs. Ferari), 98-99
Conway, William Hopkins, 93
Conway and Seacoast Railroad, 72, 75, 109
Conway Board of Health, 164
Conway Boat Landing, 42
Conwayborough (Conwayboro), 9, 10, 22, 44, 46, 106, 111, 171, 173; lots sold, 9; Musterfield, 174; name changed to Conway, 22, 47; occupation after the Civil War, 173, 174
Conwayborough Academy, 127, 142, 143; Conwayborough Academy Association, 144
Conwayborough Township, 50
Conway Branch Library (black), 155
Conway Chamber of Commerce, 122, 128, 165
Conway City Hall, 22, 46, 49-50, 106, 116, 153; portraits of mayors, 50; Conway watch, 99; earthquake rods, 116

211

Index

Conway Field, 139
Conway High School, 134, 157
Conway Hospital, 48, 165–67; auxiliary, 167
Conway Light Company, 168
Conway Marina, 173
Conway National Bank, 43
Conway Telephone Company, 53
Conway Township, 165, 166
Cook, Waterman, 73
Cooke, Catherine Carolina Ayers (Mrs. Henry B.), 132
Cooke, Henry B., 132
Cooke, Henry Kemper ("Kemp"; "Backwoods Statesman"), 132–33
Cool Spring, 72, 129, 180, 181
Cooper, Mary Harriet Beaty (Mrs. Timothy), 107, 110
Cooper, Thomas, 53
Cooper, Timothy, 107, 110, 127
Cooper River, 18
Corinth, Miss., 171
Cornwallis, 6
Correct Mispronunciations of Some South Carolina Names (Henry and Neuffer), 19
cotton, 10, 53
courthouses and jails, 22–27; first, 22–24, 46, 96, 98; second, 24–25, 46, 49–50, 106, 116; third, 26–27, 46
Coventry, Conn., 113
Cowpens, Battle of, 38
Cox, Jerry, 195
Cox, Jerry, Company, 195–97
Cox, Walter, 195
Cox-Lundy, 195
Craven County, 37
Crawford, Dan E., 141
Crawford, Robert, 104
Crescent Beach, 88, 89, 156
Cronkhite, Philip, 57
Cross, John, 96
Crowson, Thomas, 98

Cuckon, William Kelland, 41, 162
Currie, Frances Elizabeth Cooper (Mrs. William), 111
Currie, William, 111
Cushing, William B., 41
Cyclopedia of Eminent and Representative Men of the Carolinas of the Nineteenth Century, 107

Daggett, Mary A. Tillman (Mrs. Thomas W.), 117
Daggett, Thomas West, 115–17, 177–79
Dagnall, W. A., 146
Dahlgren, John A., 115, 178
Daisy community, 52, 62
Daniell, Robert (Landgrave), 93, 94
Daniels, Rufus J., 194
Dargan, Ervin E., 82
Darien, Ga., 115
Daughters of the American Revolution (Peter Horry Chapter), 26
Davis, Capt., 41
Davis, William F., 157
Dawsey, Carlisle, 73
Dawsey, John, 74
Dawsey, Thomas, 97
De Quincey, Thomas, *Confessions of an English Opium Eater,* 190
Deep Gully, 126
DeLettre, U. A., 144
Democratic party, 119, 176–79
Depression (1930s), 12, 13, 28, 56, 62, 64; banking holiday, 125
Derham, Edgar McGougan, 54
Derham, Ida Bryan, 118
Derham, John Pickens, 26, 54, 117–20, 121
Derham, Joseph Henry, 117, 118
Derham, Lula Jackson McGougan (Mrs. John Pickens), 118, 120
Derham, Mary Hoban (Mrs. Michael), 117
Derham, Michael, 117, 118

Index

Derham, Sallie Enzor (Mrs. Joseph Henry), 117, 118, 119
Derham, Sarah Amanda Bryan (Mrs. Joseph Henry), 118
Derham, William Patrick, 118
Derham family, 117-20
Dicks, John, 23
Dillon County, 37
doctors, 12, 67, 68
Dog Bluff School, 141
Dog Bluff Township, 128
Dolphin, John, 189
Dover Plantation, 91
Dow, Lorenzo, 113-15
Dow, Peggy Holcomb (Mrs. Lorenzo), 114
Doyle, B. K., 183
Draughan's Business Schools, 52
DuBois family, 74
Dubose, D. O., 163
Duke Endowment, 165, 166
Dunbar, Elisha, 187
Dunlap, W. M., 133
Dunn, John, 23
Dunn, Thomas C., 42, 44
Dunn Sound, 36
Durant, Henry, 23, 25, 126-28
Durant, John, 126-27
Durant, John Wesley, 25
Durant, William, 126-27
Durant land case, 126-28
Dusenbury, Charles, 183, 187
Dusenbury, J. E., 144, 165
Dusenbury, J. S., 163
Dwight, Origen, 97
Dynamite Hole, 43
Dysinger, J. H., 146

East, J. Kenyon, 157
Eastern Carolina Junior College, 13
Eddy Lake, 163, 168
Edge, Mitch, 173
Edge, R. Marvin, 88

Edge, Robert L., 89
education, 8, 10, 121, 140-50; for blacks, 149, 150-52
Edwards, Gabe, 73
Edwards, John T., 52
Egerton, Mrs. Effie Burroughs, 110
Electoral College, 105
electric lights, 13, 168
Elizabeth City, N. C., 151
Ellerbe, Gov., 121
Elliott, Alexander, 144
Ellis, Georgia, 34
Ellis, Ralph H., 157
Ellsworth, Kenneth C., 79, 80
Elrod, N. C., 69
Elvington, P. L., 169
Emory University, 130
Emptage, A. L. ("Roy"), 80
English settlement, 2, 3
Enterprise Landing, 192
environment, 17
Epps, Florence Theodora, 34, 35, 135-37, 193; house, 135
Epworth League (Conway Methodist Church), 190
Eva Mae (steamboat), 61
extension agents, 12
Eykner (Eynner; Ikner), Jacob, 73

Fair Bluff, N. C., 118, 132
Faircloth, Esther, 164
Fairfield Enterprise (newspaper), 128
Farm, Field and Fireside, 188, 189
Farmers Bank, 54
Farmers Day, 49
farmers market, 57
Farmers Warehouse, 52, 62, 71
farms and farming, 11, 55, 56, 74, 76, 81, 113, 168
Fashion Center, 58, 61
Fayetteville, N. C., 108
Fearwell, Thomas, 22, 23
federal law enforcement agents, 69

213

Index

Fenegan, Luther W., 88
Ferari, Susannah Beaty Crowson Conway (widow of Robert Conway), 99
Fine Arts Club, Conway, 194
Finney, E. A., 139
Finney, Ernest A., Jr., 139
fires (in Loris), 53
First United Methodist Church, Conway, 106, 114, 175, 190
Fisher, Alan, 192
fisheries, 43, 86, 87
fishing and fishermen, 32, 82
Flagg, Henry Collins, 102
Flagg, Rebecca Allston (Mrs. Henry Collins), 102
Fleming, P. K., 88
Fleming's store, Georgetown, 97
Floral Beach, 82
Florence, S. C., 88
Florence County, 37, 184
Florida Power and Light Company, 169
Floyd, J. Bryan, 89
Floyd, J. W., 163
Floyd, Samuel F., Jr., 22
Floyd, Wallace, 133
Floyds High School, 148, 153
Floyds Township, 138, 139, 152
Forgaty, John, 141
Fort Randall, 41, 45
Fort Sumter, 28
Fort Ward, 115
Foxworth, Samuel, 22
Fredericksburg, Va., 101
freedmen, 19
Freeman, O. D., 56
Freeman, W. R., 143, 144
free range law, 121
Free School Commissioners, 141
French Huguenots, 18, 19, 21, 38, 91, 102
Frisino, James, 49
Fuller, J. A., 83
funerals: Beaty, 123-24; Stackhouse, 137-39
Furman College (University), 132, 152, 153
Futch Beach, 87
Futch Island, 86

Gaddis, Mrs., 4
Galbraith, Archibald Hector James, 163
Galivants Ferry Baptist Church, 133
Galivants Ferry, 82, 132, 177, 182; school, 141
Gapway School, 141
Gardner and Lacy Lumber Company, 42
Gary, Ernest, 183
Gasque, Ralph, 185
Gate City. *See* Loris, S. C.
Gates, Horatio, 91
Gause, Benjamin, Jr., 24
Gause, Mansie, 169
Gause, William, 8, 101
Gause, William, Sr., 86
Gause family, 86
Gause's Landing, N. C., 8
Gause's Swash, 86
Gay, Josiah, 141
General Education Board of New York, 151
George Peabody College for Teachers, 149
Georgetown-Conway Road, 174
Georgetown County, 37, 45, 66, 86, 172
Georgetown Court of Inferior Jurisdiction, 7
Georgetown District, 21, 37, 46, 91, 95
Georgetown Judicial District, 7
Georgetown Methodist Church (Orange and Highmarket Streets), 98, 99
Georgetown Rifle Guards, 170
Georgetown, S. C., 3, 5, 8, 20, 21, 37, 42, 86, 97, 102, 114, 115, 173, 193
Georgia, Florida, and Alabama Railroad, 128, 129

German prisoners of war, 78
Germans, 18, 19
Gerrald, Levi, 141
Gillespie, I. T., 177
Gillespie, Thomas F., 143
Gilmore, J. R., 111
Gilmore, James Clifford, 188
Gilreath, Mrs. Morgan B., 157
Godfrey, Lucille Burroughs (Mrs. S. G.), 75, 190
golf, 12, 77, 78, 83, 90
Goodbee, Alexander, 93
Goodman, Eli T., 89
Gordon, Robert K., 84
Gore, Daniel, 85
Gore, Emory, 85
Gore, Le Grant, 85
Gore, Walter Porter, 54, 57
Grace Hotel, 26
Graham, J. D., 53
Graham, John, 141
Graham, John, Sr., 22
Graham, W. I., 144
Graham, William, 73
Graham, W. L., 143
Grainger, D. M., 169
Grainger, Harmon D., 182
Grainger, Sarah (Mrs. Harmon D.), 182
Grand Strand, 3, 12, 13, 45, 47, 78, 90
Grand Strand Branch Library, 156
Grand Strand Regional Hospital, 167
Granger, G. B., 141
Grant, J. H., 173
Grant, John, 162
Grantsville community, 110, 162, 188
Gray, Wil Lou, 13
Great Pee Dee River, 27, 29
Greater Conway Chamber of Commerce, 49
Green Sea Baptist Church, 118
Green Sea community, 52, 62, 88, 117-20, 163
Green Sea Township, 50

Green Sea-Floyds High School, 153
Green, Dove Walter, Jr. ("Sonny"), 157
Green, Nathanael, 102
Green, Richard, 98
Green, Richard, Sr., 21, 23
Greenville, Miss., 134
Greenville, N. C., 101
Gregg's *History of the Old Cheraws,* 93
Grice, George, 157
Griffith, James E., 160
Grimball's Causeway, Battle of, 172
Guignard family, 26
Gully Store, 131, 164
Gurganus, B. H., 143, 144
Gurley community, 52

Haarlem, Netherlands, 134
Hagan, William Franklin, 153
Hagley Plantation, 109, 170
Halfway Branch School, 141
Hamilton, Alexander, 99
Hammer Lumber Company, 42
Hampton Institute, 151
Hampton, Wade, oak, 124, 177
Hampton Plantation, 103
Hampton, Wade, 116, 119; campaign of 1876, 119, 124, 176
Hardee, Henry, 143, 144
Hardee, Jennie (Mrs. R. P.), 58-59
Hardee, Oliver, 49
Hardee, Roy, 60
Hardee, T. C., 169
Hardin, H. E., 139
Hardwick, Clifford Hugh, 54
Hardwick, Dan W., 52, 53, 54, 55, 57
Hardwick, Jennings W., 55-56
Hardwick, N. E., 52
Hardwick, Nathan, 71
Harlee, William, 39, 50, 81
Harper, Mrs. Aleen Paul, 34
Harrell, John T., 88
Harrell, Joseph F., 143, 144, 162, 163

Index

Harrelson, Doc D., 52, 54, 57
Harrelson, Newsome, 49
Harrelson, Sims, 52
Harrelson, W. L., 78
Harris, James B., 88
Harris, John, 141
Harrison, E. T., 127
Harrison, T. J., 83
Harrow School (England), 170
Hart, M. G., 162
Harvest Moon (U.S. vessel), 115-16, 178
Haworth, England, 190
Hayes, Shelton T., 160
Hebron United Methodist Church, 112
Hemingway, William, 9, 22, 23, 49; Hemingway map of Conwayborough, 22, 49, 94
Hendersonville, S. C., 110
Heniford, D. O., 55, 61, 66
Heniford, Katherine Hammack ("Kate"), 66-67, 168
Heniford, Lewis Lafayette ("Fate"), 61-62
Heniford, Thomas, 172
Heniford family, 58; cemetery, 172
Henrietta (sailing ship), 112, 125, 187-88
Hewitt, D. L., 183
Heyward, C. D., 184
Heyward, Thomas, Jr., 103
Hickman, O. E., 54
Hickman, Sam, 56
highway transportation, 44, 47, 87, 90
Hill Chapel, 139
Hillsboro, N. C., 91
Hipp, James C., 157
historic preservation, 17
History of Marion County (Sellers), 179
Hodges, Charles Edward, 54, 57
Hog Inlet, 86, 87
Holliday, George J., 82

Holliday, J. W., 143, 144
Holliday, Joseph W. (grandson of J.W.), 157
Hollings, Ernest ("Fritz"), 14
Holmes, Mrs. Hal, 194
Holmes, Hal B., 165, 166
Holmes, Thomas H., 143, 144
Holt, Boss, 51
Holt, John, 54
Holt, W. K., 54
Home Rule, 15, 16, 57, 58, 80
Homewood Colony, 47, 110, 188-90
Homewood Farm Association, 189
Hooks, W. C., 152
Horry, Daniel, 91
Horry, Elias, 91
Horry, Harriott Pinckney (Mrs. Daniel), 103
Horry, Hugh, 91
Horry, John, 91
Horry, Magdaline, 91
Horry, Margaret, 91
Horry, Margaret Guignard (Mrs. Peter), 92-93
Horry, Peter ("Stuttering Pete"), 9, 19, 21, 46, 91-93; biography of Francis Marion, 92; portraits, 26, 125
Horry community, 148, 152
Horry County Board of Education, 149, 154
Horry County Colored Hospital and Training School, 165
Horry County commissions, 15
Horry County Conservation Foundation, 160
Horry County Council, 16, 73
Horry County Court of Common Pleas Judgment book, 1804-1829, 97
Horry County Development Board, 14
Horry County government, 15, 16
Horry County Higher Education Commission, 14, 158, 159

Index

Horry County Historic Preservation Commission, 17, 34
Horry County Historical Society, 17, 30, 33-35, 194
Horry County Legislative Delegation, 13, 14, 15, 56, 57, 153, 165, 167
Horry County Medical Society, 163
Horry County Memorial Library, 83, 134, 153-56, 157, 158, 191; branch libraries, 156; commission, 16, 154, 155
Horry County Museum, 17, 122
Horry County National Bank, 57
Horry County News, 71
Horry County School District, 161
Horry County Survey of Historic Places, 130
Horry County: Our Independent Republic (Tricentennial pageant), 194
Horry Cultural Arts Council, 17, 49
Horry District Board of Commissioners, 9, 22, 23, 24, 98, 140
Horry District Commissioner of Locations, 9
Horry District, 10, 21, 39, 42, 91, 95, 141; created by S. C. General Assembly, 21; first petition to form (1793), 9, 21; petition to form (1801), 9, 19, 21, 95
Horry Electric Cooperative, 13, 169, 194
Horry Georgetown Technical College, 14, 153
Horry Herald, 25, 26, 53, 54, 55, 139, 147, 166, 173
Horry Hussars, 119
Horry Industrial School, 121, 147, 152
Horry Land and Improvement Company, 76, 126
Horry School District 19, 146-47
Horton, S. F., 56, 160, 167
Howle, James Patrick, 169

Huckabee, Blue, 83
Hucks, Lacy K., 73
Hucks, W. G., Jr., 73
Huger, Mrs. Elias, 91
Huger, Benjamin, 21, 95
Huger, Francis Kinloch, 21, 95
Huger, Isaac, 74
Hugerborough, 20, 21, 22, 46, 95
Huger family, 21
Hughes, W. J., 53, 64
Huguenot Church (Charleston), 172
Hunter, William, 4
Hurl (Hearl) Rocks, 74
hurricanes: Hazel (1954), 44, 78, 87, 88, 89; Hugo (1989), 78, 83

illiteracy, 13
Independent Republic (nickname of Horry County), 28, 29
Independent Republic Quarterly, 34-35, 73, 137, 194
industry, 14, 55, 56, 58
influenza epidemic (1918), 54
Ingle, Ronald R., 159
Ingram, Charles N., 88
Ingram, James, 104
Ingram Beach, 88
Inman, Elizabeth, 127
Intracoastal Waterway, 29, 44, 77, 79, 81, 191-93

Jackson, J. Blakeney, 88
Jackson, Mary Emily Platt (Mrs. Nelson II), 83
Jackson, Nelson, II, 83
Jackson, William, 100
James Island, 172
Jameson, Mr., 103
Jane Eyre (Charlotte Brontë), 190, 191
Jeanes, Anna T., Fund, 149, 150, 151, 152
Jeanes teachers, 150-51
Jefferson, Ella (Mrs. Tom), 66

217

Index

Jefferson, Thomas, 24, 99, 99, 100, 135
Jefferson, Tom, 66
Jenkens, Thomas, 141
Jenrette, John Wilson, Jr., 54, 57
Jernigan, F. W., 183
Jerry Cox Company, 195-97
Jet Magazine, 139
Jewish merchants, 66-67
Johnson, Mrs. C. A., 183
Johnson, Charles, 110
Johnson, Commander, 182-84
Johnson, Dick M., 83
Johnson, H. L. W., 173
Johnson, Horace, 165
Johnson, Hugh, 73
Johnson, J. W., 163
Johnson, Margaret Ellen Cooper (Mrs. Charles), 107, 110; *Memoirs,* 108, 110, 142, 181
Johnson, Monroe, 183
Johnson, Robert, 2, 20
Johnson, U. A., 169
Johnson, V. M., 169
Johnson, W. A., 53
Johnson, Warren, 110
Johnson, Waterman, 173
Johnston, Ernest W., Jr., 160
Johnston, W. H., 143, 144
Johnston, Sheriff W. H. ("Hickory Bill"), 181
Johnston, William, 24
Jones, C. A., 165
Jones, Henry Wallace, 112, 175-76
Jones, William H., 127
Jordan, A. Elbert, 88, 89
Jordan, Daniel William, 39
Jordan, Joseph, 4
Jordan, Laura Quattlebaum (Mrs. E. E.), 34, 179, 193
Jordan, W. J., 169
judiciary, 16, 17

Kaminski, H., 116
Kelly, Peter C., 84
Kidd, William, 36
King, B. R., 51
King, Jim, 52
King, W. H., 183
King, W. Hal, Jr., 169
King, William Eugene, 163
King family, 58, 74
King's Highway, 3, 81, 101, 102
Kingston (village), 4, 6, 7, 20, 21, 45, 46, 94, 105; name changed to Conwayborough, 9, 95, 114
Kingston Bluff, 45
Kingston District, 7
Kingston Hotel, 131
Kingston Lake, 94, 109, 122, 123, 126
Kingston Lake Baptist Association, 138
Kingston Parish, 141
Kingston Pointe Development Corporation, 49
Kingston Presbyterian Church, Conway, 97, 106, 134, 143, 177; cemetery, 97, 98, 116, 117, 122, 123, 124
Kingston Street, Conway, 122
Kingston Township, 3, 4, 20, 37, 45
Kirby, H. T., 163
Kirke, Edmund, *Among the Pines,* 111-12
Kiwanis Club of Conway, 165
Klugh, J. C., 183
Knauff, Miss Leo, 194
Knight, John M., 146
Knights of Pythias, 121

LaBruce, John, 144
Lafayette, Marquis de, 21, 95
Lake Swamp, 50
Lake Swamp Farms, 132
Lake Swamp School, 141

Index

Lakeside Cemetery, Conway, 110, 121, 126, 131, 134; Causey mausoleum, 131
Lake Waccamaw, 30
land grants, 3, 6, 7, 9, 20, 86, 94, 126
Lane, S. M., 183
LaRue, James, 193-95
Last of the Bighams (Zeigler), 186
Laurel Hill plantation, 40, 115
Lay, George M., 56
Lee, Jesse M., 157
Legette, Golden, 66
Levister, B. F., 165
Levister, Nellie Adelaide Burke (Mrs. B. F.), 151
Levister Elementary School (renamed Aynor Elementary), 151
Lewis, A. D., 163
Lewis, Mrs. Catherine H., 34, 193
Lewis, Josiah, 23
Lewis, W. R. ("Bill"), 26, 88, 127
Lexington, Battle of, 38
Libbert, Joe, 67
Liberty District, 7
libraries: Methodist Church, 190; public, 153-56
Lincoln's Commando (Roske and Van Doren), 115
Little, H. P., 26
Little Pee Dee River, 3, 6, 11, 17, 27, 30, 72, 75, 116, 152, 178
Little River (stream), 29, 36, 39, 191
Little River (village or community), 3, 4, 8, 17, 18, 34, 36-45, 77, 85, 86, 115, 118, 120, 141, 162, 178, 194
Little River Blue Crab Festival, 18
Little River Committee of Safety, 5, 37, 38
Little River Hotel, 43
Little River Inlet, 192
Little River Methodist Church, 43

Little River Neck, 37, 38, 41, 43, 63, 86, 90
Little River Neck Road, 90
Live Oak community, 113, 172
livestock, 12, 25
Livingston, Harry, 88
Livingston, Jennings, 89
Livingston, Thomas, 22, 23
Lloyd, Sarah Buck, 165
Long, Ike, 50
Long, Jefferson M., 55
Long Bay, 74, 86
Lords Proprietors, 2, 20, 37
Loris, S. C., 11, 38, 43, 50-74, 87, 113, 117, 167, 168; name, 51; nickname "Gate City", 53; attempts to secede from Horry, 54
Loris Baptist Church, 67, 70
Loris Board of Trade, 54, 56
Loris Bog-Off, 18, 58
Loris Boosters Club, 56
Loris Branch Library, 156
Loris Chamber of Commerce, 56
Loris City Hall, 64
Loris Civitan Club, 56, 57, 69
Loris Community Hospital, 56, 68-69, 167
Loris Drug Store, 57, 67, 68
Loris Fair Association, 62
Loris Grammar School, 60
Loris High School, 72, 148
Loris Industrial Developers, 56
Loris Merchants Association, 56
Loris Methodist Church, 62
Loris News, 53
Loris Observer, 55
Loris Presbyterian Church, 51, 61
Loris schools, 19
Loris Sentinel, 71
Loris Supply Company, 53
Loris Telephone Co., 53

Index

Loris Tobacco Warehouse Co., 52
Loris Town Council, 53
Loris Training School, 151
Loris Wood Products, 56
Loruhamah (Young), 128
Loughre County, Galway, Ireland, 117
Lovell, S. George, 194
Ludlam, L. M., 183
lumber industry, 9–10, 12, 39, 40, 42–43, 46, 47, 50, 55, 75, 111, 112–13, 129, 189
Lumber River, 27, 30
Lupo, C. A., 56, 167, 169
Lutheran Church of the Risen Christ, 80
Lythgoe, Robert, 103

MacDill Field, Tampa, Fla., 134
Mace, Sam, 163
Magrath, L. D., 165
Maham, Hezekiah, 92
Mahoney, James, 143, 144, 175, 176
Malet, William, *An Errand to the South in the Summer of 1862,* 171
Malloy, Charles F., 143–44
Manigault, Arthur Middleton, 172
Manigault, Charlotte Drayton (Mrs. Joseph), 172
Manigault, Edward, 172
Manigault, Gabriel, 103
Manigault, Joseph, 103
Manigault, Joseph, 172; House Museum, Charleston, 172
Manning, Richard I., 120
Maple community, 162
Maple Swamp, 29
March, Fredric, 72
Margraten, Holland, 134
Marion, Francis ("the Swamp Fox"), 6, 19, 21, 38, 39, 91
Marion, Isaac, 5, 38
Marion, S. C., 72, 152, 184
Marion County, 37, 120, 121, 127, 152, 179

Marion District, 23, 132
Marion family, 86
Marion Star, 41, 42, 71, 175, 176
Marlow, Martha. *See* Patterson, Martha Marlow
Marlowe, Joseph J., 143
Marshall, Mrs. Virginia Burroughs, 131
Martin County, N. C., 108
Martin (doctor), 68
Martin, Roy, 49
Masons, 101, 111, 118, 119, 121, 129, 144
May, T. E., 146
Mayo, John A., 130, 146
McClellanville, S. C., 83
McCormick, A. P., 146
McDougal, John, 4
McDowell, John, 37
McGhee, Zach, 146
McIver, E. R., 34
McLeod, K. V., 88
McLeod Infirmary, Florence, S. C., 68
McMillan, Hoyt, 165
McNeill, D. M., 110, 127
McQueen, Frances Currie (Mrs. Y. P.), 111
McQueen, John, 141
McQueen, Sam B., 160
McQueen, Y. P., 51, 52, 53, 111
McRae, A. W., 24
McSweeney, M. B., 121
Meares, E. M., 152
Medical College of South Carolina, 67, 134, 164, 165
Medical College of Virginia, 66
medicine, 8, 12, 53, 67, 68, 162–67
Medlen, Hester (Mrs. Woody), 194
Medlen, F. W. ("Woody"), 26
Meher Spiritual Center, 81
Memories of the Southern States (Collins), 170
methodism, 7, 40, 113. *See also* names of churches

Index

Methodist Conference, 152
Mexican War, 172
Middle Georgia and Atlantic Railroad, 129
midwives, 12, 55
migration from Horry, 10, 11
Miller, Fenton, 71
Miller, Franklin F., 175
millinery, 131
Mills, Robert, 21, 24, 39, 46; *Statistics and Atlas,* 38, 44, 46, 50, 81, 141
Mishoe, A. J., 54
Mishoe, K. L., 133
Mitchell, John Hampton, 152
Mitchell, Nicholas, 158-59
Mitchell, Thomas, 96
Mitchell Street, Loris, 61
Monticello, 24
Moore, Bryant, 173
Moore, Henry, 173
Moore, Maurice, 39
Moore, M. Herndon, 146
Morrall, Daniel, 86
Morrall's Inlet, 86
Morris, Mrs. Flossie Sarvis, 187
Morris College, 138, 139
Morris Island, 172
Moses, Franklin J., Jr., 118
Moultrie, William, 103
Mt. Vernon, 101, 104
movies, 71-72
Muenly's, 85
Mullins, S. C., 53, 72, 152
Mullins Academy, 120
Mullins Hospital, 68
Munro, Robert, Jr., 143, 144
murals, 49
murders, 180-86
Murrells Inlet, 3, 29, 37, 86, 121
Mustershed School, 44
Myrtle Beach, S. C., 12, 13, 74-79; chartered, 78; name, 75, 110; sale of lots, 76

Myrtle Beach Air Force Base, 77, 78, 83, 154, 155
Myrtle Beach Farms Company, 12, 76, 77, 110
Myrtle Beach News, 77
myrtle, wax (shrub), 12, 75, 110

Nash, Francis, 37, 38
National Bank of Savannah, 130
National Geographic Society, 192
National Register of Historic Places, 26, 112
NationsBank, 125
Native Americans, 1, 4, 19, 36, 86, 114
natural history, 29-33
Naugher, R. E., 55, 64
naval stores industry, 9-10, 39-40, 42, 46, 47, 51, 75, 118, 189
Negro Rural School Fund, 150
Nesmith, John, 21, 95
Nettles, James, 82
Neuffer, Claude Henry and Irene, *Correct Mispronunciations of Some South Carolina Names,* 19
New Bedford, Mass., 115
New Bern, N. C., 40, 101
New County Movement, 54-55
New England, 44, 100, 112, 187
New Town (renamed Myrtle Beach), 12, 75, 78, 110
New Year's Day 1740, 3, 85
New York, 85
newsmen, 70-71
Nichols, Arthur Bell, 191
Nichols, Charles Melvin, 188
Nichols, Jonathan C., 187
Nixon, C. D., 87, 88
Nixon, J. M., 183
Nixon, Nicholas F., 40, 44
Nixon, Nicholas F., Jr., 88
Nixon, Nicholas F., Sr., 87
Nixon Crossroads, 44, 87
Nixon family, 87

Index

Norman, James H., 144, 162, 163, 173
Norman, Sir Joshua, 105
Norman, Joshua S., 24, 105, 106, 107
Norman, Sarah Jane Beaty (Mrs. Joshua S.; "Aunt Jane"; "Aunt Norman"), 24, 105-07, 143, 144
North and South Main Streets, Aynor, 73
North Carolina, 2, 5, 6, 7, 11, 93, 101, 188
North Island, 21
North Myrtle Beach, 39, 84, 85-90, 156, 193; consolidation 89
North Sea, 134
Norton, Edward Robinson ("Miss Ed"; Mrs. James Arthur), 133-35
Norton, Edward Robinson, 133-35
Norton, Evan, 134, 146, 163, 177
Norton, J. Ovander ("Van"), 154
Norton, James, 119
Norton, James Arthur, Jr., 133-35
Norton, James Arthur ("Dr. Jamie"), 7, 133-35, 154, 163, 164; "Narrative of Horry County History", 98
nullification controversy, 28
Nussey, Ellen, 190-91
Nussey, Henry, 191

Oakdale, 62
occupation by federal troops, 115-16
Ocean Drive Beach ("O. D."), 88, 89
Ocean Forest Hotel, 12, 77
Ocean View Memorial Hospital (later Grand Strand Regional Hospital), 167
O. D. *See* Ocean Drive Beach
Ogilvie, J. W., 50
Oglethorpe Savings and Trust, 130
Old Brunswick Town, 39
One of the Blue Hen's Chickens (Young), 128
Owens family, 74
oysters: canneries, 43; cookery, 63

Pad, The, 88
Paddlewheel steamers, 11
Page, Cordie, 132
Page, Emily Frances Derham (Mrs. Samuel Daniel), 118
Page, Pearly S., 169
Pamplico, S. C., 185, 186
Parham, Mary, 154
parishes, 7, 46
Parker, Jacob, 141
Patterson, Elizabeth Chapin, 76
Patterson, Elizabeth Smith, 51
Patterson, James Gould, 50, 51
Patterson, John, 51
Patterson, Martha Marlow, 51
Patterson & Toon, 51
Patterson Cemetery, Loris, 51, 67
Patterson Street (later Main Street), Loris, 51, 61, 62
Pauley Jail Company of Washington, D. C., 26
pavilions, 76, 82, 88
Pawley, Anthony, 23, 162
Pawley, George, 102
Pawleys Island, 71
Pawley Swamp School, 141
Pee Dee Academy, 147, 152-53
Pee Dee Historical Society, 121
Pee Dee region, 6, 152
Pee Dees, 36
Pee Dee Times, 99
Penobscot Marine Museum, 187
Peoples National Bank of Conway, 125, 126
Perkins and Barnhill, 127
Perrin, J. W., 88
Perry, James, 141
Petersburg, Va., 101
Philadelphia, 99, 101, 104
Pickens, Francis ("The Fighting Elder"), 6

Piece of the Fox's Hide (Boling), 186
Pig Pen Bay School, 44
Pinckney, Charles, 103
Pine House (near Ridge Spring), 104
Pine Island Cut, 192
Pine Lakes International Golf Club, 12
"Pioneers," 170
pirates, 36
planning and zoning, 17
plantations, 10, 86
Platt, V. F., 82, 83
Playcard Environmental Education Center, 17, 159-62
Playcard Swamp, 29, 159-60
Pleasant Meadow community, 113
Pleasant Meadow Swamp, 29
politicians, 11, 42, 54, 70, 74, 177-79; black, 175-76
Pope, Samuel, 143
population, 15, 46, 58
Port Harrelson, 128, 129, 187
Porter, Amelia Conway, 93, 94, 96, 98
Porter, Benjamin, 96
postal service, 57, 64; offices, 38, 40, 64; Conway post office, 126
Pot Bluff, 187
Potomac River, 101
Pratt Institute, New York, 190
pre-European period, 1
Pridgen, Carl, 88
Prince (Weston slave coachman), 171
Prince, Burroughs H. ("Buck"), 55, 70
Prince, C. D., 54
Prince, Cornelius J., 54
Prince, Daniel, 183
Prince, Eldred E., 56, 167
Prince, E. W., Sr., 56, 167
Prince, J. C., 53
Prince, Nicholas, 105
Prince, P. C., 52
Prince, R. M., 183

Prince, William Armagy, 54, 55
Prince, P. C., Company, 53
Prince George Winyah Parish, 7, 21, 46, 95, 98; church, 74, 93, 170
prohibition, 44, 87
Prospect Hill Plantation, 91
public health service, 12, 55
Purrysburg, 103

Quattlebaum, C. P., 26, 177-79
Quattlebaum, Paul, 1, 2, 133, 168, 193

Rabon, ("Little Abe"), 180-81
Rabon, Abram, Sr., 180-82
Rabon, Duke, 180
Rabon, Willis, 180
radio, 71
Ragan, B. T., Sr., 56
railroads, 11, 12, 42, 47, 50, 51, 69, 72, 75, 128-30, 191; railroad comes to Conway, 51, 124; tram roads, 42, 43, 50
Rainbow, A. L., 165
Rainey, Joseph H., 175
Randall, Thomas, 144
Rankin, Harry W., 165
Rankin, Watson Smith, 165, 166
Ratcliffe, Cecil, 83
Reconstruction, 42, 176
Red Bluff community, 62, 162, 176
Red Hill, 42
Redmon (Readman), John, 141, 143
Reese, Harold S. ("Jack"), 157
religion, 37, 106, 118
Republican party, 118, 175, 177-78
retirees, 15, 78, 83
rice, 10, 20
Rice, James Henry, 77
Richardson, Edward Ernest, 33
Richardson, George, 67
Richardson, Huger, 53, 54, 67, 163

Index

Richardson, Jack, 67
Richardson, Katherine, 60-61
Richardson, Margaret Butler (Mrs. Huger), 67
Richmond, Va., 66, 69, 101, 168
Richwood, J. J., 143
Ridge Spring, 104
Riley, A. B., 146
Roach's Beach (renamed Floral Beach), 81
roads, 11, 29, 44, 77, 78, 80, 85, 87
Roberts, Ed, 49
Roberts family, 88
Robinson (doctor), 163
Rogers, George C., Sr., 157
Rogers, Harold S., 157
Rogers, John, 126
Rogers, John, Sr., 96
Rogers, Wilbert Kenneth, 68, 167
Rogers Clinic, Loris, 68
Rogers Company, Fostoria, Ohio, 193
Roosevelt, Franklin D., 168
Roseland, Tangipahoa Parish, La., 188
Rosenwald, Julius, Fund, 149, 150, 152
Roske, Ralph, 115
Ross, Andres McGilvery, 188
Rothmaler, Erasmus, 21, 95, 97
Rougham, England, 134
Round Swamp, 43, 163
Rouquie, S. W., 116
Rowe, William J., 148
Royals, M. A., 183
Rucker, Millard, 85
rumrunners, 87
Rural Electrification Administration, 168
Rush, A. M., 88
Ruth (steamboat), 131
Rutledge, Mrs. J. T., 26
Rutledge, John, 91
Rutledge, John, Jr., 103

St. Philips Parish, 93
St. Thomas and St. Denis Parish, 102

Salem, N. C., 104
Salisbury, N. C., 104
saltworks, 40-41, 86
Sampit River, 103
Sanders (steamboat), 43
Sanderson, E. L., 53
San Miguel de Gualdape, 2
Santee Cooper, 169
Santee River ("French Santee"), 18, 91
Saratoga, N.Y., 112
Sarvis, John, 126, 141
Sarvis, Mack, 161
Sarvis, W. G., 57
Sasser, James Archibald, 165, 166
Savannah, Ga., 3, 103, 129
Sawyer, Ben, 133
Scarborough, Charles R., 121
Scarborough, Henry L., 121, 164, 165, 166
Scarborough, Lewis, 120
Scarborough, Mary J. Jones (Mrs. Robert Bethea), 120, 121
Scarborough, Robert Bethea, 119-22
schools, 10-11, 13, 44, 52, 55, 60, 62, 140-50, 177; libraries, 156; lunches, 63; textbooks, 60
Scott, Robert F., 118
Seabrook, J. W., 84
Searsport Sea Captains, 188
Searsport, Maine, 187-88
Seaside Inn, 75
Seawell, Randolph, 162
secession, 10, 28, 112, 122
Seiler, L. L., 189
seining, 86
Selective Service Board, 121
Sellers, W. W., *A History of Marion County,* 179
servants, 65-66
Servis (Sarvis), John, 24
Sessions, B. J., 182, 184
Sessions, G. W., 173
Sessions, Josias T., 141

Sessions, J. M., 173
Sessions, Robert, 141
Sessions, S. T., 164
Sessions, Silas, 142
Sessions, W. J., 173
settlers, 4, 5, 20, 21, 36, 37, 45, 50, 86, 102, 105, 114
Shakespeare, William, 135
Shelley, John, 73
Shelley Point Plantation, 42
Sherman's March (through S. C.), 117
Shiloh, Battle of, 163
shipbuilding, 112, 122
Siege Train, Co. B., Heavy Artillery Battalion, 172-73
Simmons, Charlotte, 182-84
Simmons, John Mark, 85
Simmons family, 74
Simpson Creek, 29, 57
Simpson Creek Township, 50
Sing, John, 126
Singleton, Richard, 23, 24
Singleton Swash, 8, 102, 109
Sixth Congressional District, S. C., 119, 121
Sixth Infantry Battalion, S. C. Volunteers, 172
Skene, Alexander, 7, 20, 45
Skipper, Abijah H., 131
Skipper, Colie, 49
Skipper, James Holloway, 49
Skipper, Norman E., 49
Skipper, Sarah Caroline (Mrs. Abijah H.), 131
Skipper, William Taft, 49
Slater, John F., 151
Slater Fund, 149, 150, 151, 152
slaves, 10, 20, 28, 81, 111
Sloan, R. G., 43, 163
Smith, Benjamin, 39
Smith, B. F., 143
Smith, Jeremiah, 26, 127, 164
Smith, Jesse T., 49

Smith, Paul, 165
Smith, R. Cathcart, 157
Smith, Thomas (landgrave), 93
Smith, Tom, 186
Snider, Evelyn Mayo, 130
Snow, William, 22, 23
snowbirds, 78
Snow Hill (Burroughs homesite), 109, 171
Socastee, 10, 74, 77, 78, 140, 141, 191, 193
Socastee Academy, 148
Socastee Bridge, 44
Socastee Swamp and Creek, 29, 44, 191
South Carolina, A Guide to the Palmetto State, 28
South Carolina, University of, 14, 157, 158, 159
South Carolina Baptist Association, 152, 153
South Carolina College (later University of South Carolina), 172
South Carolina Comptroller General, 42, 120
South Carolina Constitutions; 1868, 112, 175-76; 1895, 119, 128, 147
South Carolina Department of Archives and History, 173
South Carolina General Assembly, 7, 8, 15, 16, 17, 34, 46, 47, 58, 92, 95, 97, 98, 104, 141; House of Representatives, 21, 40, 54, 55, 95, 117, 122, 128; Senate, 21, 38, 42, 54, 55, 112, 116, 131
South Carolina Highway Department, 133
South Carolina Library Association, 153
South Carolina Line, 5
South Carolina militia, 91, 92, 97, 98, 115
South Carolina Provincial Congress, 91
South Carolina State Department of Education, 151

Index

South Carolina State Superintendent of Education, 151
South Carolina State Technical Education Commission, 14
South Carolina Supreme Court, 127, 139, 183
South Carolina Tax Commission, 120
South Carolina Tricentennial Celebration, 193–95
South Santee, 172
Southern, Ernest F., 157
Southern Association of Colleges and Universities, 159
Southern Baptist Seminary, 152
Southern Workman, 190
Spanish American War, 11, 189
Spanish explorations, 1
Sparrow, Rod, 56, 71
Spartanburg Female Academy, 107
Spivey, Collins A., 82, 126
Spivey, Doc Allen ("Dock"), 26, 52, 76, 110, 122, 124–26
Spivey, Frances C. Hughes (Mrs. William Alexander), 125
Spivey, John C., 26, 126, 164
Spivey, Mary Essie Collins (Mrs. Doc Allen), 125
Spivey, Victor, 69–70
Spivey, William Alexander, 125
Spivey, William H. ("Hop"), 125
Spivey's Beach, 76, 126
Spring Branch community, 117, 118
Springs, Louise W., 79
Springs, Pauline K., 79
Squires, Louise Chestnut, 82
Squires, Robert L., 160
Stabler, B. K., 56
Stackhouse, Andrew Washington, 137–39
Stalvey, John Kelly, 163, 165
Stanley, Edgar, 67, 70
Stanley, Golda (Mrs. Edgar), 67, 70

Stanley, M. M., 54
Stanley, Nell Winesett (Mrs. Tom), 71
Stanley, Thomas W., 56
Star Bluff ferry, 87
State Hospital for the Insane, 121
Statesboro, Ga., 130
steamboats, 46, 49, 116, 131, 178
Stephens, Arden L., 160
Sterrit Swamp School, 141
Stevens, Frances (Mrs. Isom), 65
Stevens, H. E., 169
Stevens, Isom, 65
Stevens, James Price, 13, 14, 54, 57, 111
Stevenson, S. M., 144
Stilley, W. A., Sr., 165, 166
Stogner, H. Otis ("Tab"), 169
Stokes, W. S., 146
Stone, J. A., 43, 143
Stone, W. H. ("Willie"), 43
Storm of 1798, 142
Suggs, Lorenzo Dow, 113
Sumter, Thomas ("The Gamecock"), 6
Sun Fun Festival, 18, 78
Sun News, 139
Sunday schools, 64
Sunny South colony, Chadbourn, N. C., 188
Surfside Beach, 81–84
Swampfest, 161
Sweet, Silvius, 23
Sweet Home, 62
Szekes, John, 26

Taber, Charles Rhett, 163
Tabor City, 72
Tampa, Fla., 134
Tampico Plantation, 128
Tarleton, Banastre, 6
Taylor, J. P., and Company, 129
Taylor, Thomas, 103
Taylor, W. H. B., 128, 143, 144
Taylor, W. J., 143, 144

Teach, Edward ("Blackbeard"), 36
Tenth Regiment, South Carolina Volunteers, 163, 170, 171
Thaggard, S. W., 84
Theatre of the Republic, 135
Thirteenth Regiment, 172
Thomas, J. D., 53, 54, 67, 163
Thomas, Mrs. Manning, 34
Thompson, A. C., 166
Thompson, Augustus Reeves, 175–76
Thompson, Austin Charles, 110
Thompson, Emma Cooper (Mrs. Austin Charles), 110
Thompson, Frank A., 57, 154
Thompson, M. A., 89
Thompson, Steven H., 176
Thurmond, J. Strom, 120
tidal wave of 1893, 82
Tilghman Beach (estates), 87, 88
Tilghman Point, 41, 43
Tillman, Benjamin A., 117
Tillman, Benjamin T., 121
Tillman, John M., 81
tobacco: cooperatives, 52; crop, 52, 53; culture, 11–12, 13, 28, 47, 55, 58; markets and warehouses, 11, 47, 52, 53, 55, 73
Todd, Boyce, 59
Todd, Carolyn, 59
Todd, Edith, 59
Todd, Gertrude, 59
Todd, Mrs. Grier H., 59
Todd, Grier H., 59
Todd, Hazel, 59
Todd, Hugh R., 52
Todd, O. E., 53
Todd, Rudolph, 59
Todd, William, 141
Todd, W. Leamon, 88
Todd family, 74
Todd's Ferry, 50
Todd's Ferry Road, 50, 51

tokens, 9, 28, 40, 47, 113
Tompkins, E. B., 173
tourism, 48, 75, 76, 78, 83, 84, 87
Tower in the Desert (Young), 128
township plan, 2, 20
Treasury Building, Washington, 24
Trinity Episcopal Church Cemetery, Columbia, 93
Twelfth Infantry Regiment, 172
Tybee Hotel Company, 130
Tybee Island Beach Company, 130
Tyree, Walter, 52

U.S. Army Air Corps, 78, 134; Columbus (Miss.) Army Flying School, 134
U.S. Bicentennial celebration, 34
U.S. Corps of Engineers, 44, 191, 193
U.S. House of Representatives, 121
U.S. Weather Bureau, 70
Union Leagues, 175, 176
Upper Mill Plantation, 107, 111, 112

Van Doren, Charles, *Lincoln's Commando*, 115
Varin, Jacques, 102
Varin, Susanne Horry (Mrs. Jacques), 102
Vaught, Anzy, 162
Vaught, John, 38
Vaught, Lundy, 56, 167
Vaught, Matthias, 38
Vaught, Winston Wallace, 54, 57
Vaught family, 86
Vereen, Jackson, 102
Vereen, Jane Evans (Mrs. Jeremie), 102
Vereen, Jeremiah (husband of Mary Coachman Vereen), 102
Vereen, Jeremiah, 8, 18, 39, 101, 102
Vereen, Jeremie, 102
Vereen, J. L., 88
Vereen, Mary Coachman (Mrs. Jeremiah), 102

Index

Vereen family, 18, 38, 86
Vereen Gardens, 17, 101, 102
vocational agriculture, 55; teachers, 12, 168

"Waccamaw" (correspondent), 41–42, 175
Waccamaw Baptist Association, 152
Waccamaw Light Artillery, 115
Waccamaw Line of Steamers, 131
Waccamaw Neck, 2, 6, 8, 27, 37, 39, 40, 74, 86, 102, 106, 116, 117, 170
Waccamaw River, 3, 4, 11, 17, 20, 30, 37, 38, 43, 45, 47, 49, 50, 61, 75, 94, 97, 105, 107, 109, 116, 126, 131, 178, 191, 192; bridge, Conway, 77, 94
Waccamaws, 36
Wainwright, Grace, 74
Wait, B. Wofford, 183
Wall, E. Craig, Sr., 82, 157
Wallace, Ruben, 175
Waller, William, 126
Waller, W. W., 176
Walsh, Joseph Travis, 28, 93, 120, 121, 143, 144, 171, 173, 177
Walsh, Mary Jane Congdon (Mrs. Joseph Travis), 28
Wampee-Little River High School, 44
Wanamaker Baptist Church, 152, 153
Wanamaker community, 148, 152
War of 1812, 129
Ward Estate, 88
Warren, Russell, 24, 25
Washington Monument, 24, 39
Washington, George, 7, 18, 92, 191; southern tour of 1791, 7–8, 34, 39, 88, 99–105
Washington, William, 103
Waterman, Eleazar, 127
water transportation, 11, 12, 46, 75
Waties, William, 36, 38

Waties Island, 43
Watkins, Mance, 89
Watson, Braxton, 57
Watson, Charley, 66, 151
Watson, J. E., 165
Watson, S. P., 43, 163
Wayne County, N. C., 129
Waynesboro, Ga., 103
Webb, Henry W., 175
Webster, Charlie, 169
Weems, Mason L., 92
Weems, Parson, 19
Wendel, Douglas P., 89
Weston, Emily Francis Esdaile (Mrs. Plowden C. J.), 170
Weston, Francis Marion, 115
Weston, Plowden C. J., 116, 143, 144, 170, 171
Weston family, 109, 116
White Point Swash, 8, 86, 87
White Swamp, 6
Whitefield, George, 3, 37, 40, 85
Whiteville, N. C., 72, 88, 162, 163
Whitman, John R., 141
Whittemore High School, 13, 139, 155
Whittington, Forrest Brooks, 54
Wilder, W. J., 152
Willard, Frances 128
Williams, Cora V. Taylor (Mrs. Jesse Parker), 128
Williams, Jesse Parker, 128–30
Williams, Lloyd, 169
Williams, Rowena Olivia Outland (Mrs. Jesse Parker), 129
Williams, William, 22
Williams and Watson, 129
Williamsburg County (District), 6, 7, 37, 95
Willliamson, W. E., 183
Willson, Sam, 24
Wilmington, Chadbourn, and Conway Railroad, 51

228

Wilmington, N. C., 3, 40, 50, 56, 100, 101, 114, 189
Wilmington, Southport and Little River Steamboat Company, 43
Wilson, Mrs., 4
Winborne, W. H., 49
Windy Hill Beach, 87, 88, 89
Windy Hill Beach Corporation, 88
Winesett, Lem, 70
Winnsboro, S. C., 117, 118
Winthrop College, 153
Winyah Barony, 93
Winyah Bay, 1, 42, 44, 45, 91, 103, 115, 178
Winyah District, 7, 38
Winyah Indigo Society, 140
Winyahs, 36
Withers, Francis, 74
Withers, John, 74
Withers, Mary Esther, 74
Withers, Richard, 74
Withers, Robert, 74
Withers, William, 74
Witherspoon, David B., Jr., 88
Witherspoon, W. D., 160
Withers Swash (Eight Mile Swash), 74, 76, 126
Wofford College, 67
Wolpert, Bernard, 66
Wolpert, Bertie, 67
Wolpert, Katie (Mrs. Bernard), 66-67
Wolpert, Raphael, 67
Wolpert, Robert, 67
Woman Suffrage, History of, 128
women, 65, 105-11, 168
Women's Christian Temperance Union, 128

Women's College, Greensboro, N. C., 153
Woodhouse, Edward, 157
Woodhouse, Margaret (Mrs. Edward), 157
Woods, M. C., 146
Woodside Brothers of Greenville, S.C., 12, 77
Woodward, H. H., Sr., 26, 164
Woodward, Henry, Jr., 34
Works Progress Administration, 28, 154
World War I, 12, 46, 54, 64, 121, 128, 152, 164; armistice celebrations, 54, 62-63
World War II, 13, 49, 56, 69, 78, 84, 133-35, 149, 154, 192
Wortham's Ferry, 61, 87
Wortham's Ferry Road, 44
Wright, M. A., 165, 166, 179
Wright, Robert, 7, 20, 45
Wright Building, 169
Writers Program, Works Progress Administration, *South Carolina, A Guide to the Palmetto State,* 28
Wuthering Heights (by Emily Brontë), 190

Yadkin River, 30
Yaupon Acres, 79
Yon, J. H., 62
York County, 133
Yorktown, 6
Young, Virginia Durant (Mrs. William J.), 126-28

Zeigler, J. A., *The Last of the Bighams,* 186